IMAGES
of America

PARIS

ON THE COVER: Pauline and Ebert Powell take a stroll in their pony cart in front of their residence. The house with the turned spindles was handed down through Pauline's family to her descendants, the Kinemonds. It is likely the oldest extant house in Paris today. The photograph is undated. (Courtesy of Vivian Myers Marty, from the Doris Meyers Collection.)

IMAGES
of America

PARIS

Daniel Jay Grimminger, Ph.D.

ARCADIA
PUBLISHING

ISBN 978-0-7385-8393-8

Published by Arcadia Publishing
Charleston, South Carolina

Printed in the United States of America

Library of Congress Control Number: 2010930004

For all general information, please contact Arcadia Publishing:
Telephone 843-853-2070
Fax 843-853-0044
E-mail sales@arcadiapublishing.com
For customer service and orders:
Toll-Free 1-888-313-2665

Visit us on the Internet at www.arcadiapublishing.com

For my grandpa, Jay Alvin Lutz; my parents, Charlene and Junior Grimminger; my brother, Michael Grimminger; my nephew, Brandon Michael Grimminger; my children, Julia Anna Rebecca and Justus Abraham Friedrich Grimminger; and those older people in the village who told me the stories of the past and fostered my interest in our local history. Soli Deo Gloria.

Contents

ACKNOWLEDGMENTS

From the time I was a little boy, I heard stories from lifelong "Parisians," particularly the memories of my grandfather Jay Alvin Lutz Sr., as well as my parents, Charlene and Junior Grimminger, my aunt Marion Wilson, and others: Doris and Olen Lutz, Pastor Donald Rice, Esther and Wayne Schoner, Paul and Viola Saeger, Betty and Jim Speakman, and Eloise Wood among others. They were interesting reminders of just how much history is in Paris. These people told stories that I have never forgotten.

The commentary accompanying each picture in this book is based on both these first-hand accounts and the historical research of the books that I have listed in the bibliography at the rear of this volume. When I use a printed source in a caption or chapter introduction, I cite it in parentheses with a page number from the source. This allows the reader to read further if he or she so chooses.

The images in this volume have been brought together from several collections other than my own. I am indebted to the following people for trusting me with their pictures and historic items to scan for this book: Verla Crowl, Minerva, Ohio; Edwin Ely, Louisville, Ohio; Bob and Ruth Fisher, Paris, Ohio; Don and Barb Gram, Paris, Ohio; Charlene and Junior Grimminger, Paris, Ohio; Richard and Mary Henning, Paris, Ohio; Carol Keith, Georgia; Kay Latham, Homeworth, Ohio; Linda K. Lilly, Canton, Ohio; Vivian Marty, Canton, Ohio; Doris Myers, Paris, Ohio; Fred and Truus Monhemius, Paris, Ohio; Donna Monnot, Paris, Ohio; Lillian Munk, Paris, Ohio; Doris Myers, Paris, Ohio; Esther and Wayne Schoner, North Canton, Ohio; Betty Speakman, Minerva, Ohio; Steven Tibrea, North Carolina; Les and Audrey Wade, Paris, Ohio; Dawn and Eloise Wood, Paris, Ohio.

John Miller provided some excellent new photography for the book. The Israel United Church of Christ Consistory and Hanley and Ruth Ann Wheeler helped to collect items from church members and gave of their time to help me scan photographs. For all of the people who contributed to this book, I extend my thanks, and the gratitude of future readers, for their interest and effort in helping to preserve Paris's unique history.

INTRODUCTION

It is difficult to imagine modern-day Paris as being a one-time center of commerce and the arts. Currently there are no businesses within the village's limits, and many people moving to the area are not joining the local churches nor are they getting involved with the annual festivities like people once did. This little village, however, was booming from the 1830s to the early 1900s.

Paris's location on the state road, "The main thoroughfare of travel, gave it considerable prominence," according to one respected historian (Danner, 67). But by 1923, the oldest resident recalled just how things had changed from what he remembered in the early years of the village when his parents brought him from Pennsylvania (Howells). Paris was on the mail route from Pittsburgh to the West; the stagecoaches started to carry mail to the village, and horses were changed at Paris as early as 1824 (Kauffman, 149). According to another source, a post office was established in the village on August 22, 1822. The first postmaster was Daniel Burgett (Lehman, vol. I, 81).

Paris's founder, Rudolph Bair (d. 1820), originally came from York County, Pennsylvania, and served as a member of Ohio's Constitutional Convention of 1812, having helped to draft the first state constitution. Between coming to Paris in 1806 and the actual founding of the village in 1814, he was appointed a justice of the peace in Osnaburg Township (then Columbiana County), which took in what is modern-day Paris Township (established on April 1, 1818). He was clearly an industrious man who had vision and worked hard to attract people to his new home, for in 1812 he built the first sawmill on the Black Creek (a half mile southwest of the village) and in 1814 he built the first gristmill on the same stream "a mile up" (Danner, 67). It was likely that Bair was just interested in Paris as a moneymaking opportunity. However, he was known to "accommodate emigrants of limited means," often selling land to them "on long-time payments and though these were not always met when due, he was never known to oppress a delinquent" (Danner, 65).

William Perrin noted in his 1881 history of Stark County, Ohio, that by the 1880s Paris had two dry goods stores, one drugstore, one provision store, two hotels, one wagon and carriage factory, one wagon factory, two paint shops, two harness shops, three boot and shoe shops, two blacksmith shops, one meat market, one planing mill, one sawmill, one gristmill, and one vinegar factory. The location and its people attracted artisans like Smythe and Harmel, who were potters of remarkable stoneware and crocks that were intended to adorn kitchens and basements while storing and pickling homegrown foods. Their work was on par with the great potters of Pennsylvania and Maryland.

When the railroad came through the area later in the century, it contributed to Paris's slow demise, as did the use of highways and the turnpike in the 20th century. Further, the loss of family ties to Pennsylvania cut out a whole demographic of visitors that served as a large nucleus of future residents and tourists in the 19th century. Paris's history is nevertheless worthy of our attention, because its sons and daughters and their descendents have spread across the nation and the rest of the world; Paris's history is the history of frontier America, it is the history of how most everyone lived in this country for many years. Thus when we document it, we record American culture in microcosm.

This book is only the beginning of a larger history project. As interested people form a historical society in the village, it is this author's hope that as more artifacts and photographs surface, that their owners will either donate them to the historical society or allow us to scan and photograph them for the preservation of our common heritage. A fuller narrative history is also planned that will include all of the families and landmarks that made Paris one of the great metropolises of this part of the country in the early 19th century.

—Daniel Jay Grimminger

One

PEOPLE

Modern-day historians know little about the earliest settlers of Paris. Rudolph Bair and his brother Christopher came to Paris in 1806 to search out land that they could claim at the Steubenville land office. That fall, Bair brought his wife and baby from Columbiana County to live in his unfinished log cabin, about a half mile north of the present village. Before their arrival, legend states that Bair encountered Native Americans along the Black Creek (down the hill west of town), and they fed him gravy made with bear's hair (*Paris, Ohio Sesqui-Centennial*). Later settlers included Conrad Henning, a veteran of the Revolutionary War, who bought 100 acres from Bair in 1811 for $200. He became the first village blacksmith and his wife was the first midwife, having a record of no fatalities in over 500 home deliveries during her 30-year tenure in that capacity.

Several doctors practiced medicine in the village's history. Among them was Robert Estep, who came from Fayette County, Pennsylvania, in 1818; he was actually trained as a silversmith but became an important figure as he performed some of the earliest caesarian births in the country.

Because dairy farming became one of the main professions in Paris Township, many people in Paris were ordinary folks; they were neither notable nor significant to people outside of the area, but their story needs to be retold, because this history of common people and their lives serves as a foundation for many of society's present attitudes, beliefs, practices, and problems.

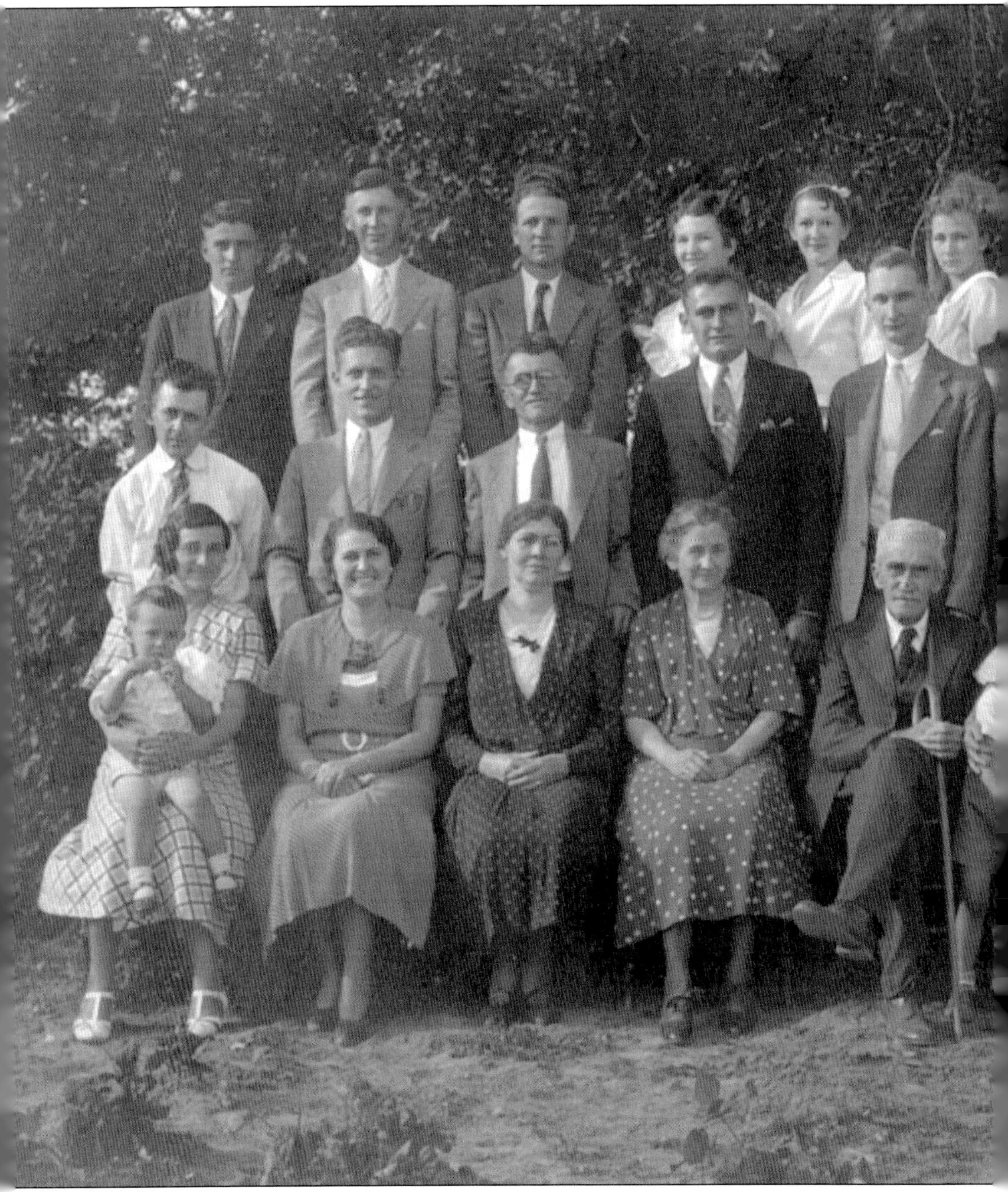

Josiah Lutz was the only child from Abraham Lutz's second marriage. He farmed, was a fine carpenter, and served as the treasurer of the Lutheran Church and the Freeburg Cheese Company. He is pictured here with his descendants (and their spouses). The children in the first row are, from left to right, Earl Stuckey, Melvin Vandegrift, Paul Lutz, Mary Ann Greenwald Linder, Lucian Greenwald, and Nelson Vandegrift. The adults are, from left to right, (first row) Dorothy Sponseller Stuckey, Irene Lutz Stier, Elva Lutz, Emma Lutz, Josiah Lutz, Ida Lutz Sponseller, Amanda

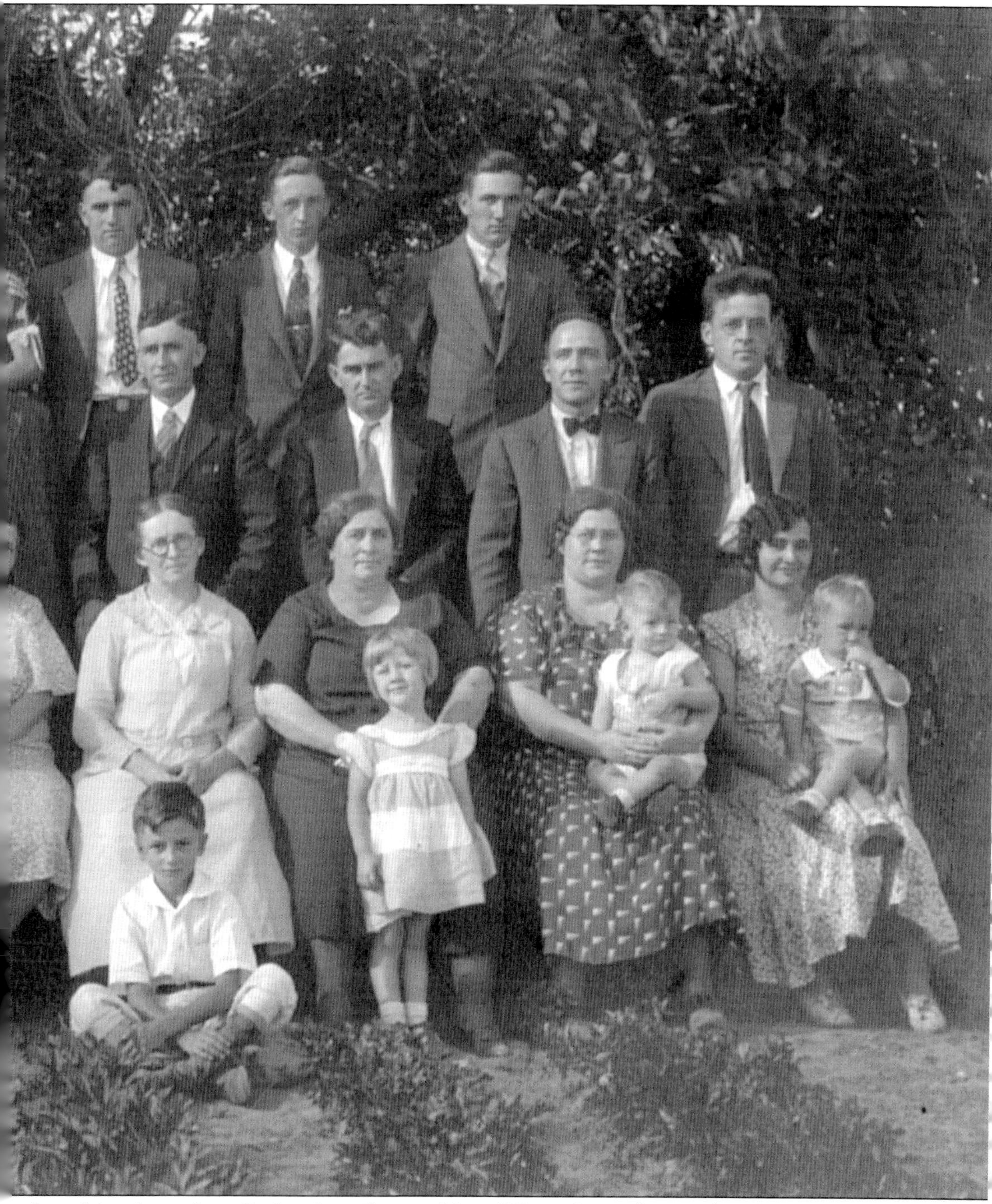

Lutz, Mary Jarvis Lutz, Pauline Lutz Greenwald, and Flossy Sponseller Vandegrift; (second row) Kenny Stuckey, Paul Stier, Edward Lutz, Herman Lutz, Arthur Lutz, Robert Sponseller, Norman Lutz, Charles Lutz, Grant Greenwald, and Lloyd Vandegrift; (third row) Ralph Lutz, Olen Lutz, Lloyd Sponseller, Pearl Lutz Zuber, Ethel Lutz Watkins, Lillian Sponseller Candle, Elva Sponseller Waltz, Jay Lutz, Mervin Lutz, and Ray Sponseller.

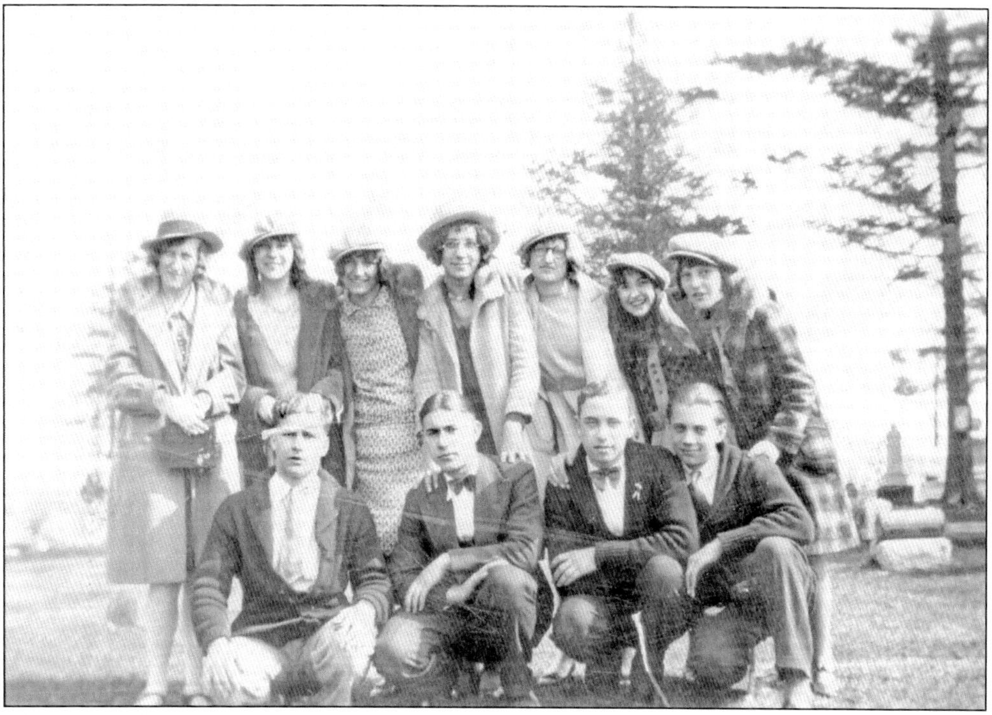

This group of young people stopped for a snapshot in front of the Paris cemetery. Pictured are, from left to right, (first row) Howard Stier, Claire Ely, Gordon ?, and Nelson Myers; (second row) Ruth Lautzenheiser, Ardes Gill, Elva Sponseller, Ruth Linhart, Rose Coleridge, Vera Gugelman, and Doris Stier. (Courtesy of Audrey and Les Wade.)

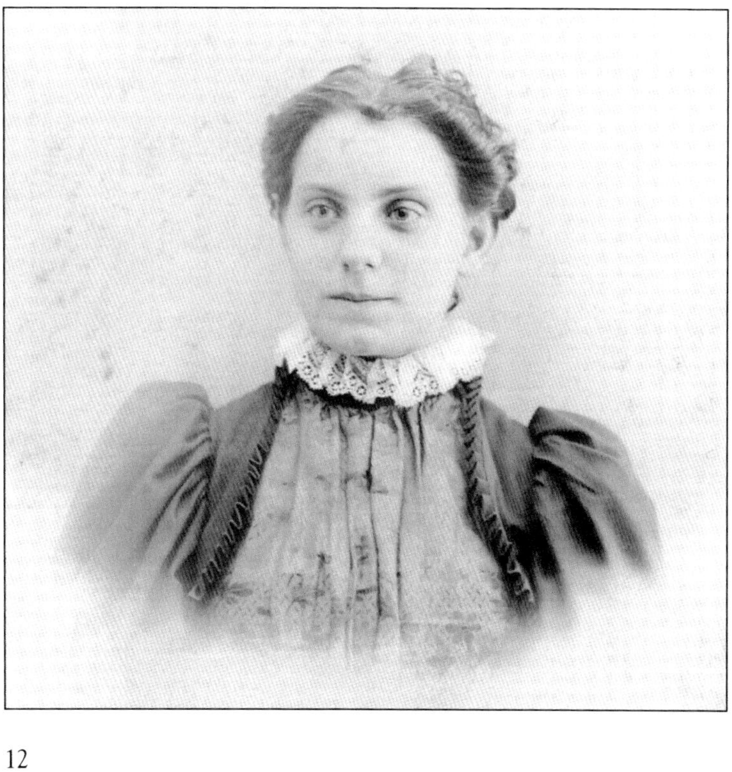

Anna Bush was possibly the sister to Bernice (Livelsberger) Bowman. There have been members of the Bush family in and around Paris since the 19th century. (Courtesy of the Linda K. Lilly Collection.)

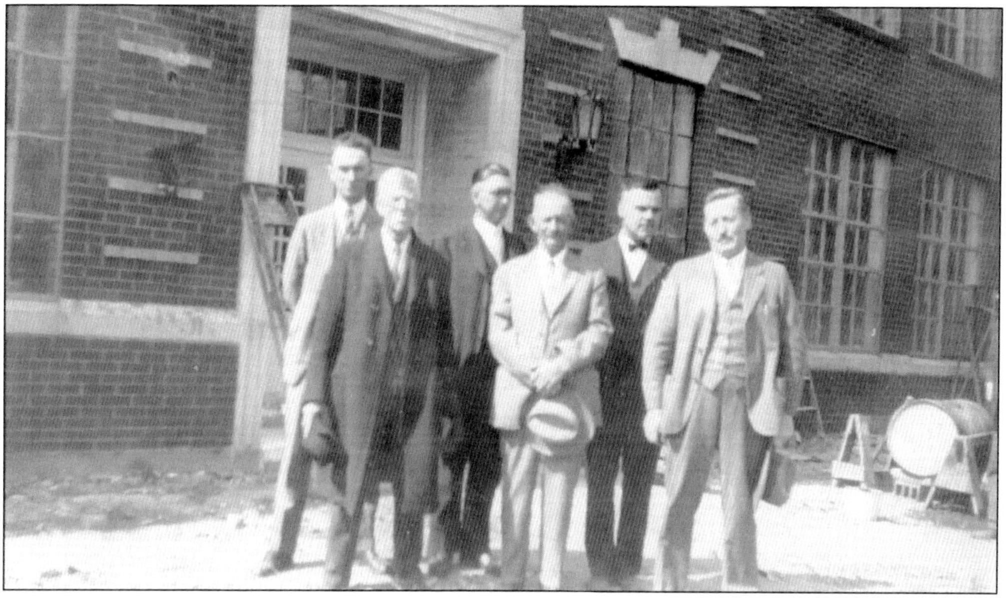

Here the Paris School Board poses proudly in front of the newly constructed school building in 1928, the third edifice to serve children in the heart of the village. Pictured from left to right are (first row) John Martin, John Stonehill, and H. E. Stier; (second row) Lloyd Pariso, Harry Watson, and Carl Dager. The two pictures of the board, with and without their hats, are part of the same private collection. (Courtesy of Audrey and Les Wade.)

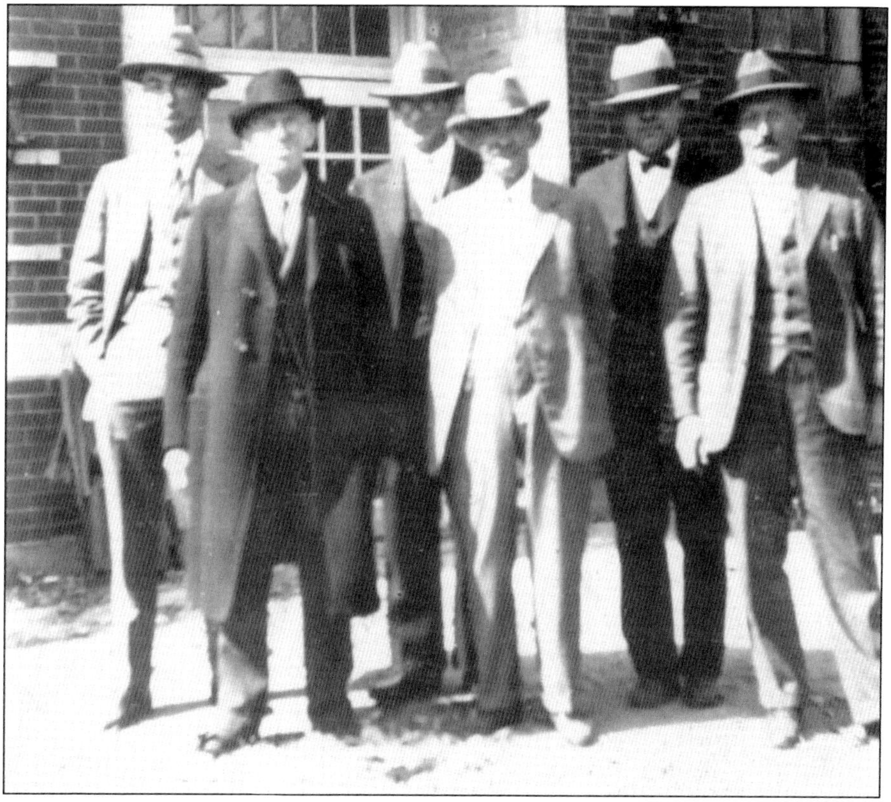

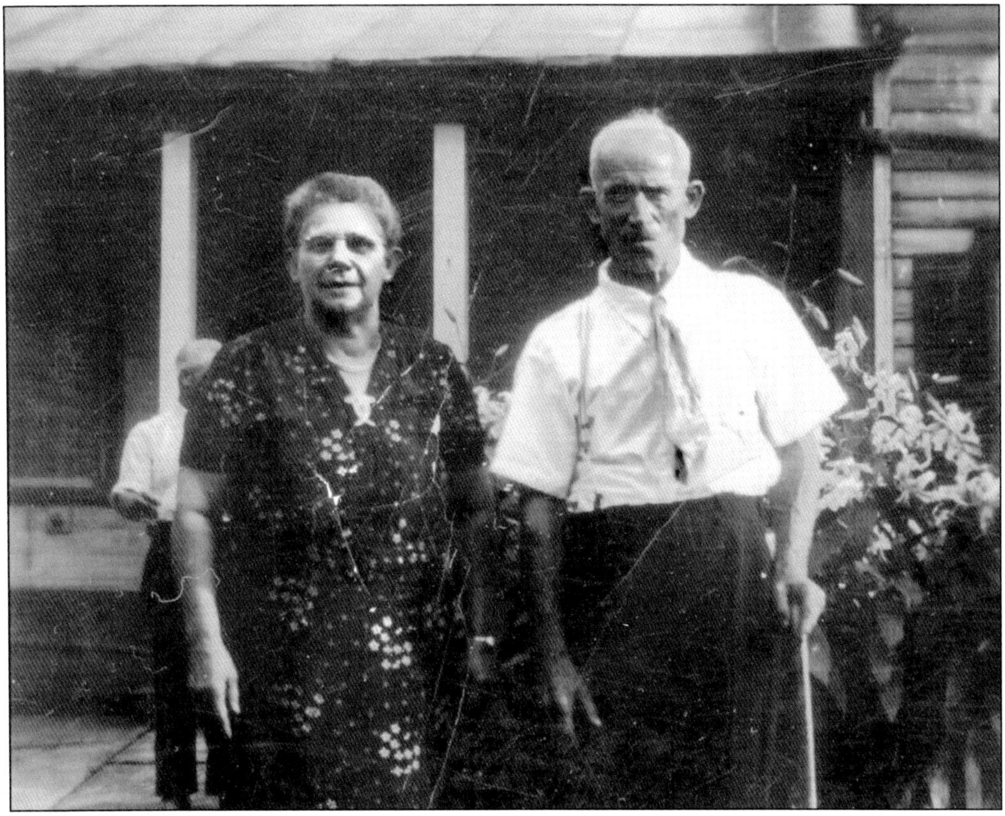

Dean and Emma Livelsberger lived just north of the Lutheran Church parsonage. They are pictured here beside their primitive house. The back porch and kitchen are visible in the background. Dean was a shoemaker and raised rabbits, and his wife was known to have an extensive rose garden in the front. (Courtesy of the Linda K. Lilly Collection.)

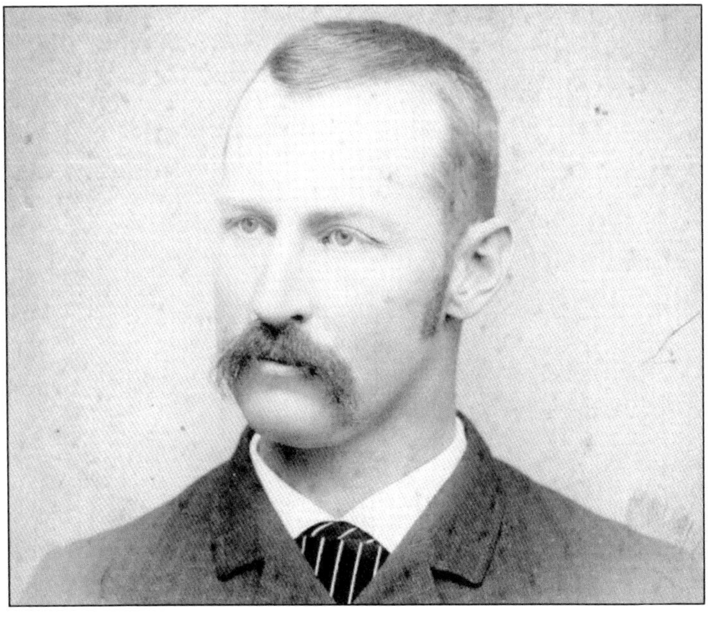

B. M. Stier (along with John Oyer) brought the cannon to Paris from the South in 1888. He is a young man in this picture. (Courtesy of Verla Myers Crowl, from the Doris Myers Collection.)

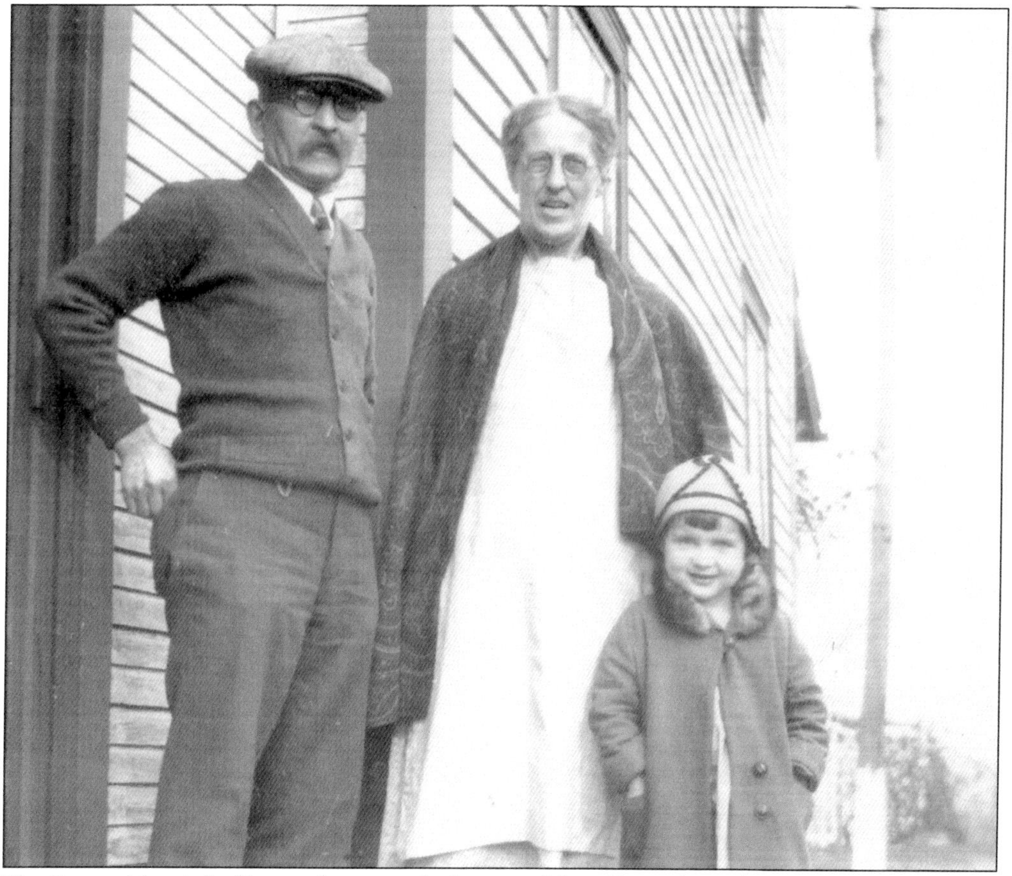

The Stimmel family had been a fixture in the history of the village. Shown here are Arthur and Alice (Shipe) Stimmel with their granddaughter Betty (Stimmel) Speakman. Arthur was a blacksmith, and they resided on the Westside of the village on Route 172. (Courtesy of Betty Speakman.)

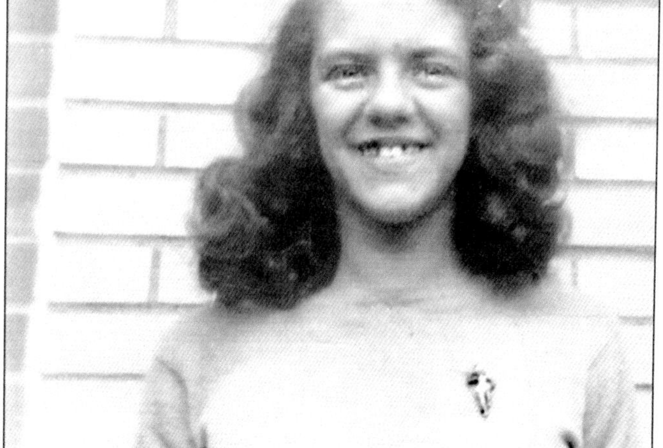

This picture shows Audrey (Gill) Wade in her teen years. She still lives in Paris and is one of the few lifelong members of the community left. (Courtesy of Audrey and Les Wade.)

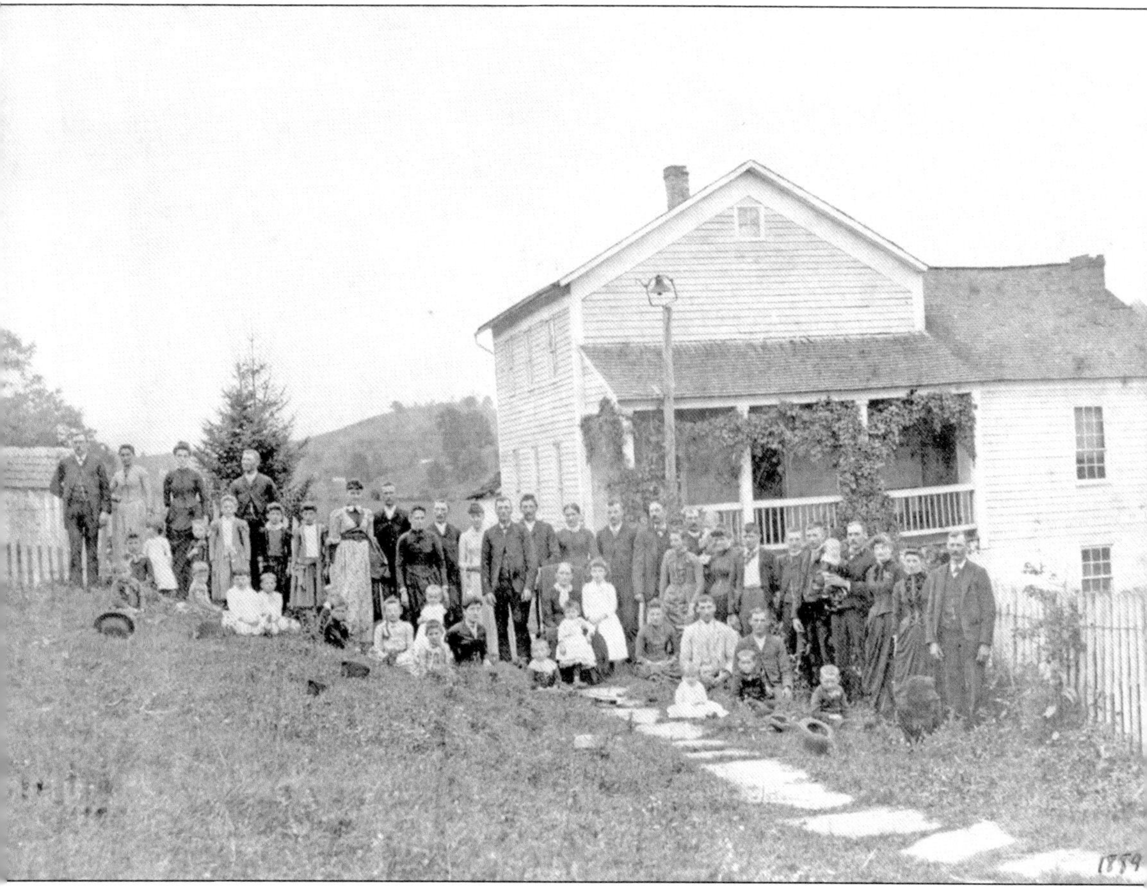

This Starkey reunion picture dates back to 1889 when it was taken on the John Starkey property on Robertsville Avenue. (Courtesy of Kay Latham.)

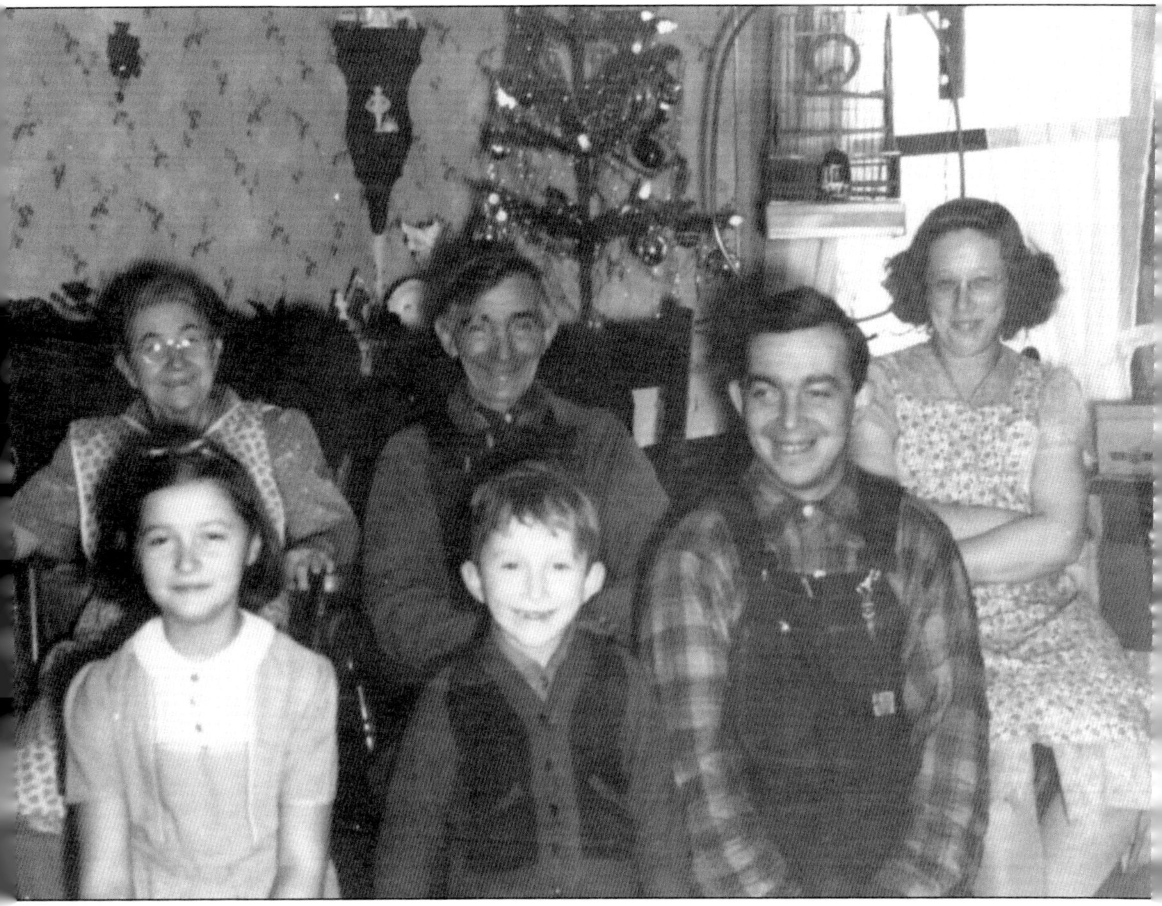

The Comforts lived on a farm on Parks Avenue on the west side of the road. A humorous Ola Comfort is pictured here with her husband, Bob, and Bob's parents, Mr. and Mrs. Abe Comfort. The two little guests from the neighboring farm to the east are Marion (Grimminger) Wilson and Junior Grimminger at Christmas time. The birdcage reveals a long passion for birds that even the author can remember when entering their house in the early 1980s. They had numerous birdcages on the first floor of their farmhouse. (Courtesy of Charlene and Junior Grimminger.)

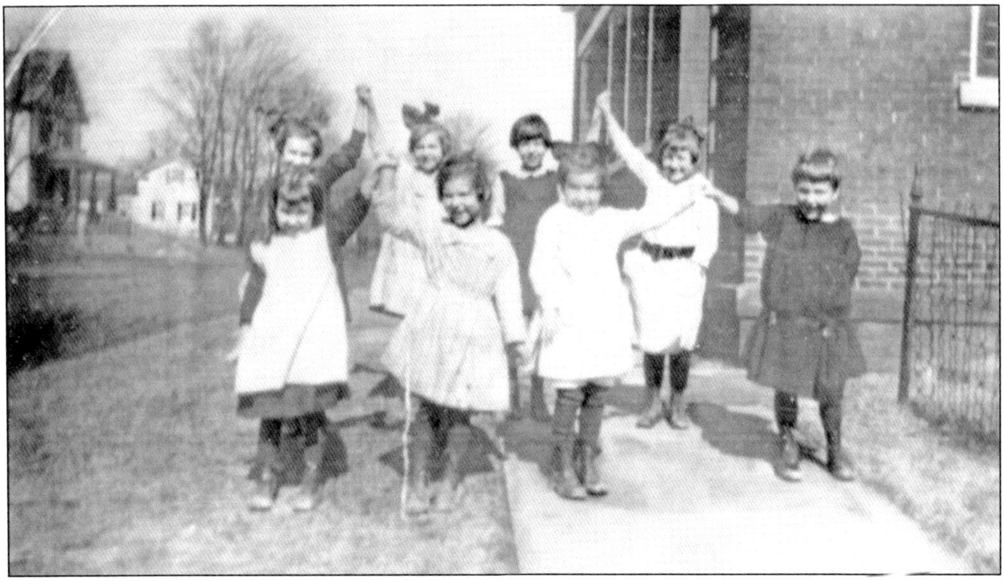

This picture shows a group of girls playing at the corner of the Lutheran Church prior to the church's addition on the south side in 1927; it probably dates to 1919 or 1920. The only child identified in the photograph is Doris (Stier) Myers, who is standing on the far right and dressed in a dark color. (Courtesy of Daniel Grimminger, Doris Myers Reproductions Collection.)

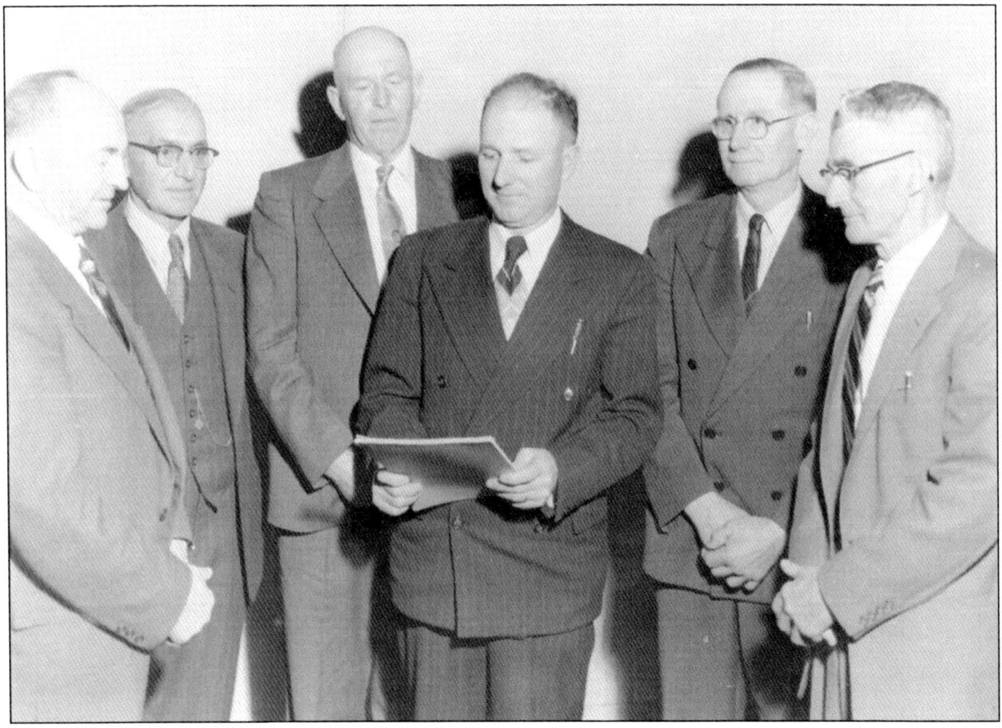

Paris farmers were influential beyond their community. In this picture are the retiring directors of the Stark County Milk Producer's Association. From left to right are Clarence J. Yost, E. J. Biery, Carl Shilling, Lloyd Sponseller, Arthur Mong, and Charles Lutz. Biery, Sponseller, and Mong were all prominent dairymen residing in the Paris area. (Courtesy of Charlene and Junior Grimminger.)

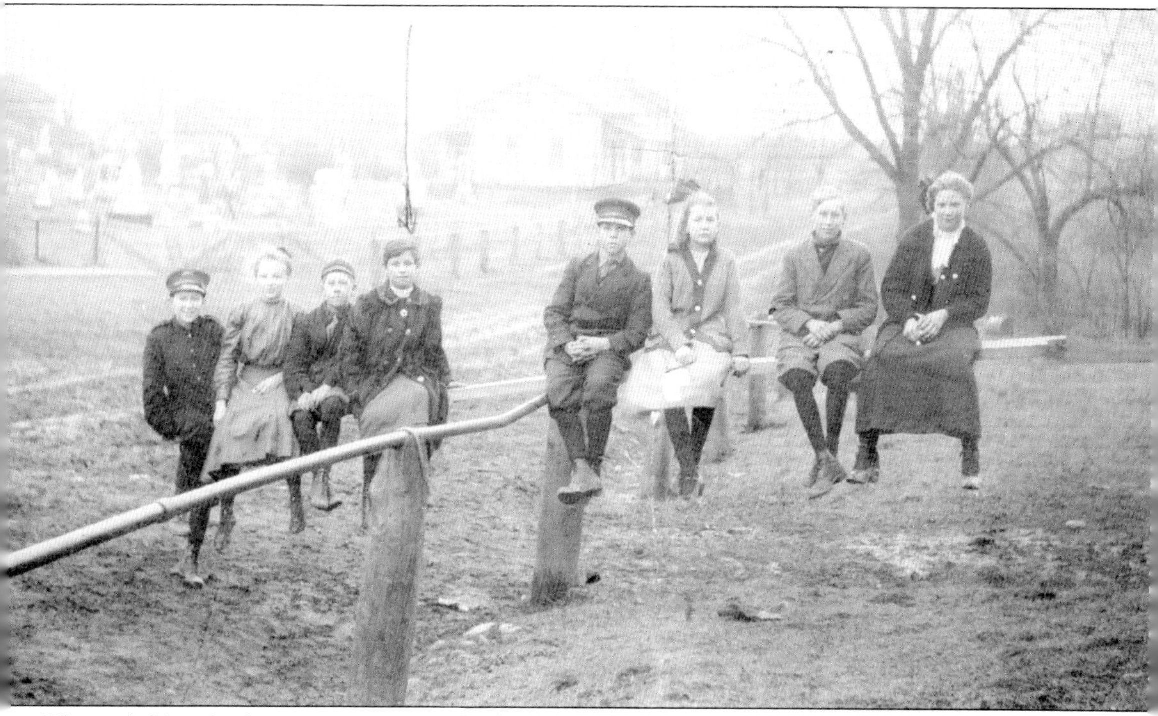

These children built a teeter-totter on the hitching rail just across the road from the Lutheran Church. Gladys Livelsberger is the child on the far right; the arrow points to the current owner's grandmother, Bernice Bowman, born a Livelsberger; the rest of the children are unidentified. The photograph predates the Paris School that many Paris residents attended and is probably from the late 19th century. At this time, there would have been about six horse stalls in a shed somewhere close to these children, and the one-room schoolhouse would be behind the photographer. (Courtesy of Linda K. Lilly.)

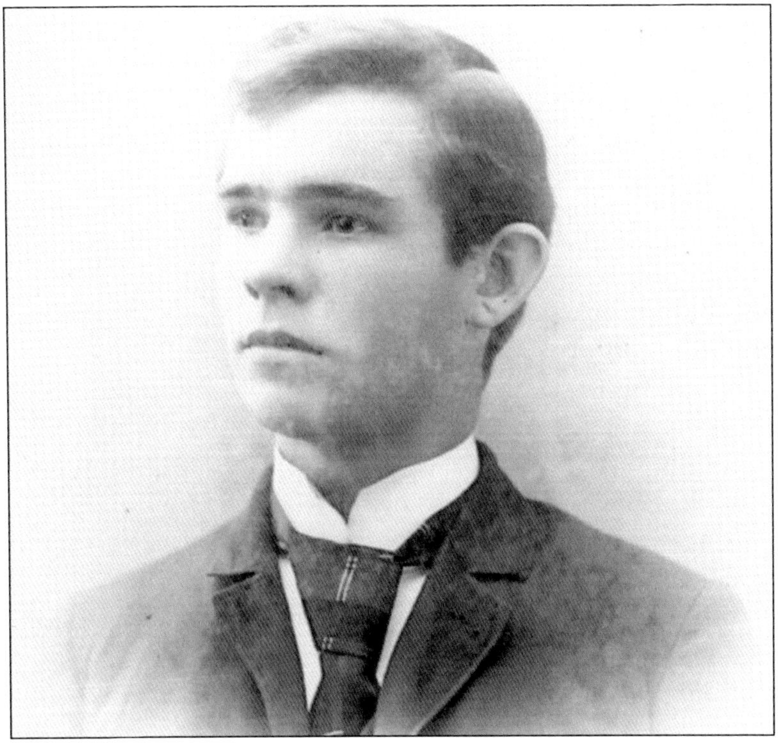

C. V. Sheatsley was born in Paris and went on to become an important theologian. It was rumored around Paris at one time that he cremated his wife in the furnace, but it is not for sure if the claim is true. He became the pastor at Christ Lutheran Church in Bexley along the campus of Capital University. (Courtesy of Steven Tibrea.)

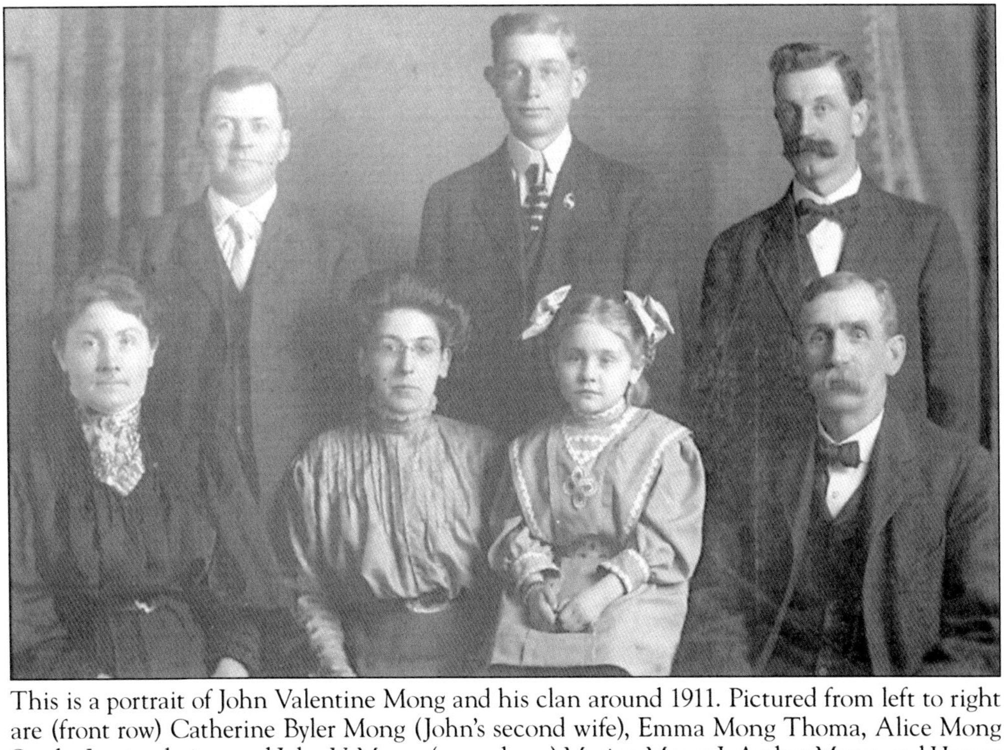

This is a portrait of John Valentine Mong and his clan around 1911. Pictured from left to right are (front row) Catherine Byler Mong (John's second wife), Emma Mong Thoma, Alice Mong Snyder Lautzenheiser, and John V. Mong; (second row) Marion Mong, J. Arthur Mong, and Homer Mong. (Courtesy of Steven Tibrea.)

Walter and Blanche (Folk) Mong lived on a farm east of Paris that is now the Jim Kiko farm. They were, along with a long line of Mongs, faithful members of the Lutheran Church. Charlene Grimminger and others still recall what a fine Sunday schoolteacher Blanche was. This picture is dated 1936. (Courtesy of Steven Tibrea.)

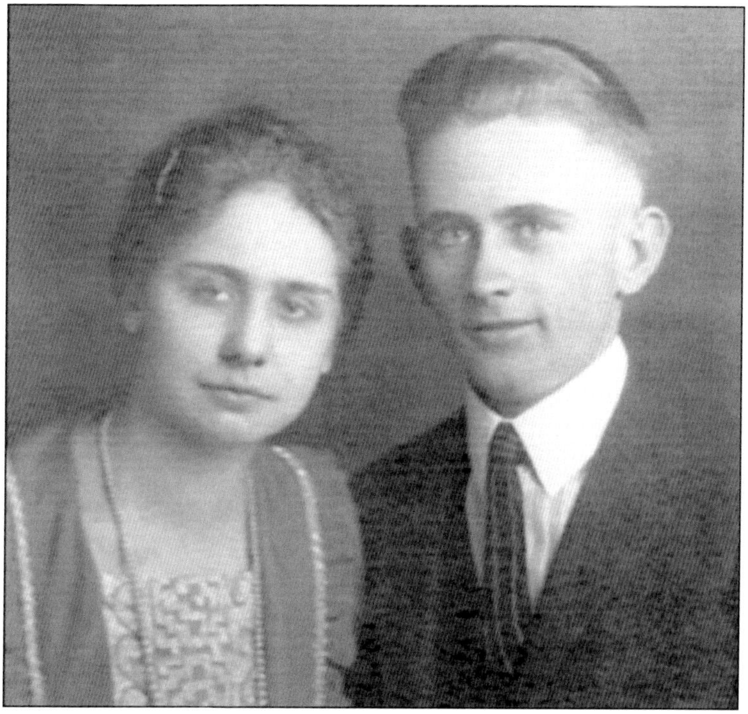

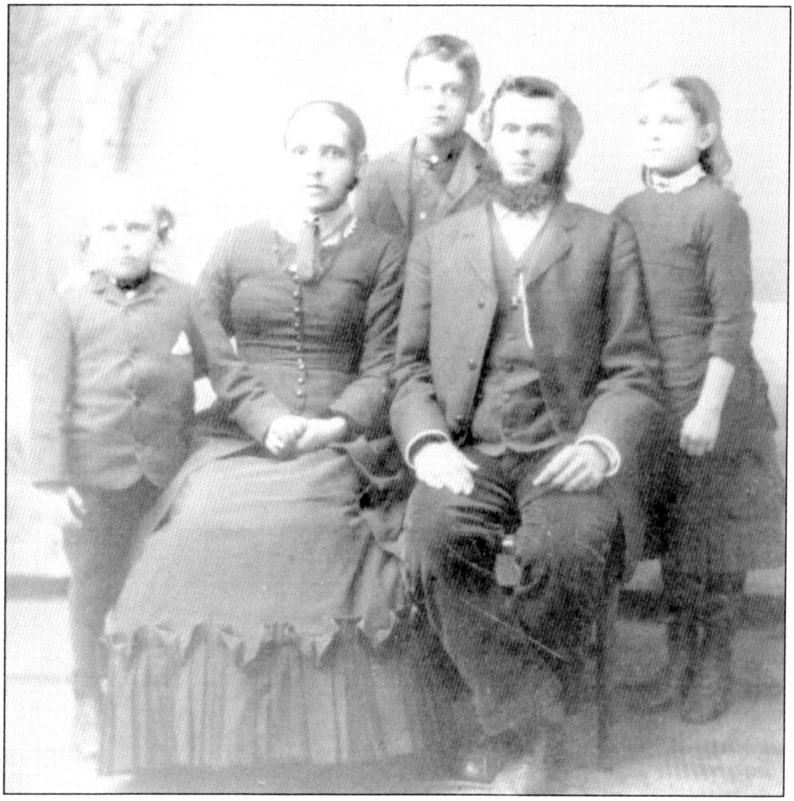

Shown here is the Tobias Stuckey family around 1880. Tobias was born in Columbiana County, Ohio, in 1845. This picture predates the birth of his daughter Bessie, who married Elmer Koontz and had one daughter, Esther Schoner. The family, from left to right, includes David, Mary Ellen, Willie, Tobias, and Katherine. (Courtesy of Kay Latham.)

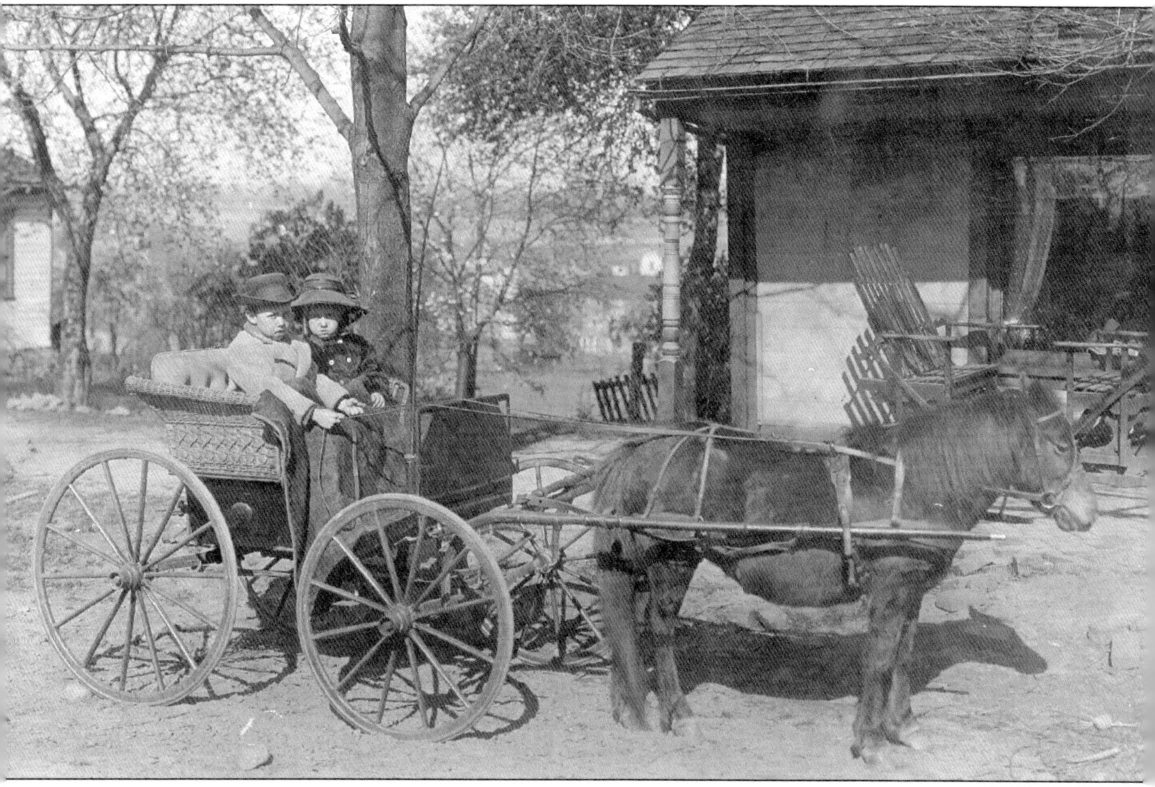

Siblings Ebert Powell and Pauline (Powell) Grossman went for a ride on the town with this pony cart. This early influence, without a doubt, instilled a love for equestrian pursuits, as Ebert later had a horse farm on Pleasant Valley Road. The log cabin in the background with nicely turned posts would be handed down through Pauline's descendants (the Kinemond family). (Courtesy of Vivian Myers Marty, from the Doris Meyers Collection.)

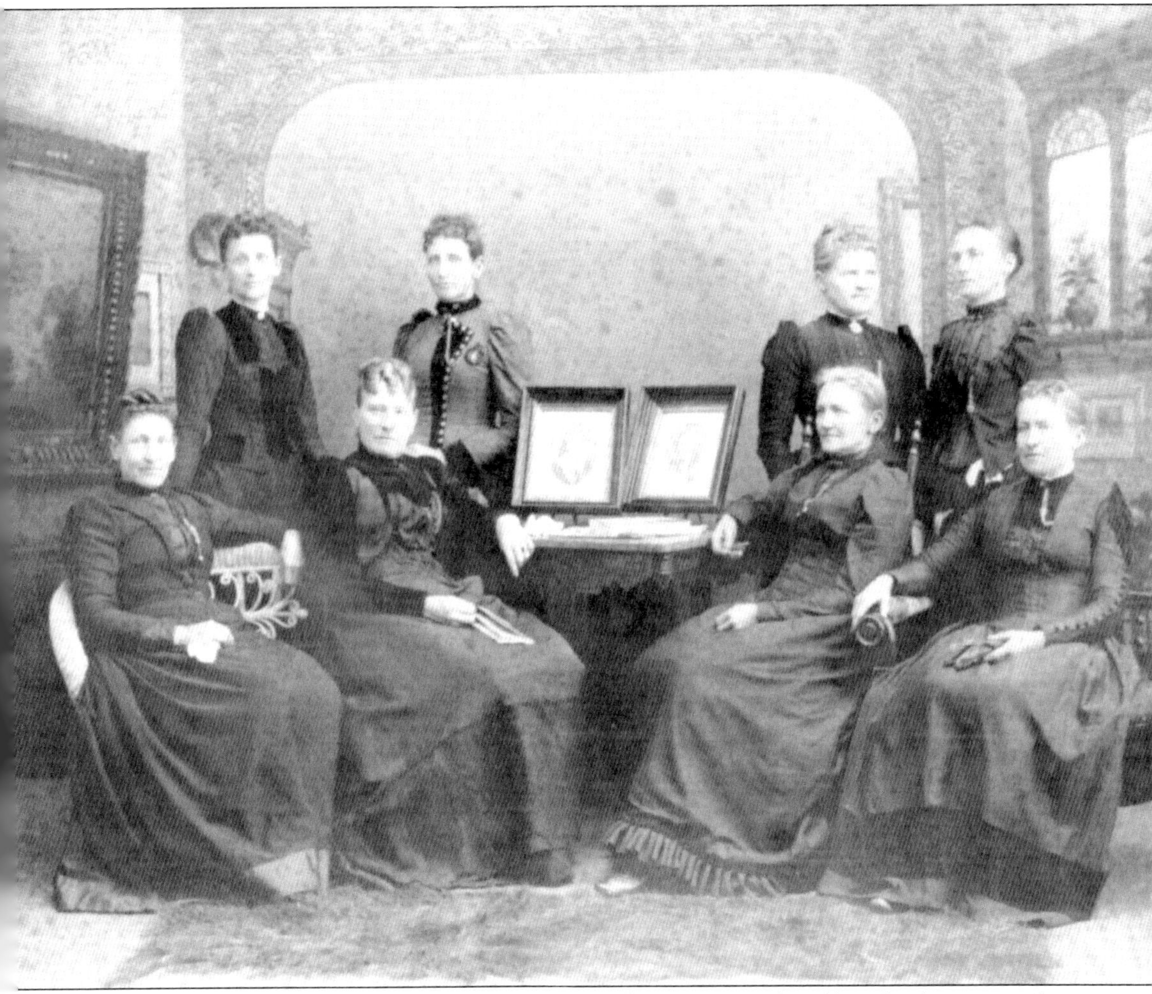

The Shearer sisters hailed from a farm just north of the village. They are listed here by their married names. From left to right they are (front row, seated) Polly Criswell, Matilda Waltz, Caroline Waltz, and Maria Snyder; (back row, standing) Isabella van Voorhis, Anna Eliza Starkey, Alice Oyster, and Cora Ake. Isabella remarried and became a Buchman. (Courtesy of Kay Latham.)

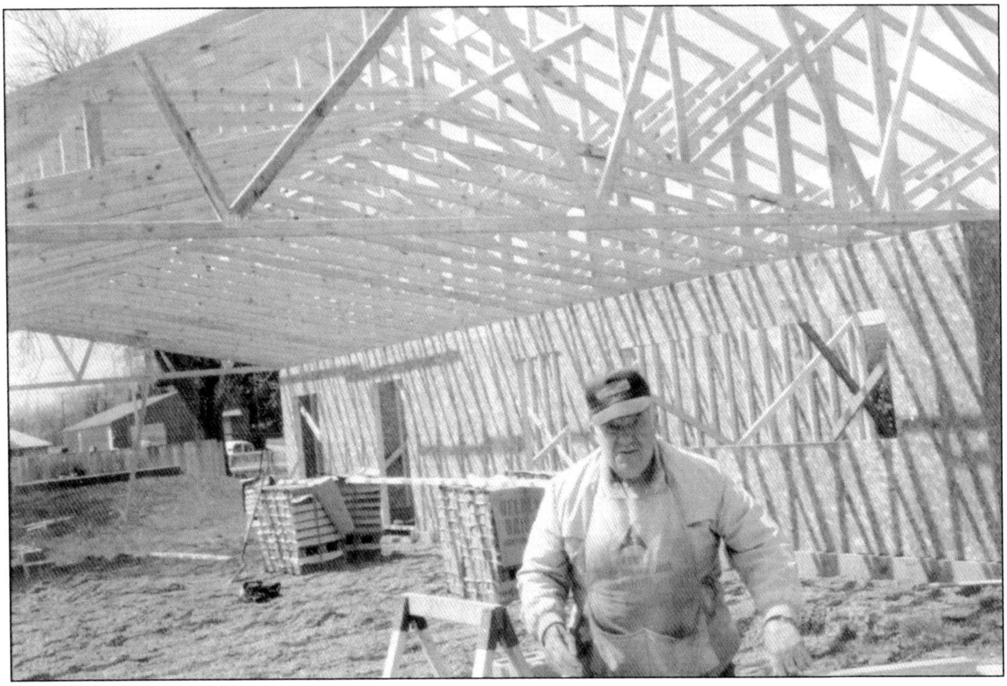

Jim Speakman came from a long line of craftsmen. He was known to have no fear of any height and could climb very high without much to hold onto. Here he is shown working on the new pavilion in the village square. He married Betty Stimmel. (Courtesy of Audrey and Les Wade.)

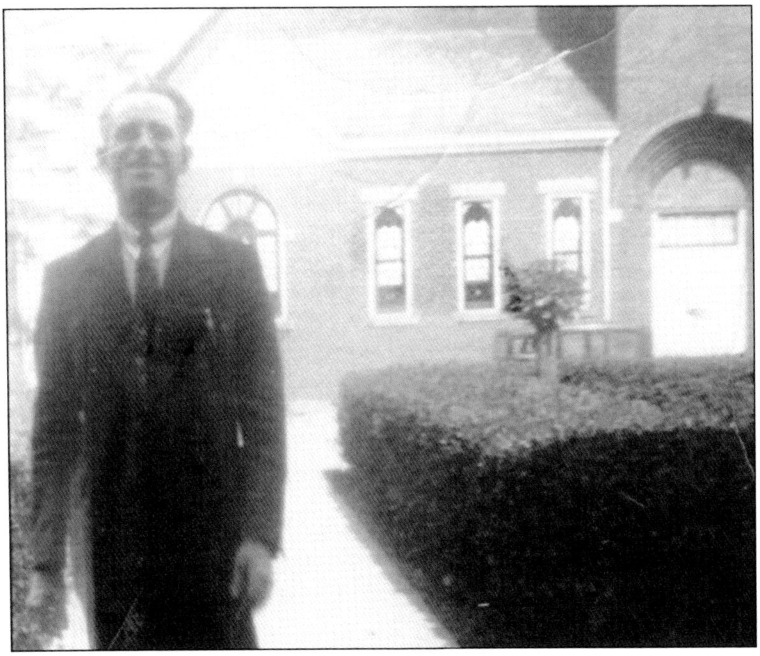

Paris schoolteachers were given pride of place in the town as they educated hundreds of young people over the years. D. I. Warner was one such teacher. He is shown here walking up the sidewalk in front of the school with the Lutheran Church at his back. (Courtesy of Audrey and Les Wade.)

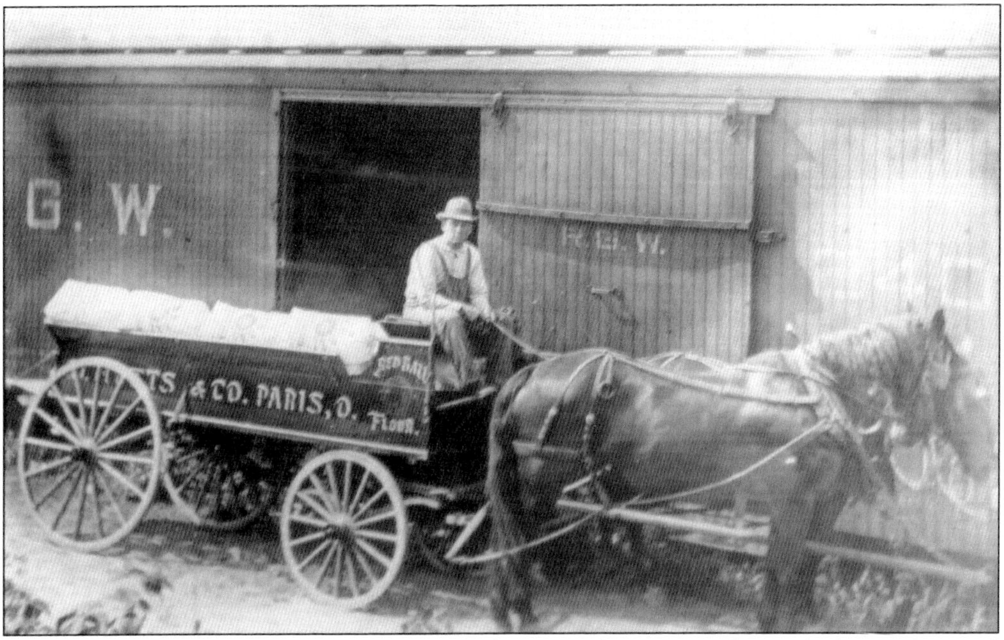

There were many people, like the unidentified man in this image, who worked in and around Paris at one time. His wagon evinces a time when Parisians could make a good living in their own village. The Motts Company sold Red Ball Flour, and here the driver shows off the flour bags he just acquired at the train tracks. (Courtesy of Daniel Grimminger, Doris Myers Reproductions Collection.)

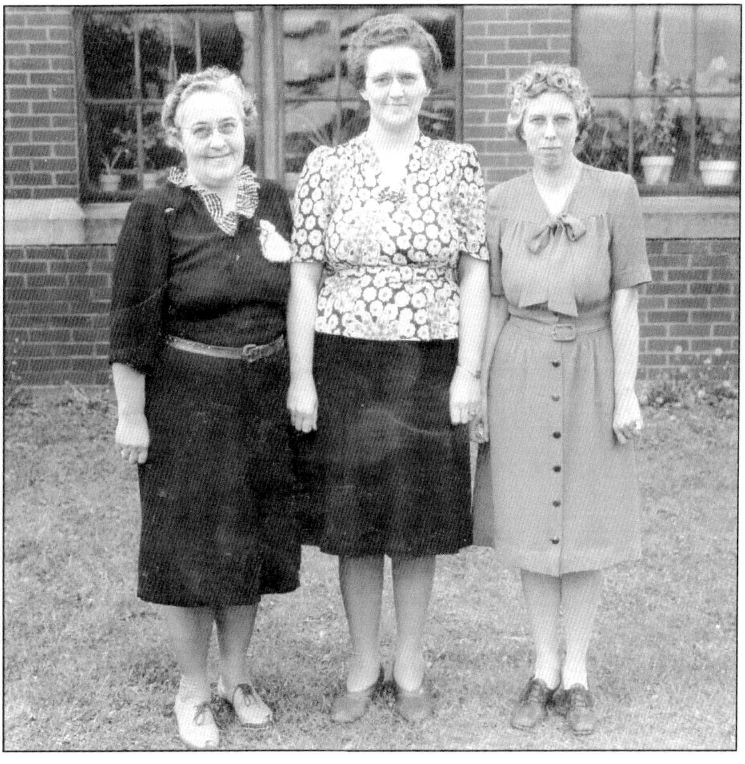

Three of the longer-serving teachers pose here for this photograph. Mamie Stimmel (left), considered by people still today to be possibly the most beloved of all Paris teachers, taught with Mabel Walker (center) and Mrs. Neidig. They are standing in front of the building for this faculty picture. (Courtesy of Charlene and Junior Grimminger.)

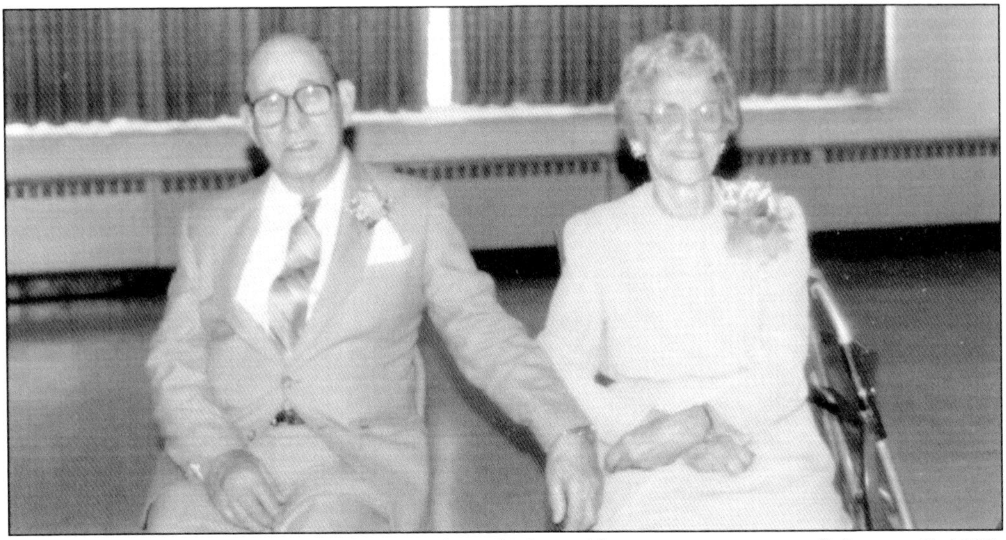

Claire and Ruth Ely are shown here at their 50th wedding anniversary on February 9, 1985. Claire's Ely ancestors lived beside the present-day Hidden Valley Lake property where they had a mine. Their son Edwin continues to be active in the Paris community even though he lives in Louisville. (Courtesy of Edwin Ely.)

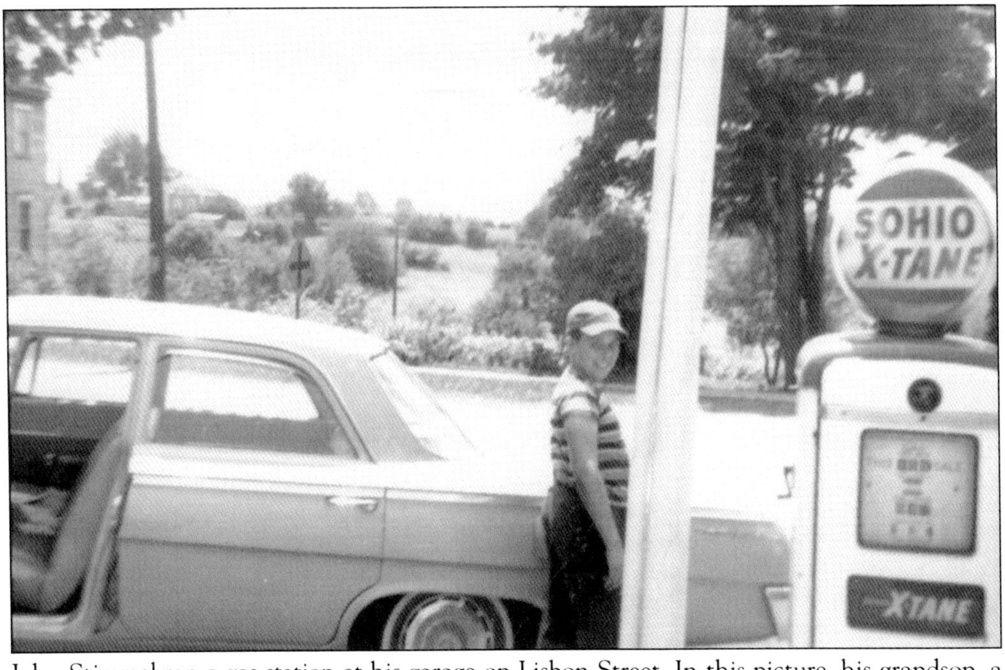

John Stimmel ran a gas station at his garage on Lisbon Street. In this picture, his grandson, a young Dave Speakman, pumps gas. The view across the street reveals a more natural landscape that predates the modern post office building in current use. (Courtesy of Betty Speakman.)

In this photograph, Emma Livelsberger holds one of her grandchildren. She was known for her large rose garden in the front of the Livelsberger property that everyone could see when passing by on Paris Avenue. There are no longer any Livelsbergers in the village or township. (Courtesy of Linda K. Lilly.)

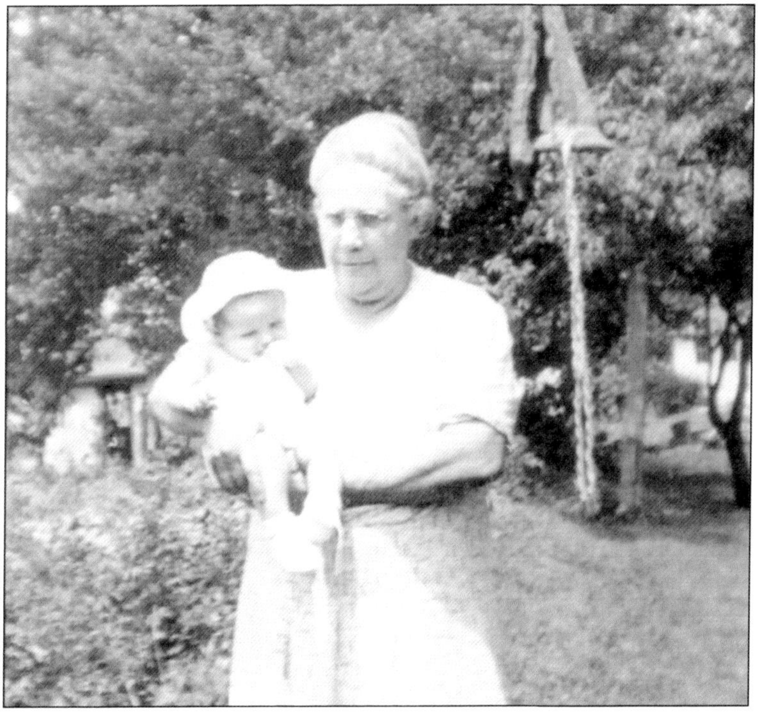

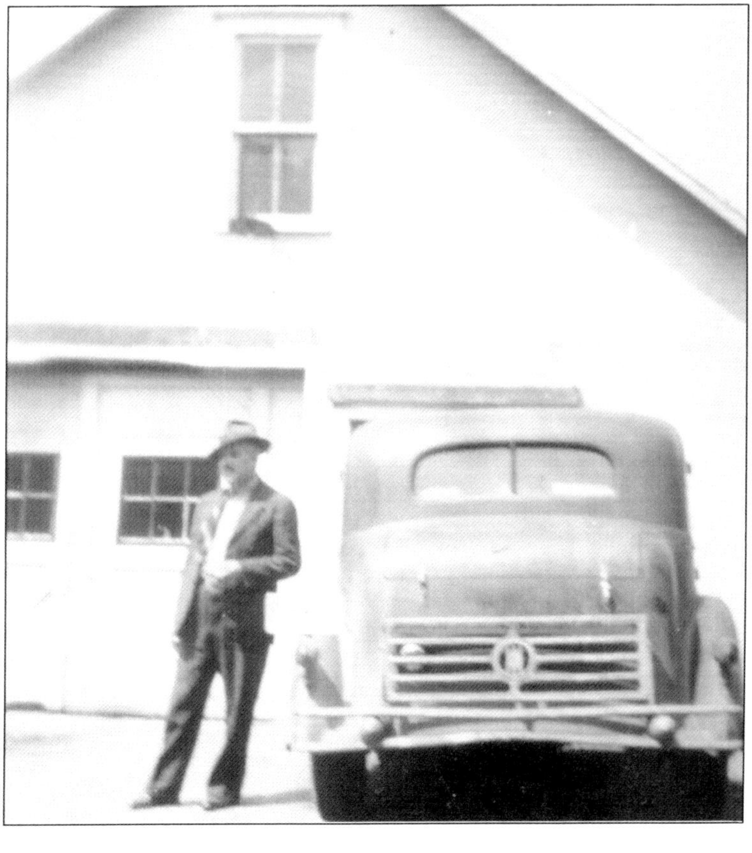

Likely the most popular figure of Paris history in recent years is John Stimmel (father of Betty Speakman). He was a mechanic who was known for fixing just about anything for a very small fee. Here he poses in front of his garage on the northwest side of the village along Lisbon Street. (Courtesy of Betty Speakman.)

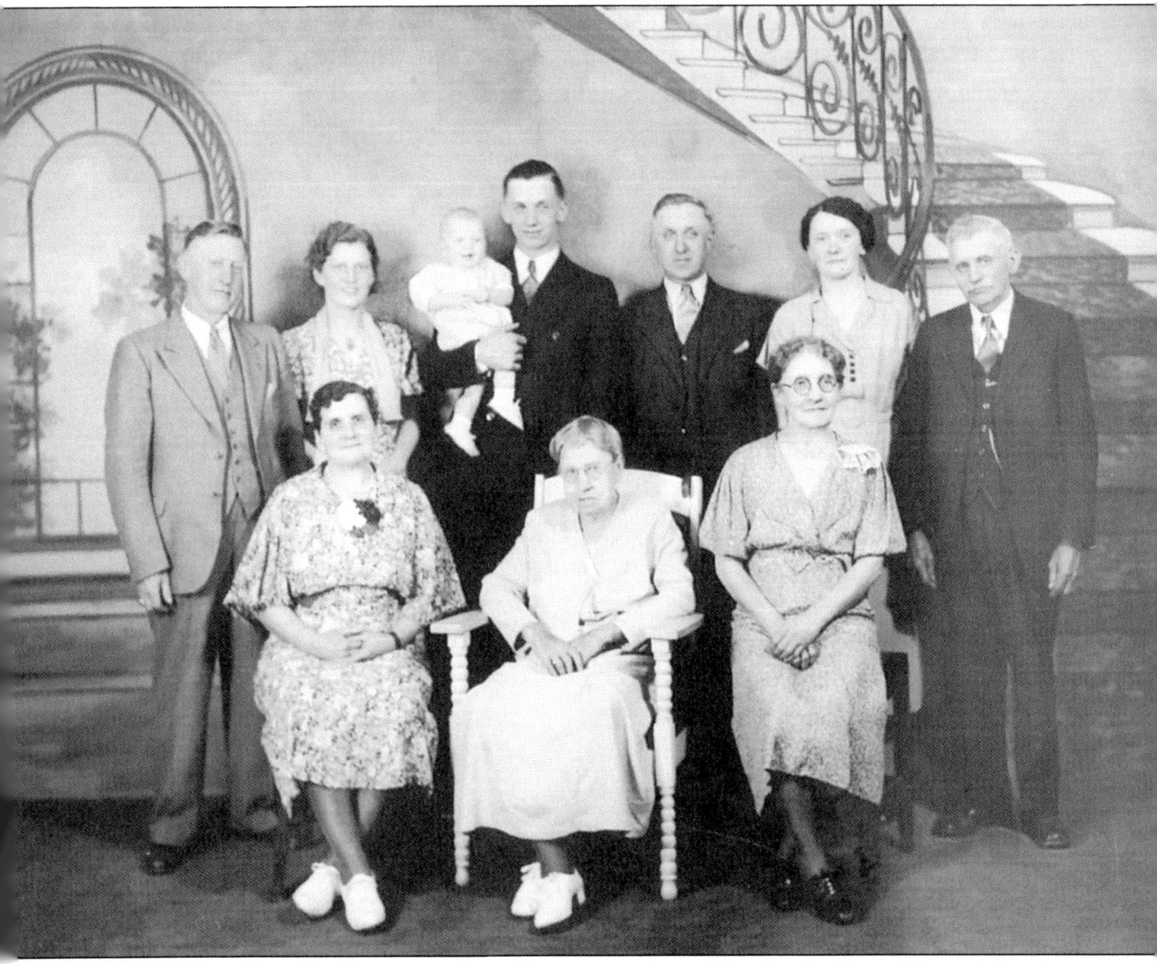

This Myers-Stier family picture shows four generations of the family. From left to right, they are (first row) Ruby Stier, Minerva Jane Stier, and Jenny Ecrement; (second row) Homer Stier, Doris Myers, baby Donny Myers, Nelson Myers, Ira Myers, Velma Myers, and Ellsworth Myers. (Courtesy of Verla Myers Crowl, from the Doris Myers Collection.)

This is one of many members of the Mong family, who were active in the Lutheran Congregation in Paris. George Henry Mong (1850–1933), pictured here, was one of the children of Valentine and Susanna. He married Charlotte Ellen Geiger (1854–1933) in 1872 and had three children. (Courtesy of Steven Tibrea.)

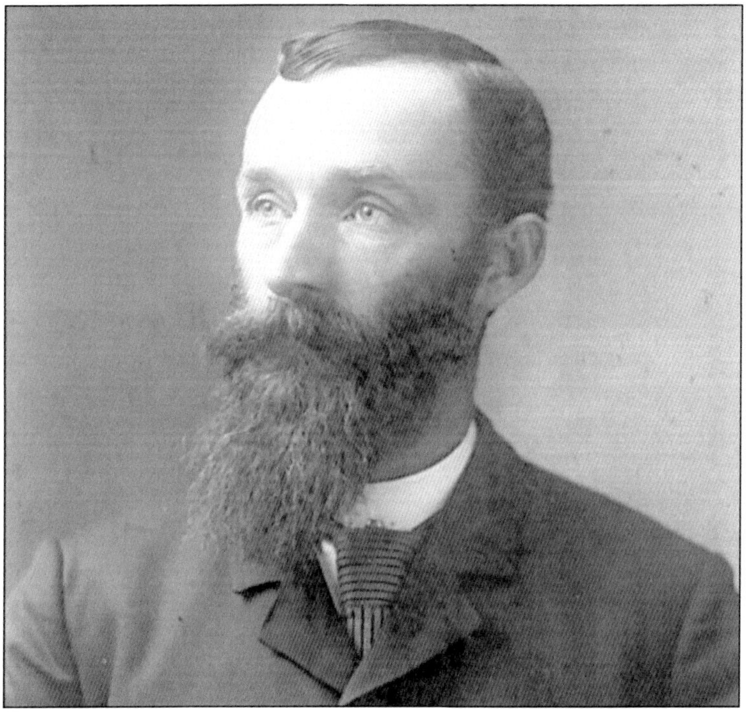

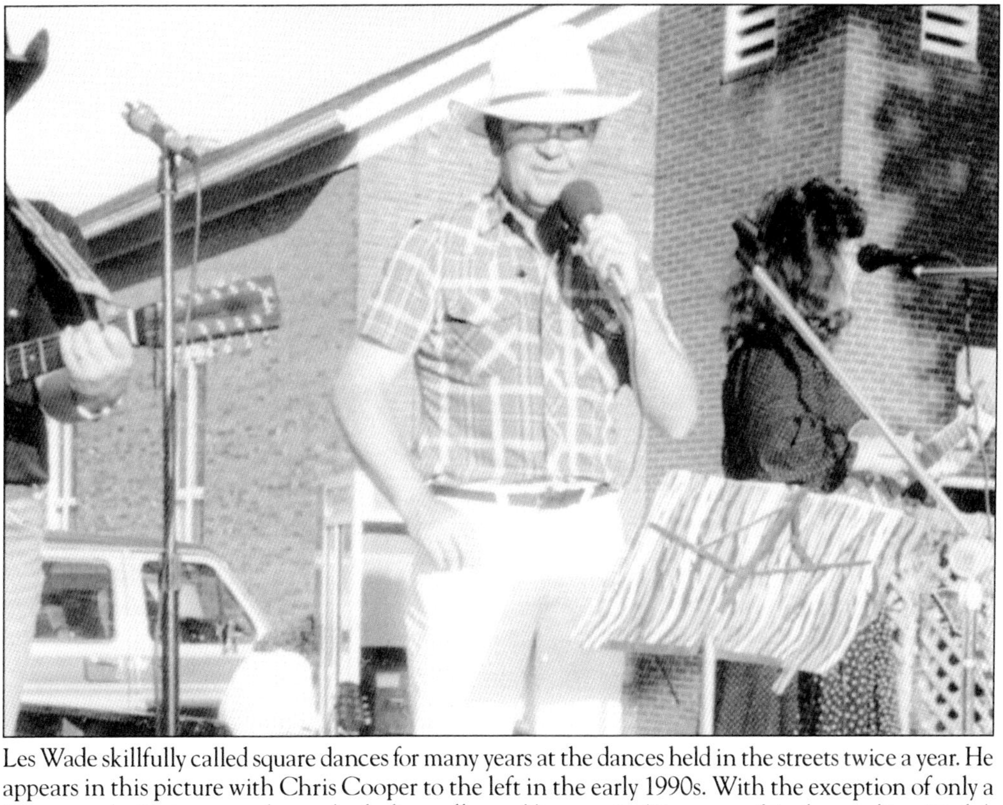

Les Wade skillfully called square dances for many years at the dances held in the streets twice a year. He appears in this picture with Chris Cooper to the left in the early 1990s. With the exception of only a few years, the Paris square dances had a live caller and live music. (Courtesy of Audrey and Les Wade.)

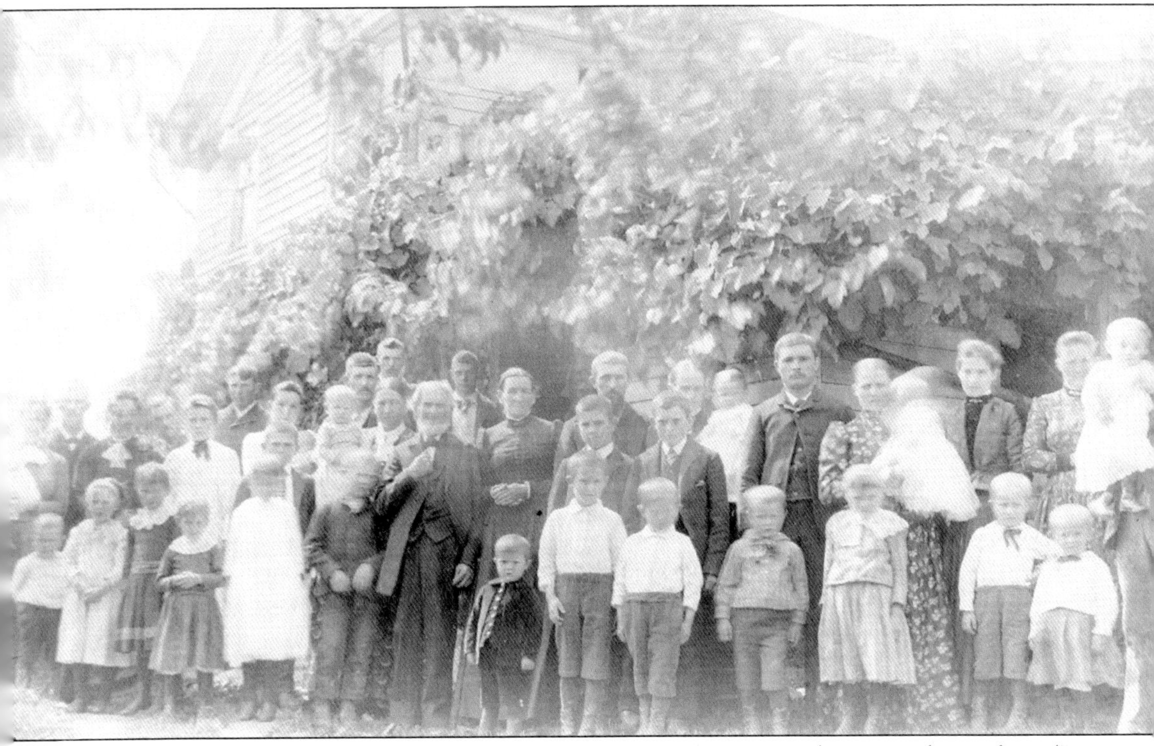

Abraham Lutz is shown here with his progeny at a gathering on the original Lutz farm (Paris Avenue almost to Louisville Street). This early photograph was taken before 1855 when Abraham Lutz, a migrant from Lancaster County, Pennsylvania, died. (Courtesy of Daniel Grimminger.)

Homer Stier was Paris's undertaker for many years. His funeral home ledger tells the details of a once-unspoken history. His daughter Doris Myers lived her whole life in the village as her parents did. (Courtesy of Vivian Myers Marty, from the Doris Myers Collection.)

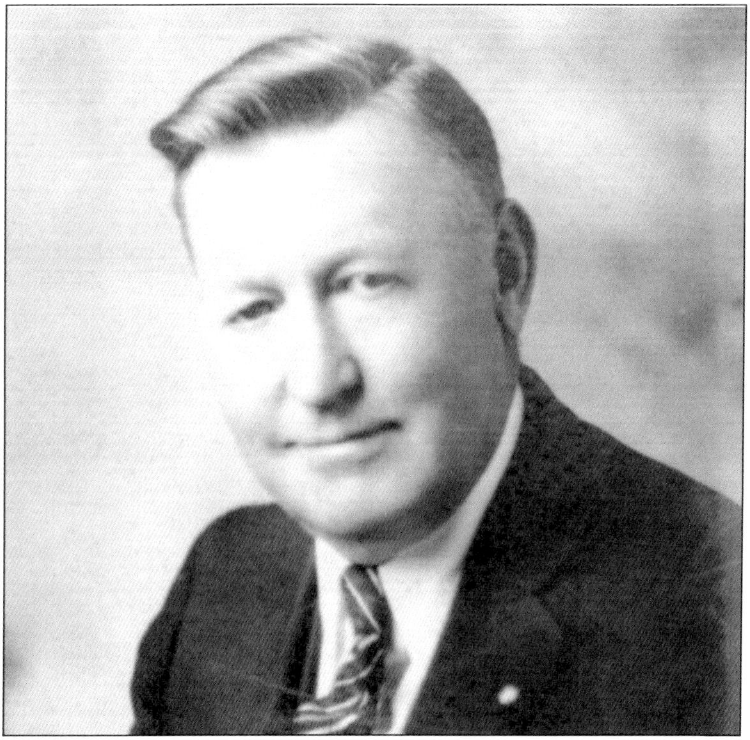

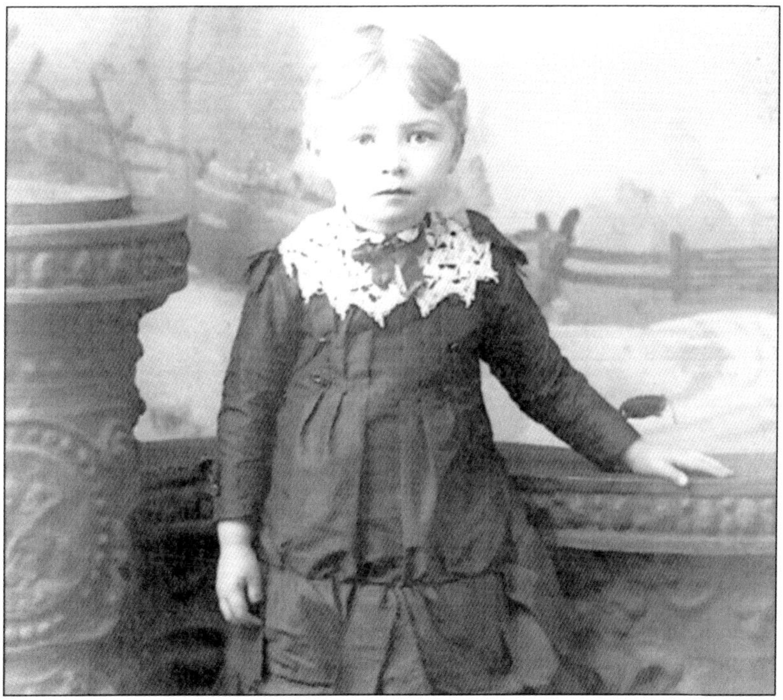

Erma Walker (1885–1970) married James Finefrock in 1909. Their descendents include Ralph, Naomi, Lela, Roy, and Dorothy. Erma is quite young in this picture. (Courtesy of Steven Tibrea.)

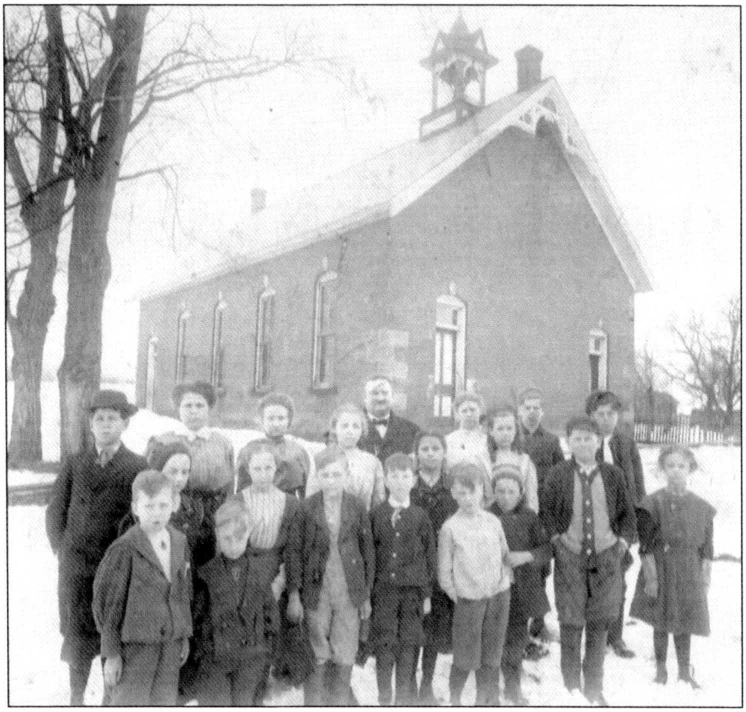

Before the newer schoolhouse was built in the 1920s (the one that most Parisians can remember), this brick structure stood just south of the Lutheran Church parsonage. It is similar to the one-room schoolhouse on the old Rohrer farm just east of the village on Lisbon Street. This is one of the earliest Paris school pictures dating from around the turn of the 20th century showing some Paris schoolchildren. (Courtesy of Audrey and Les Wade.)

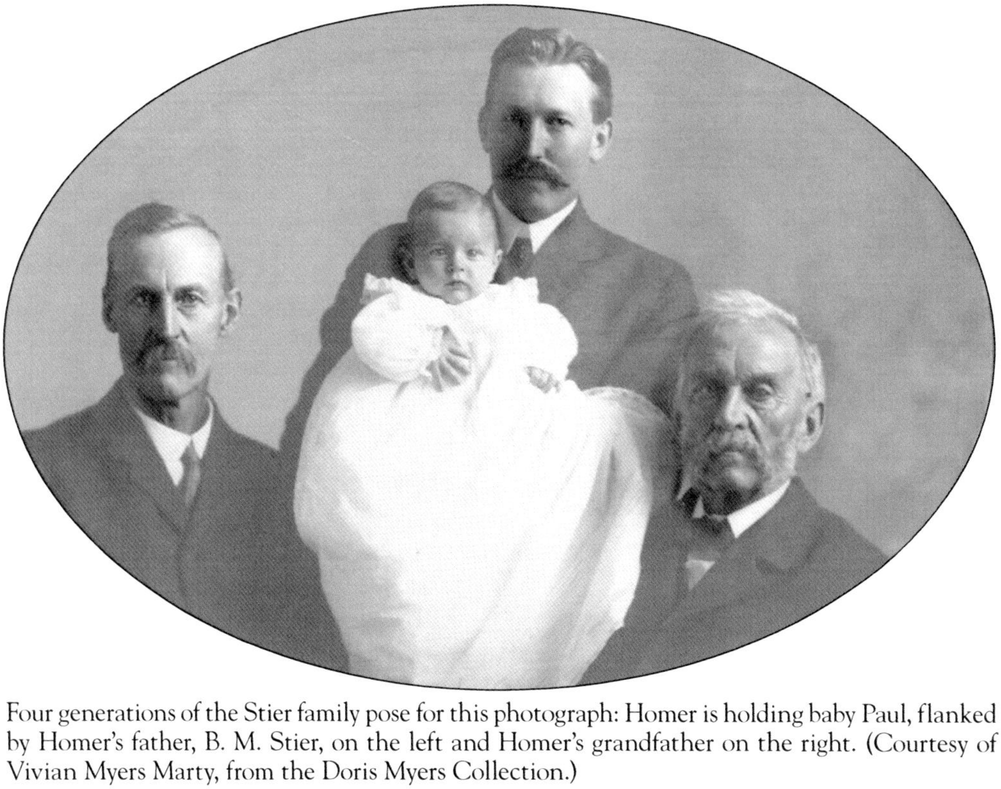

Four generations of the Stier family pose for this photograph: Homer is holding baby Paul, flanked by Homer's father, B. M. Stier, on the left and Homer's grandfather on the right. (Courtesy of Vivian Myers Marty, from the Doris Myers Collection.)

Fred Monhemius came to the United States from Holland with his wife Truus shortly after World War II. After living for a short time in Canada, they came to Paris and worked on the Arrowhead Orchard. Later they would buy the orchard from the Gotters and make it their livelihood. As a gifted horticulturist, Fred has given many people pleasure with his flowers and fruit. Here he poses on a wagon with peaches from the orchard and in front of the Arrowhead Apple Orchard truck. He later sold the establishment to Terry and Sharon Gram. (Courtesy of Fred and Truus Monhemius.)

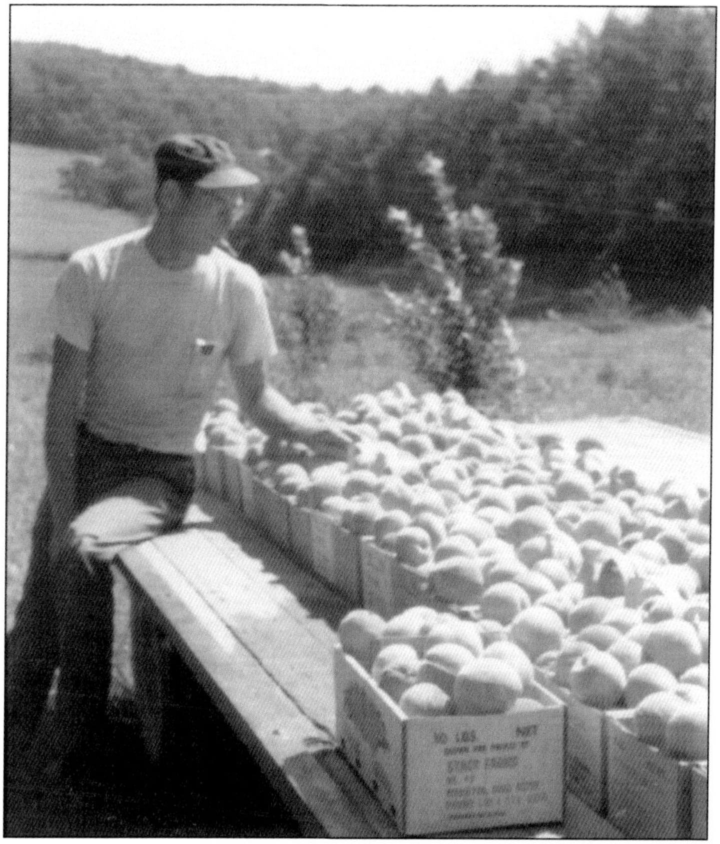

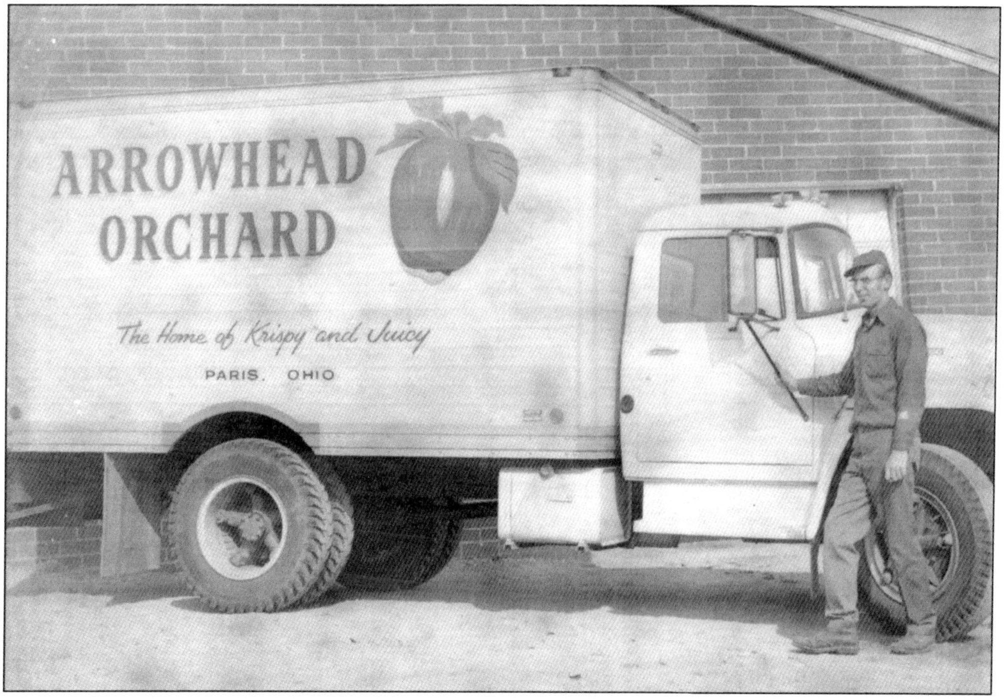

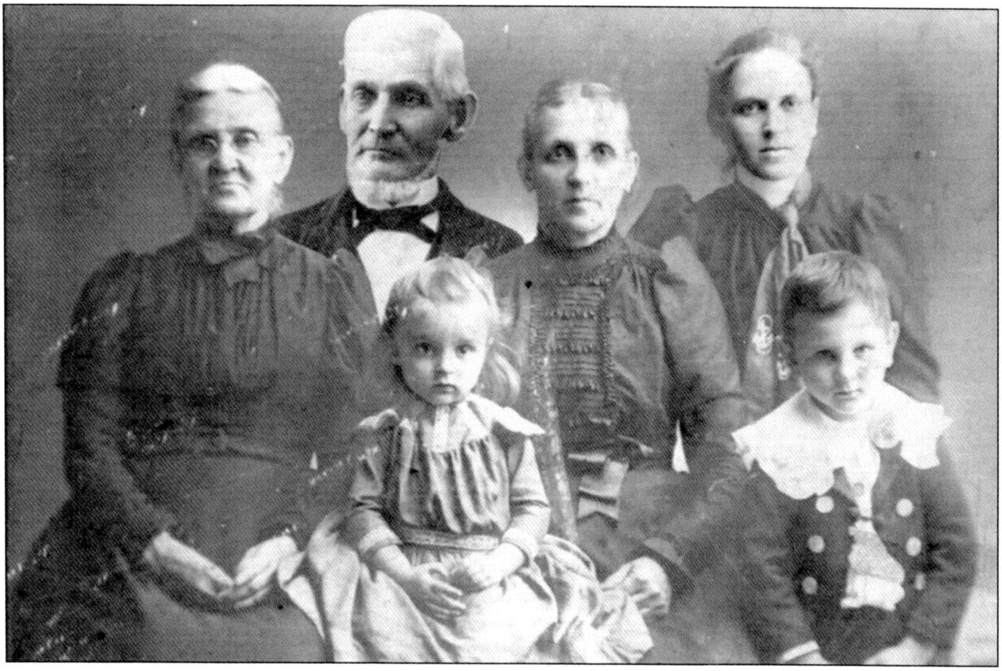

This family portrait consists of, from left to right, (front) Bessie Koontz and David Stuckey; (back) Catherine and John Meyers, Mary Ellen Meyers (Tobias Stuckey's wife), and Catherine "Katie" Starkey. There is no date on the photograph, but because John's head has been superimposed on the paper after the photograph was originally taken, it leaves room for speculation. (Courtesy of Kay Latham.)

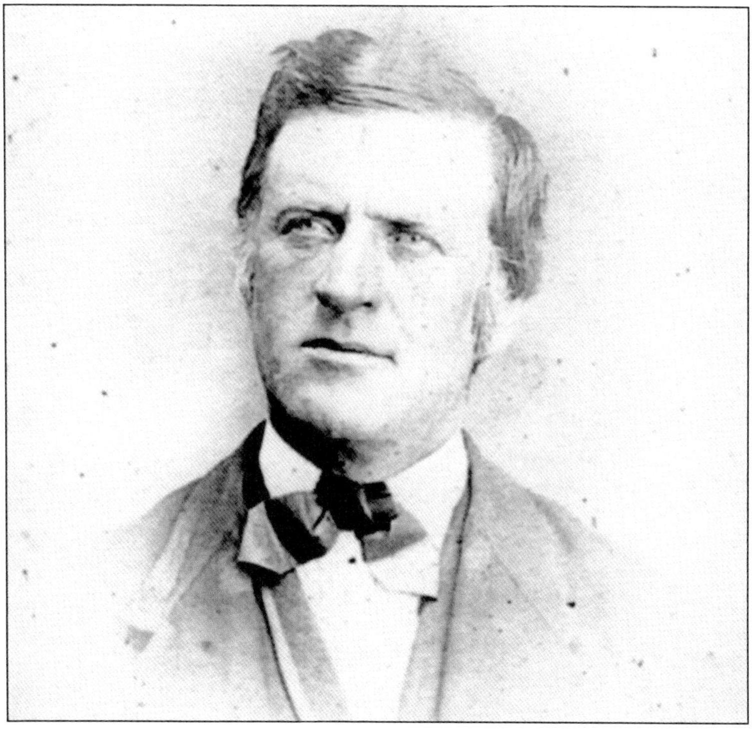

Valentine Mong (1828–1905) came to America from Germany. He met his end when he crossed railroad tracks with his carriage in Louisville and did not see the oncoming train. His gravestone stands close to the north wall of the Lutheran Church in Paris. (Courtesy of Steven Tibrea.)

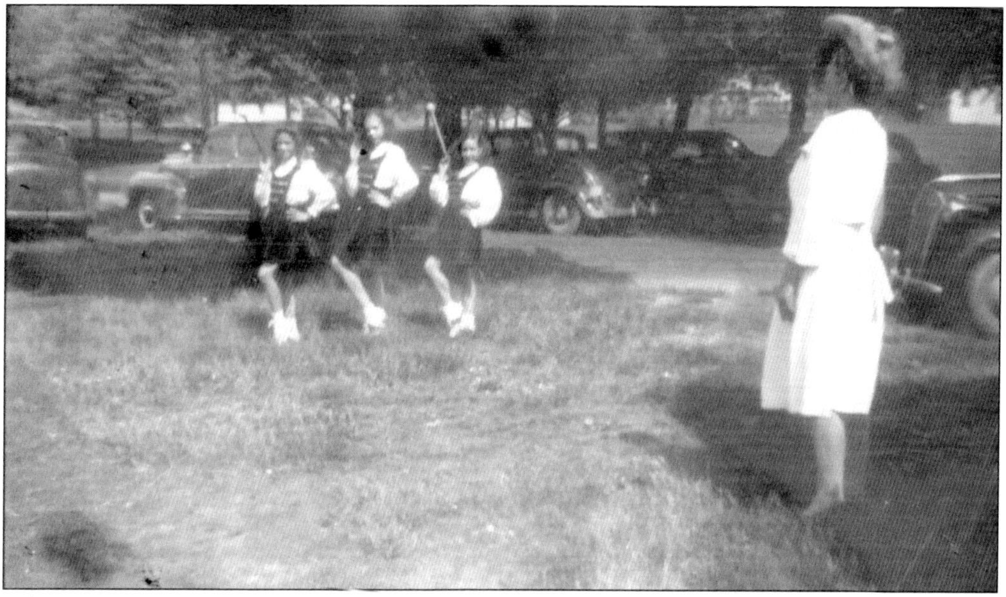

When Paris had a band, these girls served as majorettes. From left to right, they are Audrey (Gill) Wade, Janis Sefert, and Donna (Irwin) Monnot. Looking on is Maude Gill, mother of Audrey Wade. (Courtesy of Audrey and Les Wade.)

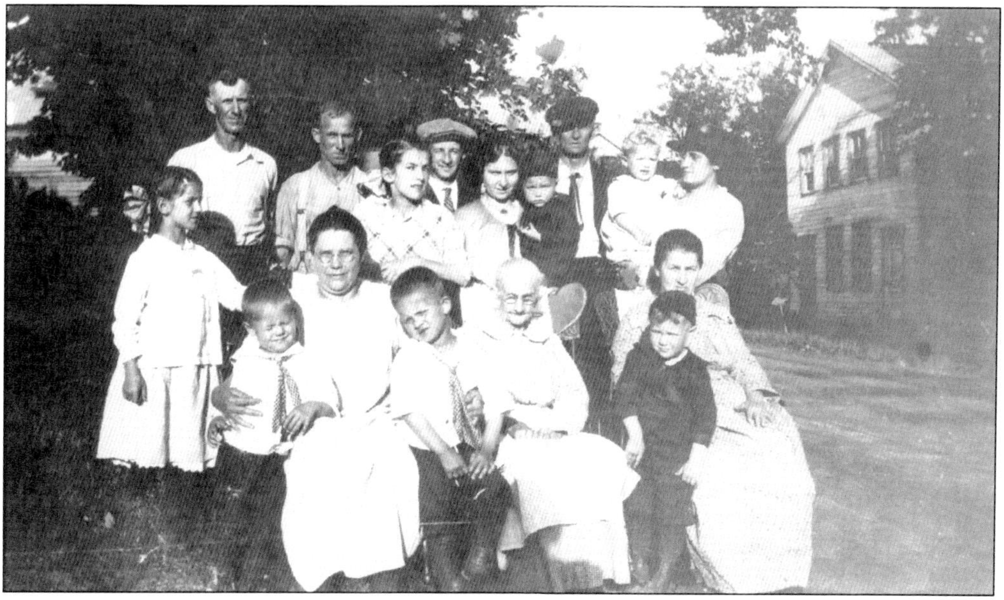

The Livelberger family members pictured here include Gayle Bowman, possibly Dean Livelsberger's mother, Gladys Livelsberger Harsh, possibly Gladys Harsh's son, Orlin Harsh (Gladys Harsh's husband), Dean Livelsberger, Demer Bowman, Charles Bowman, and Bernice (Livelsberger) Bowman. Notice the building off to the right of the people that no longer exists. (Courtesy of Linda K. Lilly.)

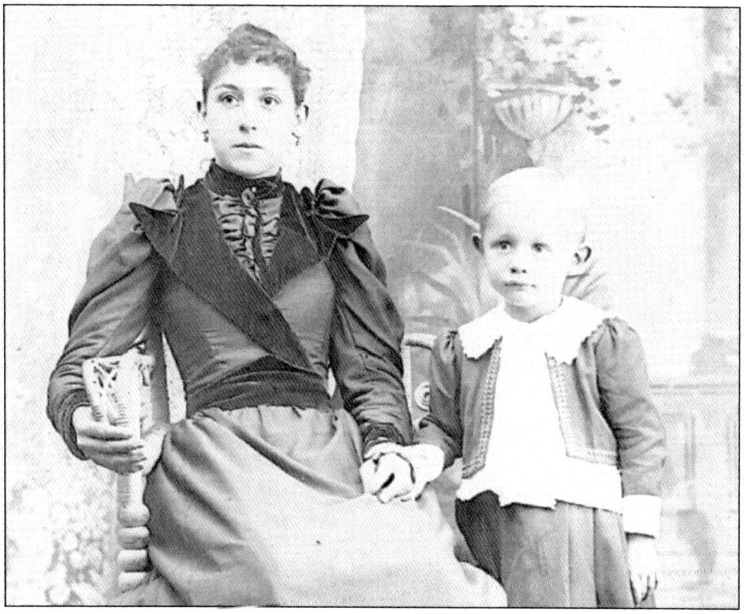

Emma Mong Thoma poses here with young J. Arthur Mong (1891–1979) at Reichard Photography Gallery in the city of Mount Union, now Alliance, Ohio. (Courtesy of Steven Tibrea.)

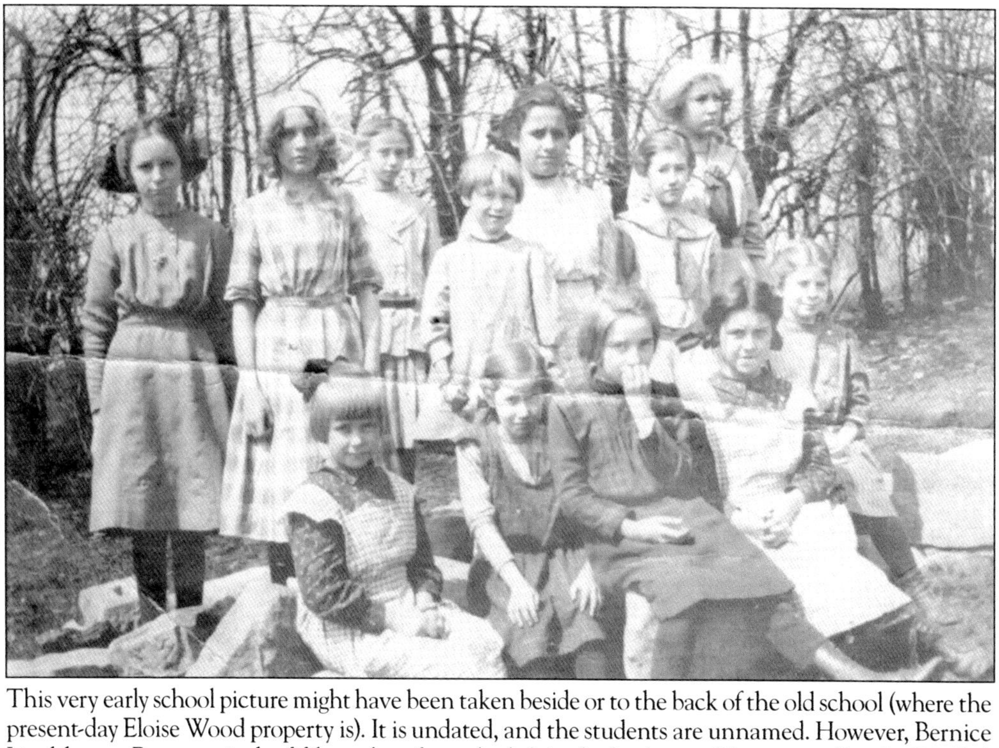

This very early school picture might have been taken beside or to the back of the old school (where the present-day Eloise Wood property is). It is undated, and the students are unnamed. However, Bernice Livelsberger Bowman is the fifth student from the left in the back row. (Courtesy of Linda K. Lilly.)

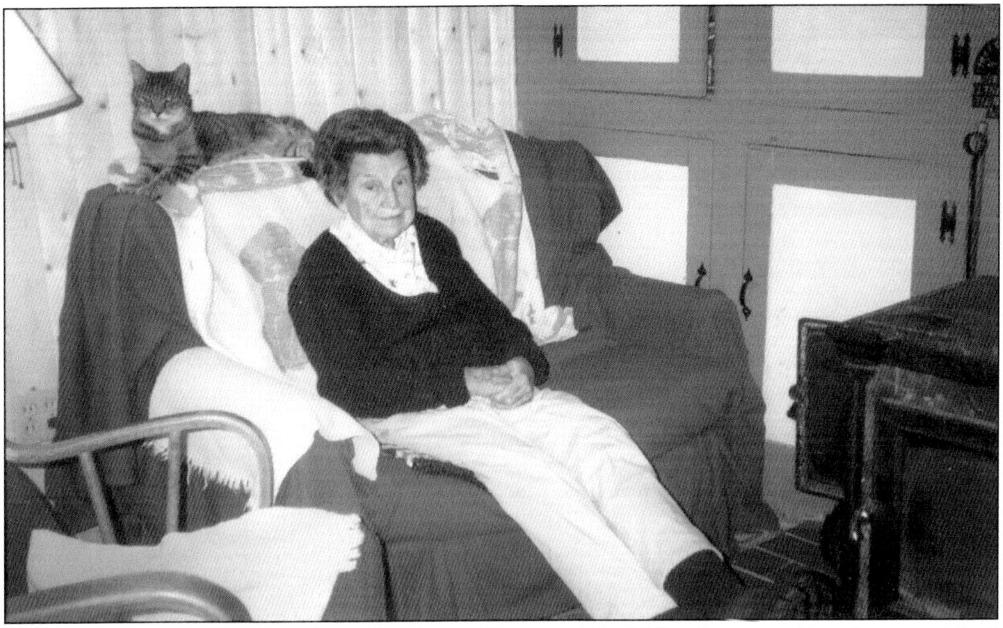

While they were not born and raised in Paris, Eloise and Paul Wood came to Paris because it had a lot to offer them as they raised their own children. They purchased the house that schoolteacher Mamie Stimmel once owned, which was surrounded by the beauties of nature. This seems very appropriate since Wood also taught in the Paris school. Today she is the oldest person living in the village. Her home remains warm not only with the heat from her wood-burning stove, but with the love she gives her friends and family. These matching pictures show Paul and Eloise as they could be seen sitting by their stove. The old cupboard behind the stove is original to the house, built in the early years of Paris's history. (Courtesy of Eloise Wood.)

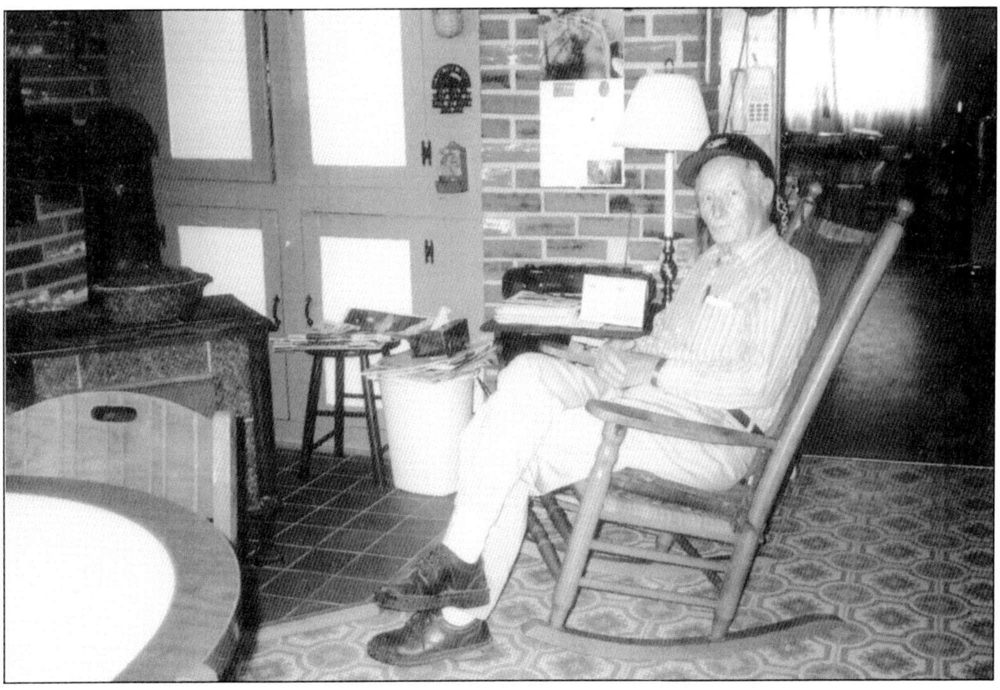

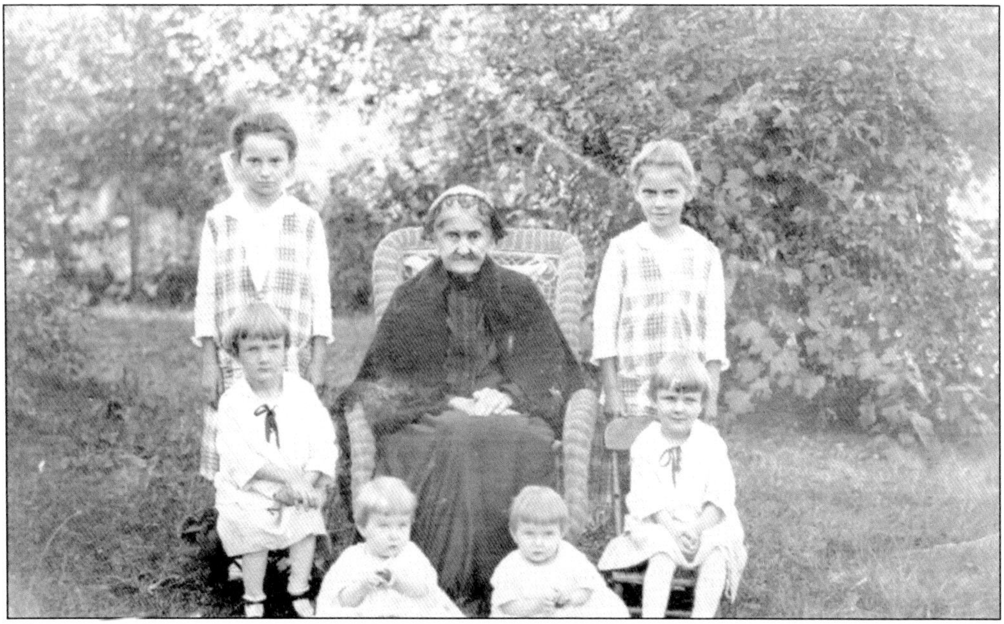

This photograph shows the three sets of twins of Mary Ellen Meyers, who is sitting in her rocking chair for this picture. The children are, from left to right, (first row) Burdella and Burdette; (second row) Beatrice and Bessie; (third row) Eva and Pauline.

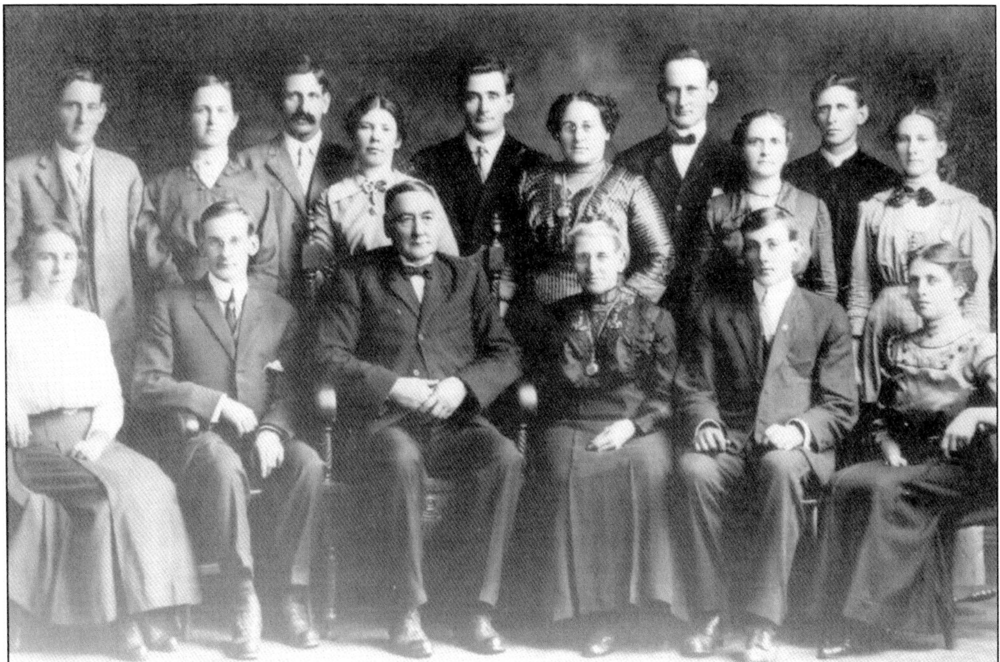

Henry Starkey was a wealthy but generous man. He built many homes in Canton for a living. Pictured here is Henry and his wife, Anna (middle, front row), surrounded by his children and their spouses, from left to right, as follows: (first row) Cecilia and Edward, Henry and Anna, and Harry and Anna; (second row) Bert and Perl, Will and Maggie Shaffer, Otto Lotz and Hulda Katura, Leonard and Katie, and David Stuckey and Viola. (Courtesy of Kay Latham.)

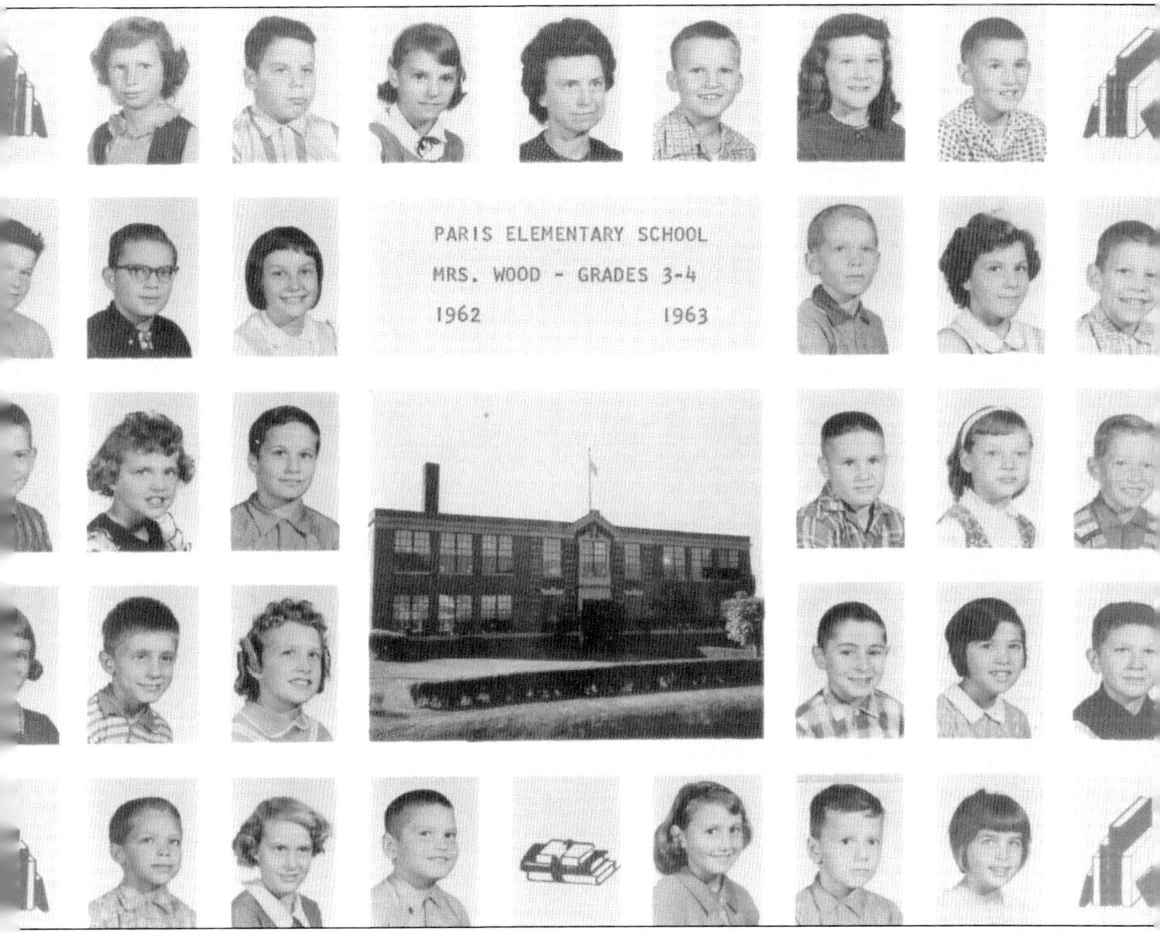

Shown here are the students in Eloise Wood's class during the 1962–1963 school year. Wood also taught vacation Bible school for many years and tutored for the Minerva School System when the Paris school was no longer in use. (Courtesy of Eloise Wood.)

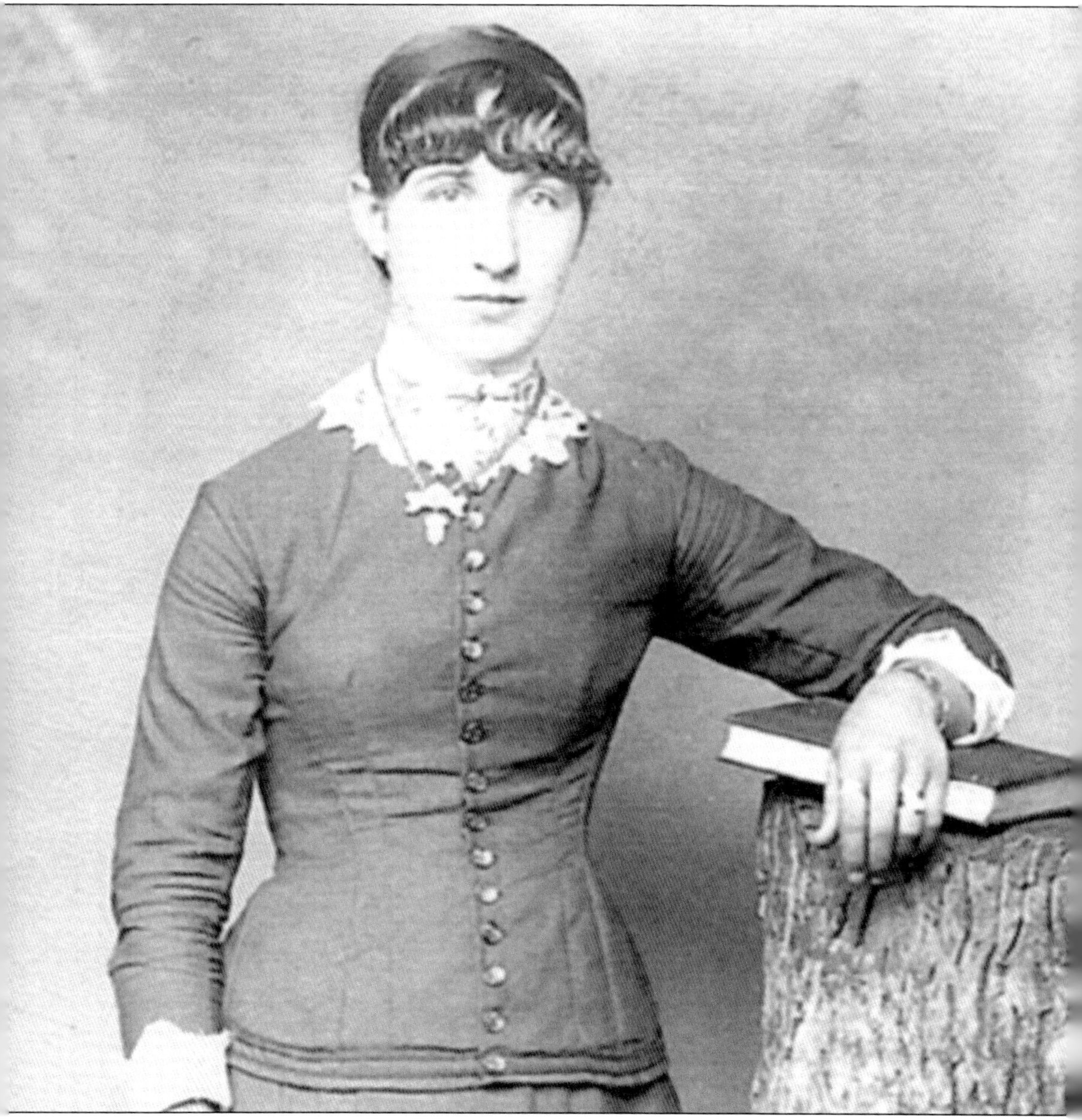

Clara Mong Walker, one of Valentine Mong's eight children with Susanna, must have been studious. In this picture she is seen with a book under her left arm. She married Jacob Walker of the historic Paris Walker family. (Courtesy of Steven Tibrea.)

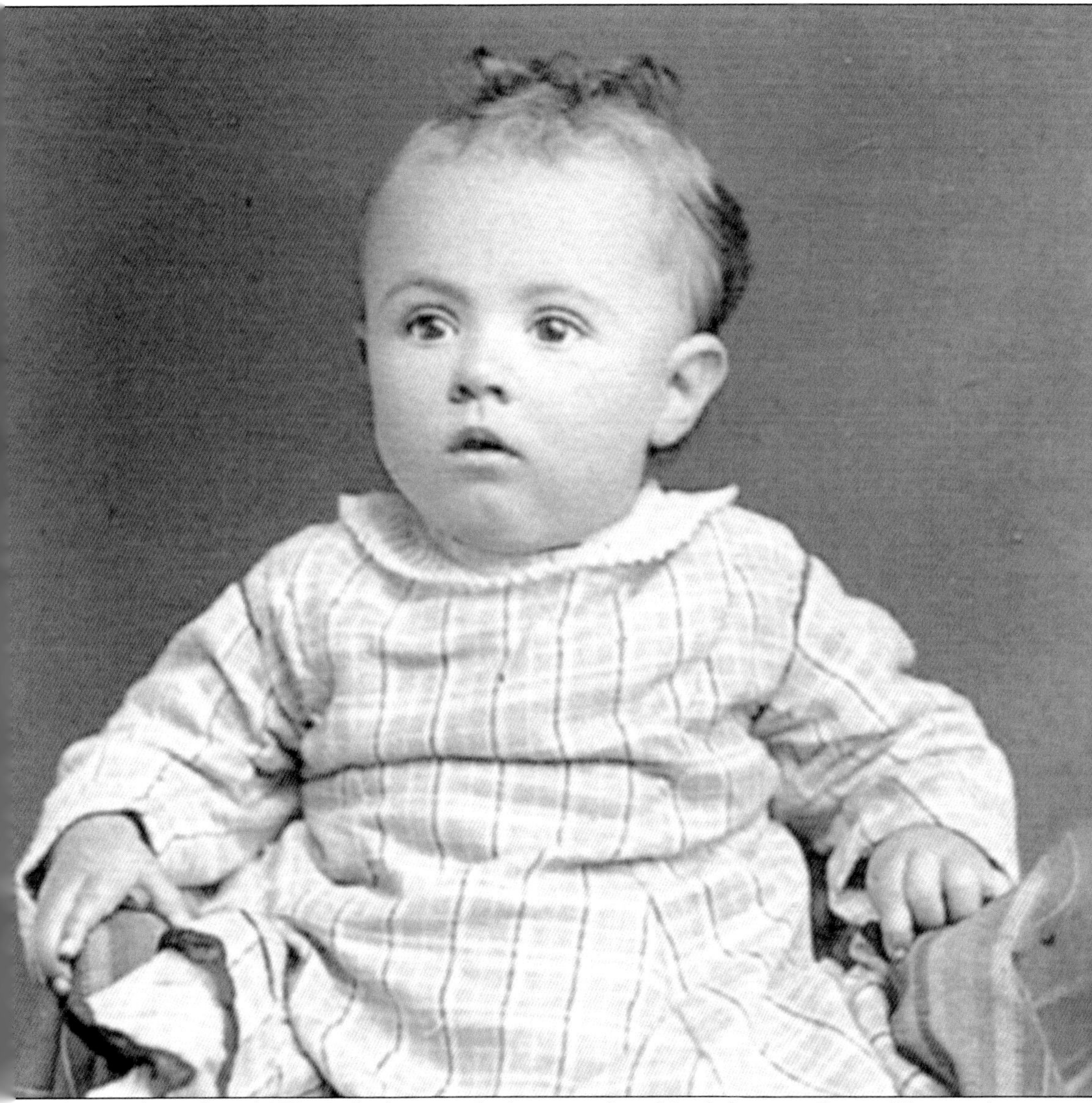

This is Clara Kleitz (1877–1916) photographed as an infant. Her father was George Kleitz and her mother was Emma Mong, daughter to Valentine and Susanna Mong. She married Adam Sponseller in 1899 and bore four children: Esther, Arthur, Harold, and Leland. The only two to live beyond childhood were Arthur and Leland. (Courtesy of Steven Tibrea.)

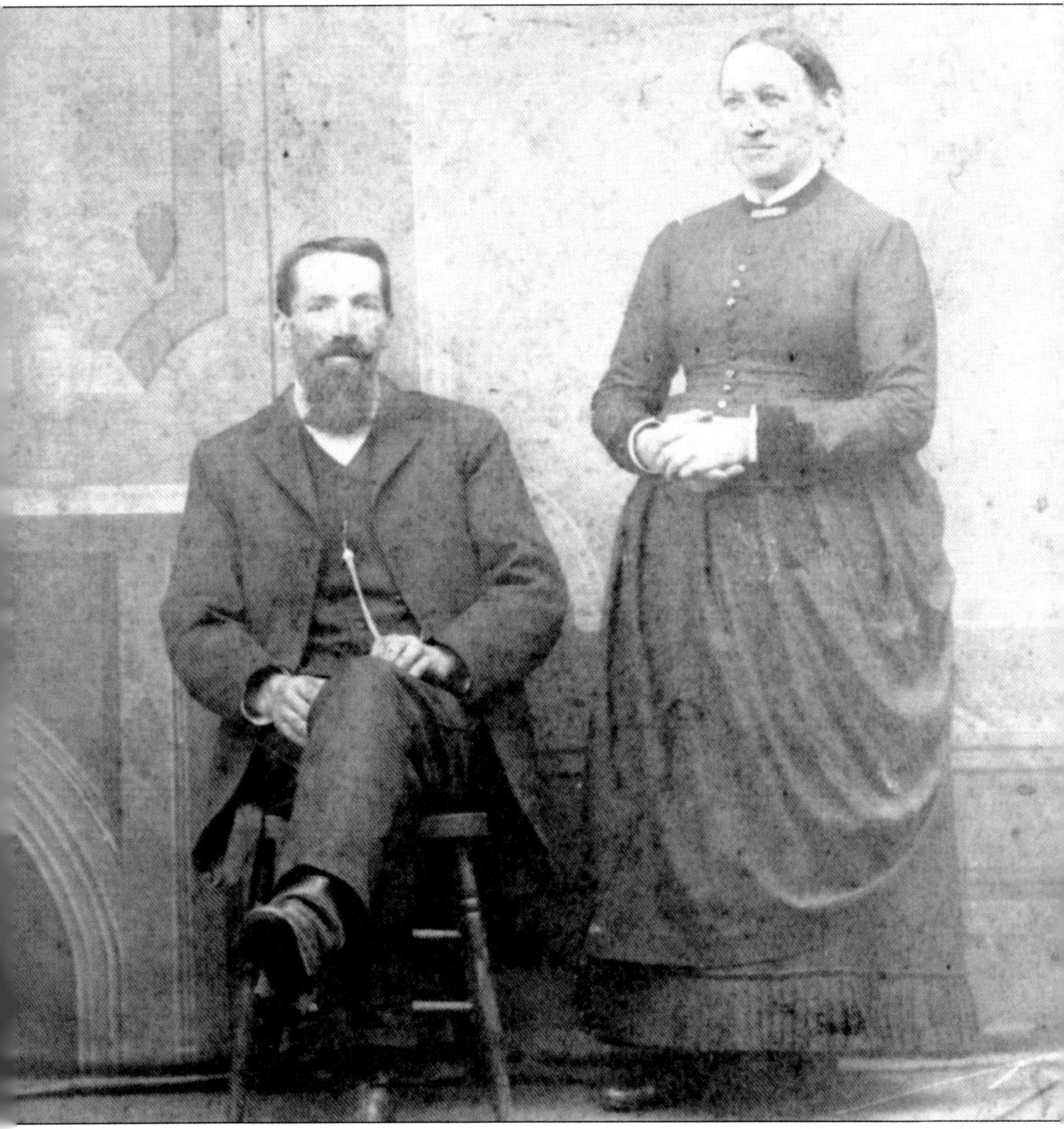

Emma Bush is shown here with her (unidentified) husband. Emma was possibly Bernice Livelsberger Bowman's sister. The original cabinet photograph has the stamp at the bottom, "C. F. Sell, Travelling Photographer." C. F. Sell was likely of the Paris Sell family, many of which are buried in the Paris cemetery. (Courtesy of Linda K. Lilly.)

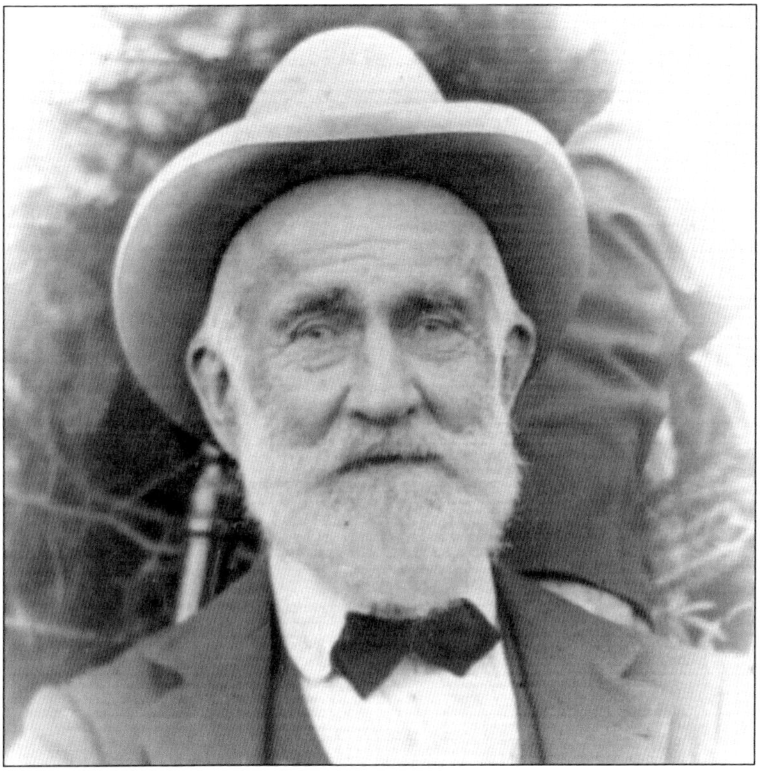

John Stimmel is the great-grandfather of Betty Speakman. Her father, the town mechanic, was likely named after the man shown here. (Courtesy of Betty Speakman.)

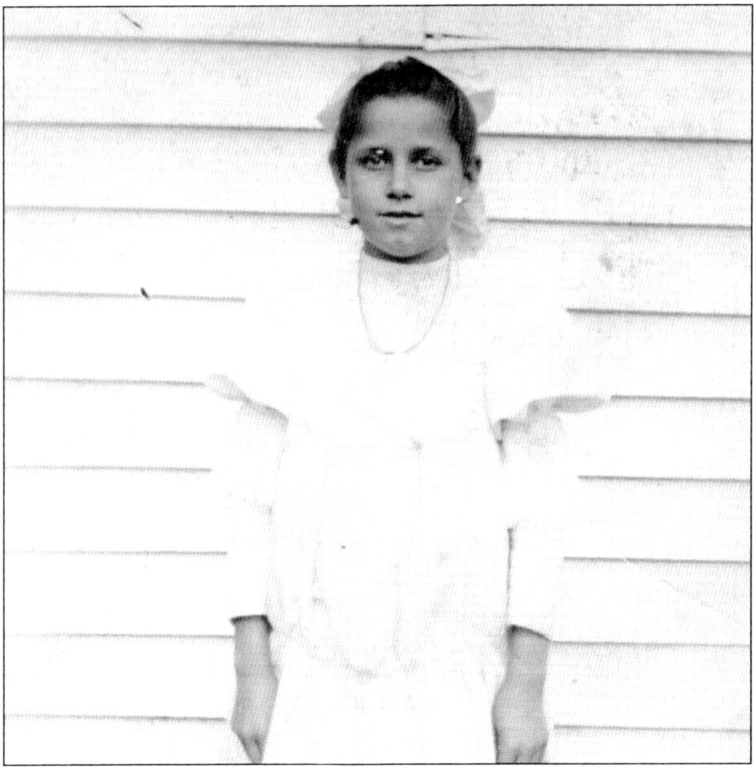

Bernice Livelsberger poses in front of the Livelsberger home next to the Lutheran parsonage. She married a Bowman. (Courtesy of Linda K. Lilly.)

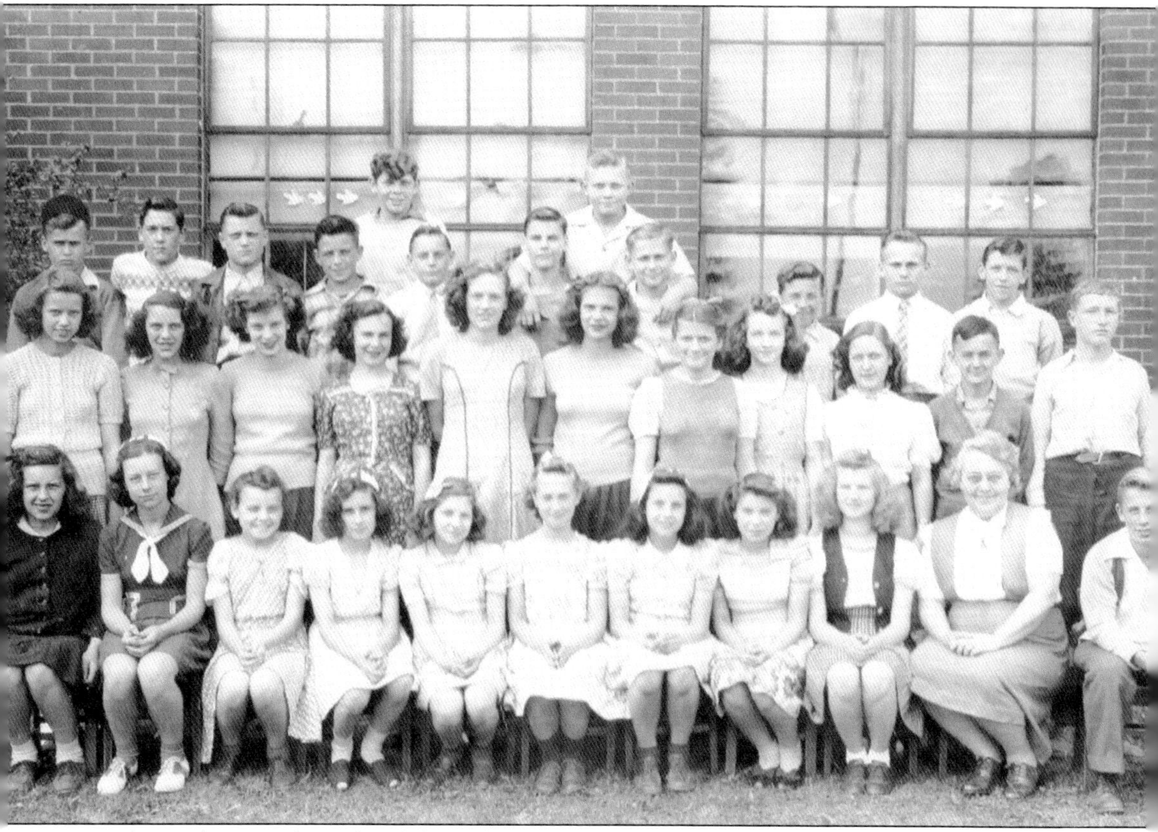

The sixth, seventh, and eighth grades of the Paris School came together for this picture. The students, from left to right, are (first row) Doris Rusher, Ann Speakman, Evelyn Clapper, Nancy Riggle, Bonni Denny, Carolyn Starkey, June Dourm, Patty Neighbor, Ruth Ann Snyder, teacher Mamie Stimmel, and Dick Sheatsley; (second row) Tom Bush, Jack Clark, Harry Coleman, Gene Anthony, Dick Dourm, Rodger Bowman, Ralph Snyder, Herbert Clapper, Paul Bush, and Richard Denny; (third row) Barbara (Kenny) Wise, Audrey (Gill) Wade, Mona Sefert, Helen Touvell, Helen Clark, Janis Sefert, Peggy Smith, Shirley Grunder, Donna (Irwin) Monnot, Earl Stuckey, and Bill Myers; (fourth row) Jim Servey and Gordon Dewey. (Courtesy of Audrey and Les Wade.)

Two

Buildings and Landscapes

It is no secret that the Kinemond house, next to the village cemetery, is possibly the oldest surviving structure. Underneath its painted shingles is an early log structure, reminiscent of the pioneer lifestyle. This house also documents the lineage of a property in continuous use by a single family.

The old stagecoach (northeast corner of the square) was owned by Samuel Unkefer, who could "spin a good yarn and furnish a square meal," which "gave his house and the town a widespread reputation" (Danner, 67). On the opposite (southeast) corner of the street stood an old hotel building, which was sitting vacant for many years. The original owner believed that Paris needed a sixth hotel but defected to Steubenville; it later became a dry goods store and then a farm implement factory. Andy Bair, the oldest village person in 1922, claimed, "The bricks are so old they are not worth anything, and shucks, it costs too much to tear down a building." But eventually it did meet its demise.

Eloise Wood lives in the Mamie Stimmel house, built in the earliest years of the 1800s. The Kintner Store and post office, once a tavern (southwest corner of the square), is likely the earliest preserved business building extant. The Meiser Store, located diagonally from Kintner's, is now just a worn shell of what it once was: a hardware and general store and later a short-lived holiness Bible college.

Many people still lament that the Lutherans tore the third Paris School (1928) down for parking space. Before that there was a large one-room schoolhouse that sat on the same lot, similar to Centerville School, Creek School, and the Thurman Rohrer School.

The Meister House (Robertville Road) is historically significant as it was part of the Underground Railroad. The Richard Hudy House is also very early and well preserved. But the square of the village itself has been the most significant place in terms of community. Up until approximately 80 years ago, there was a small white gazebo, crowned with a tall white martin house, and later a new community pavilion (1992).

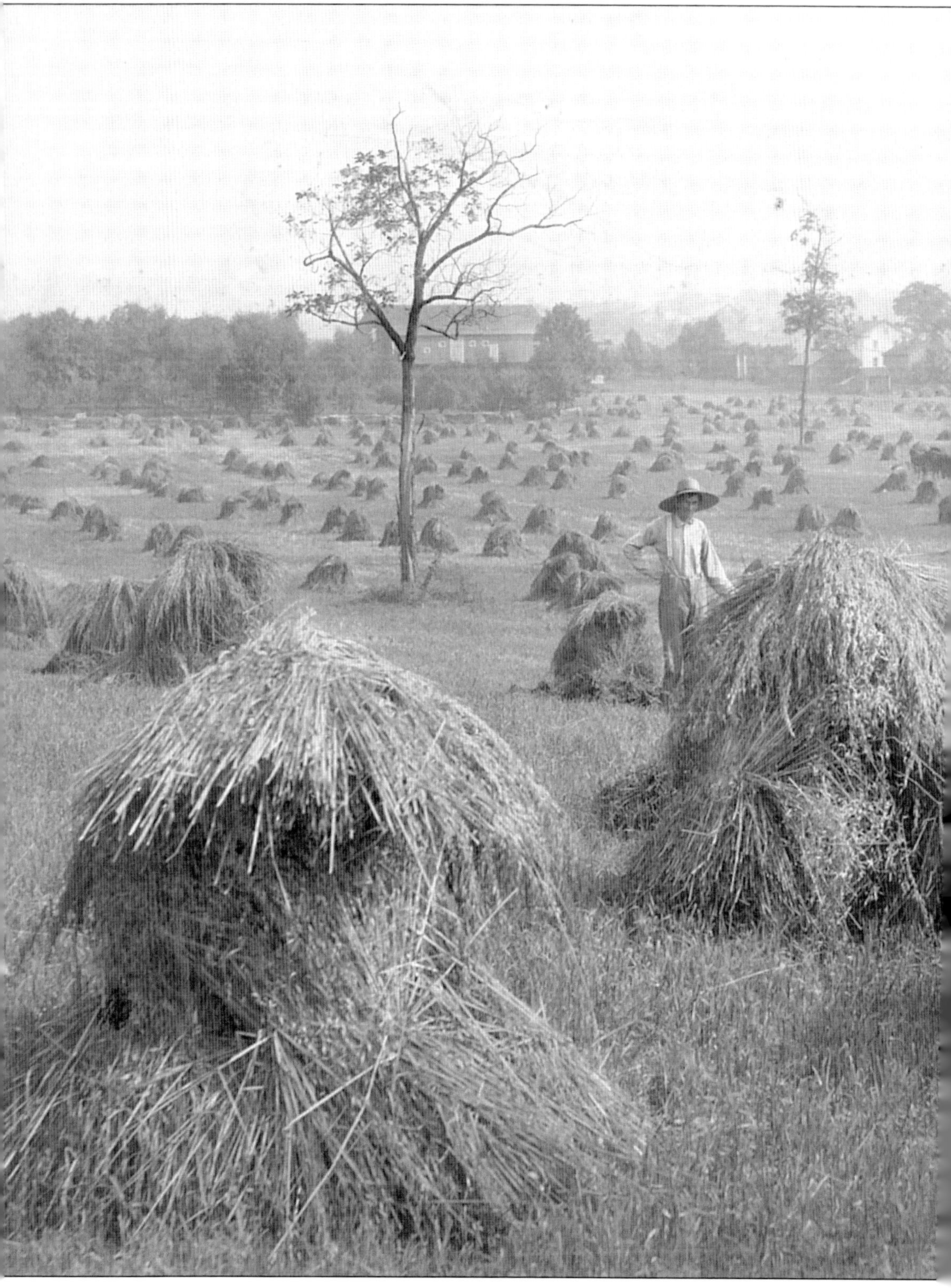

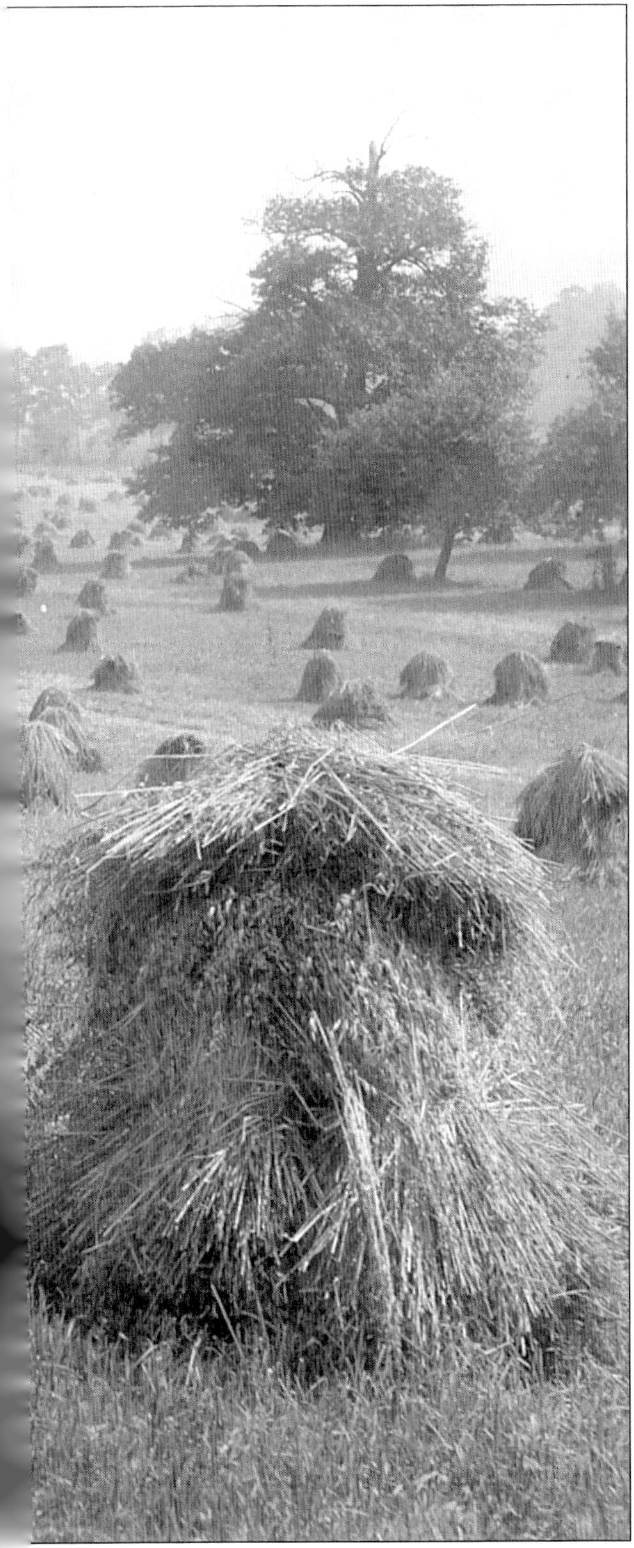

Edward "Ed" Lutz was one of the grandchildren of Abraham Lutz, who settled in Ohio in the first half of the 19th century. Even though Ed did not live in Paris or Paris Township, he and his ancestors were active in the Lutheran parish at Paris, and they would travel the short way up the road to Paris in order to do most of their business. This *c.* 1870 picture is a reminder that northeastern Ohio used to be an agricultural center in America. In the background, beyond the shocks, one can see the house (still extant), many small outbuildings, and a bank barn. The house and barn are still visible on Paris Avenue; the barn now has an addition ("straw shed") protruding toward the south and is painted white. (Courtesy of Charlene and Junior Grimminger.)

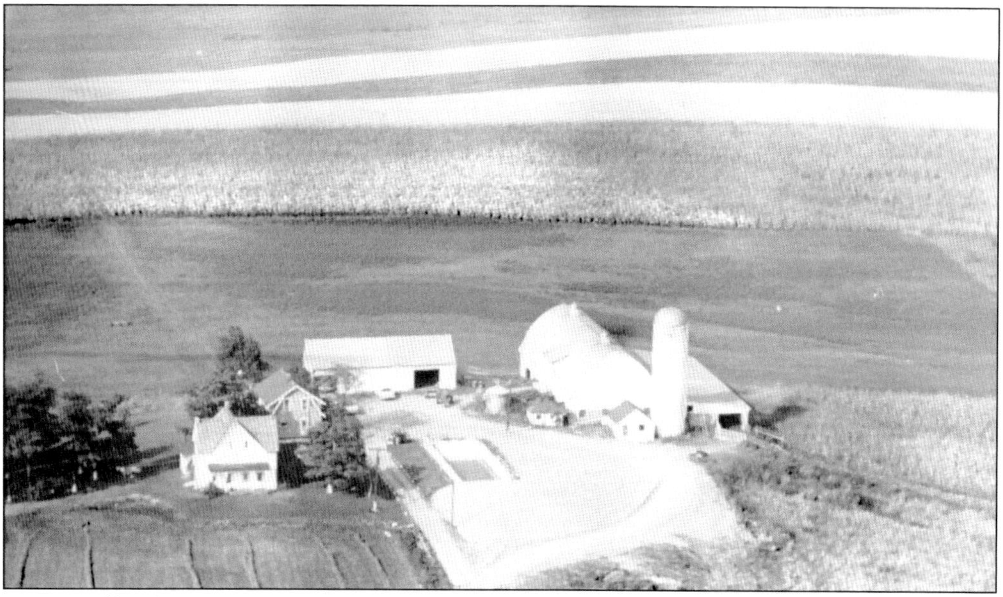

George Julliard was a native of France. In 1854, he purchased this farm just one mile west of the village on Lisbon Street. After his death, his son George A. took over the farm operation in 1876. Known by locals for many years as the Julliard farm, this property was owned for a short time by Harry Starkey, but he lost it. In 1940, Lerane Grimminger Sr. bought it to have a dairy operation. He farmed it with his son Lerane Grimminger Jr. until his son assumed full responsibility of the operation. The village post office was located for many years in the Kintner Store just west of the pavilion on the square. The c. 1950 image below shows the east doorway, a telephone booth, and the worn threshold stone at the foot of several of the long doors of the building. (Courtesy of Daniel Grimminger.)

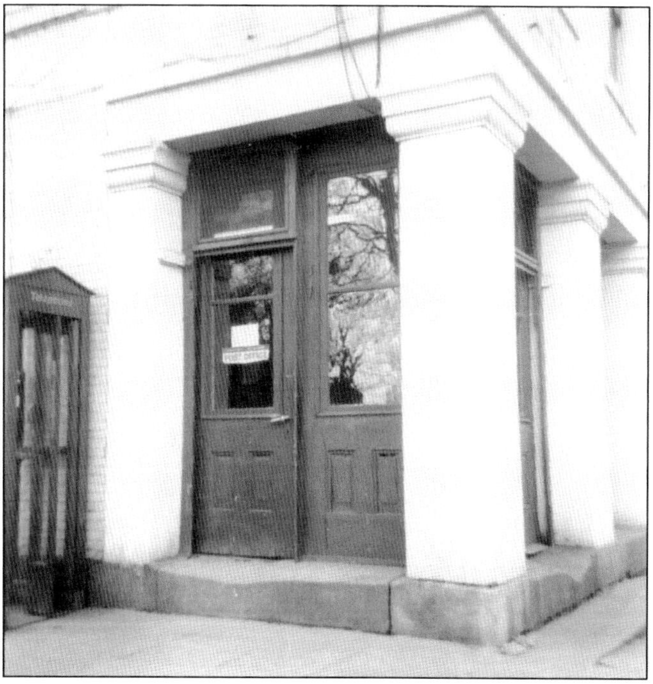

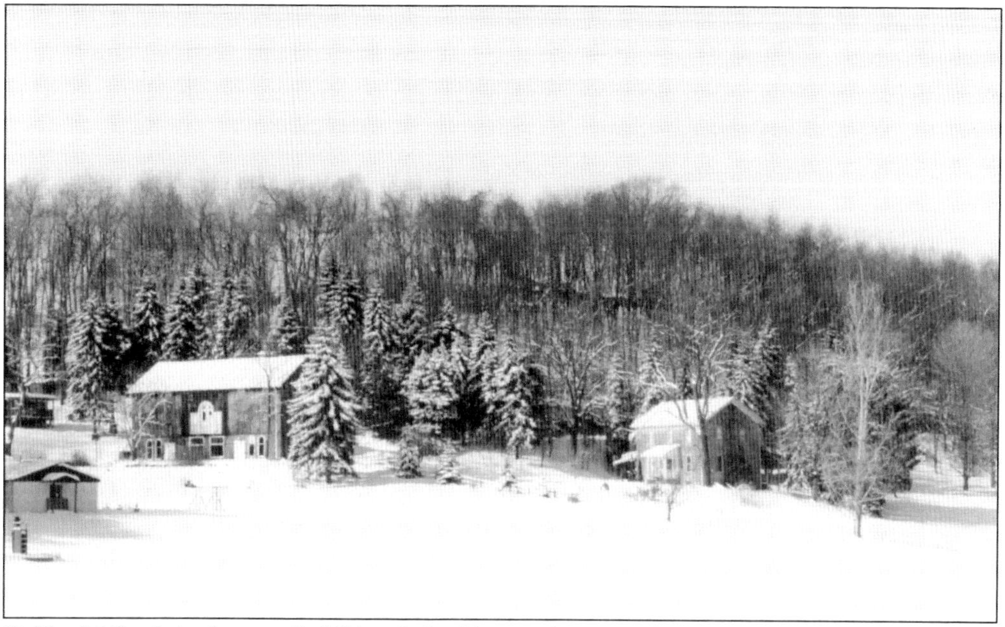

Hidden Valley Lake (once called "Vista Lakes" by some) is a very historic place. The old stone house is the oldest part of the property. Among the wildlife and beautiful foliage are a campground and a barn, where many people have gathered for church events and family camping trips. Originally owned by John Betz (1864–1915), Don Cole purchased the property with the dream of turning it into a first-rate resort. It was Cole who bought the white doors and balcony that William McKinley used when he gave his presidential acceptance speech. Cole installed them on his barn. Later Robert (Bob) Smith owned the property (1963–1976), and Dale and Ida Cumpson also owned the place (1976–1988). After a period of four more owners (1988–1992), Ruth and Bob Fisher purchased the grounds in 1992. (Courtesy of Bob and Ruth Fisher.)

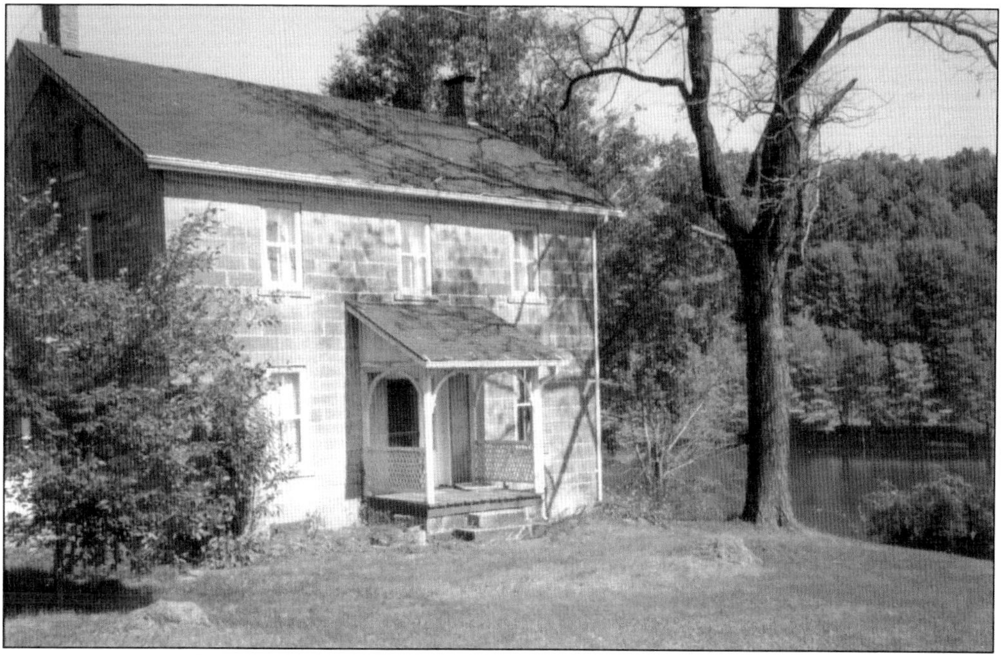

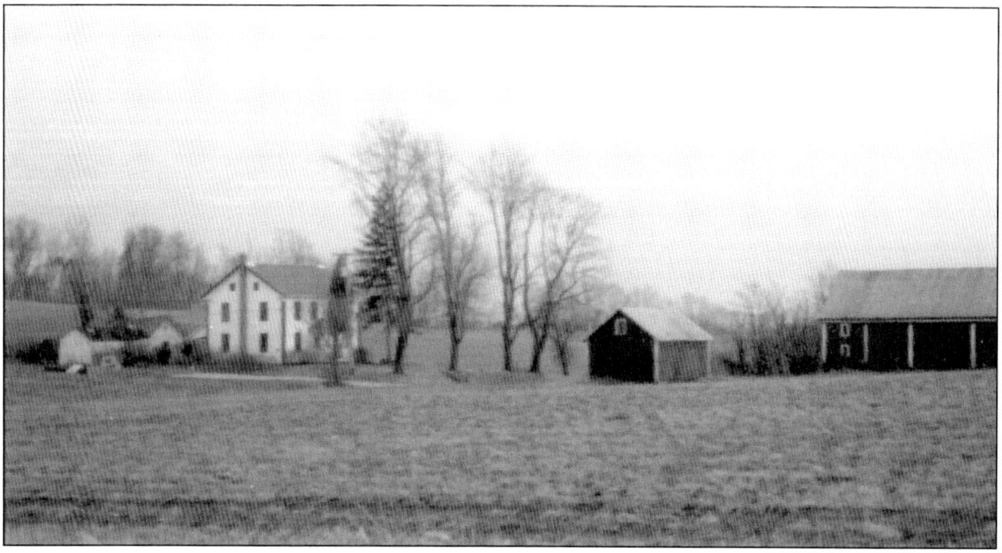

The Burget farm ran along both sides of Paris Avenue. Until it was parceled out at a public auction, it was one of the only farms around Paris to remain in one family for 150 years. Up until the last living Burget needed in-home health care in the late 1990s, the house had no running water or electricity. In the evening, one could drive past the house and only see the flicker of a candle in the back room. The outbuildings included an outhouse and original summerhouse where the summer cooking and canning would be accomplished. A quaint fruit orchard sat on a mound beyond the summer house shown in the picture above. Further, the bank barn on the far right of the picture is one of the larger historic barns in the area, and it originally bore the date 1859 on its white trim. (Courtesy of Daniel Grimminger.)

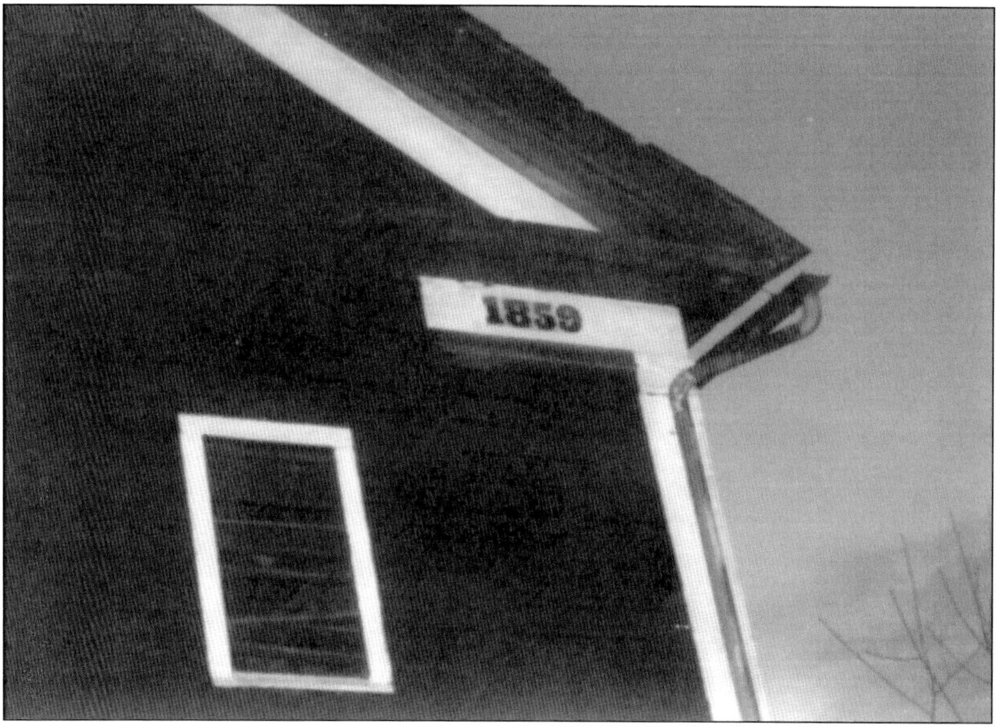

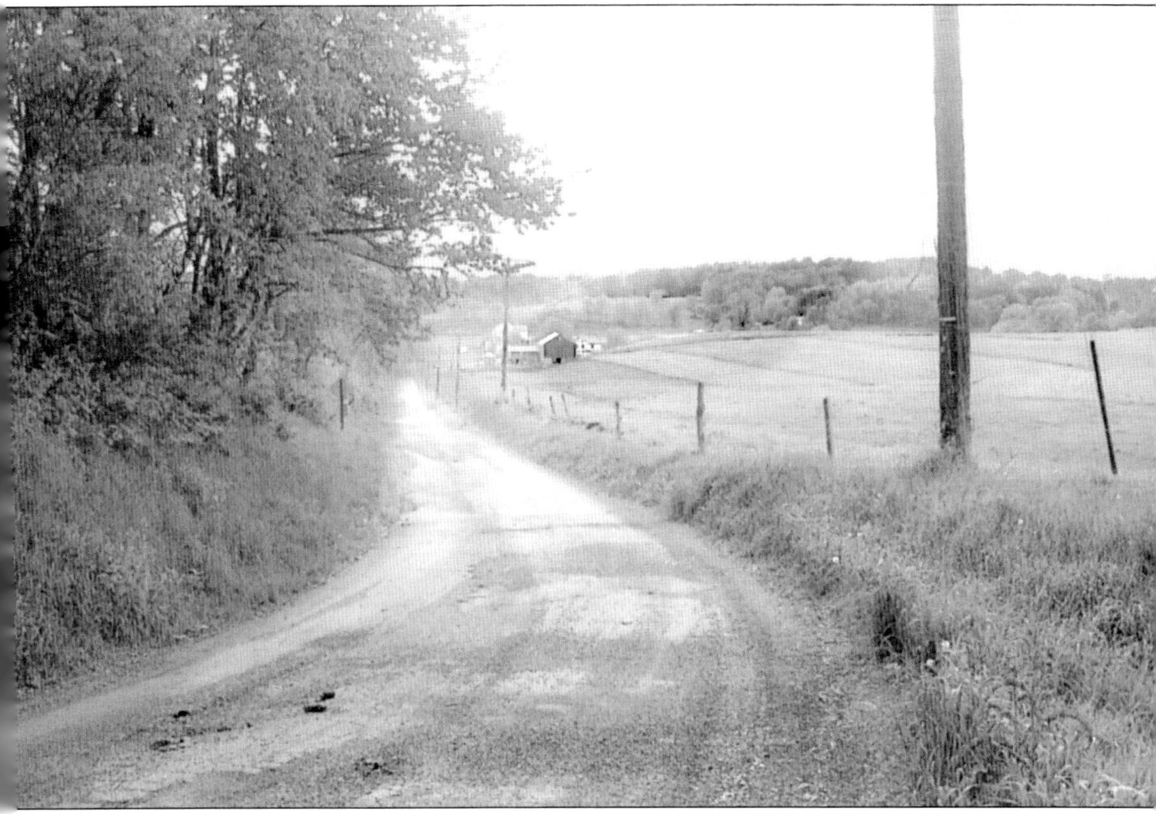

Back on the old dirt road towards Joel Snyder's farm is a beautiful sprawling landscape green with crops. The barn in the distance once housed a harness shop in its one wing. Behind the photographer on the curve is where the butcher shop was in the earliest years of the 1900s and further back into the village the old feed mill. Now that there is a modern bypass to the upper part of Paris Avenue, the old dirt road is rarely used by locals. (Courtesy of Daniel Grimminger.)

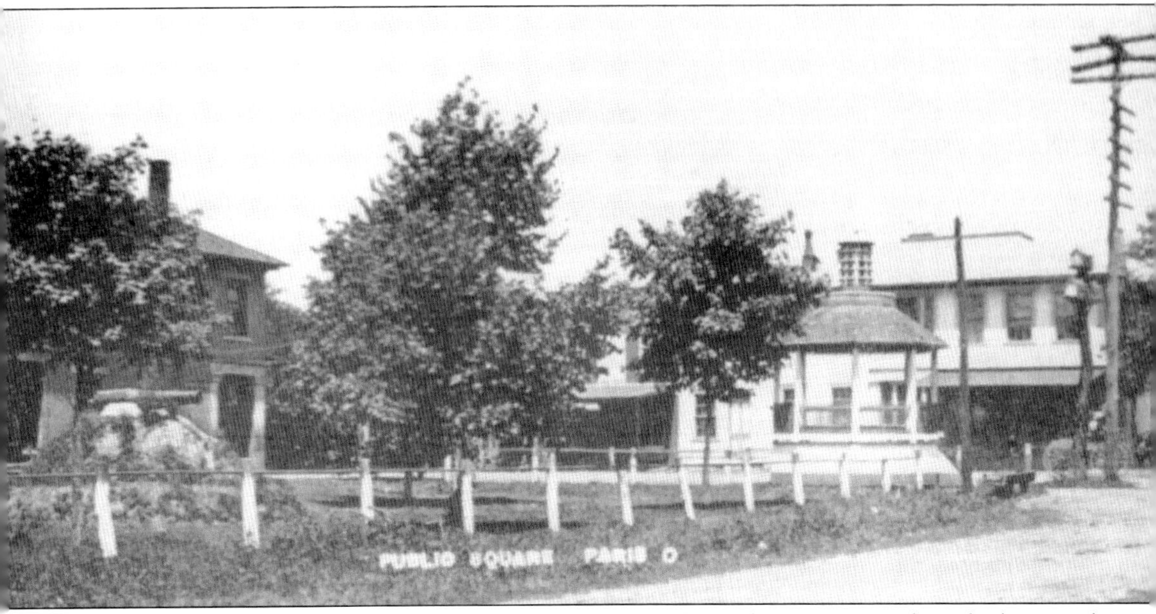

This view of the square looking north is very different from what one sees today. The horse rails and the cannon perched on the mound are two noticeable differences. The old Emma Lutz property (now owned by the United Church of Christ) is barely visible along the north side of Lisbon Street. Instead of having an exposed water pump where more recent village kids have stopped for a drink, there is a trough (and a pump?) where the horses could be watered. At the time of this picture, shutters on houses must not have been en vogue. (Courtesy of Daniel Grimminger.)

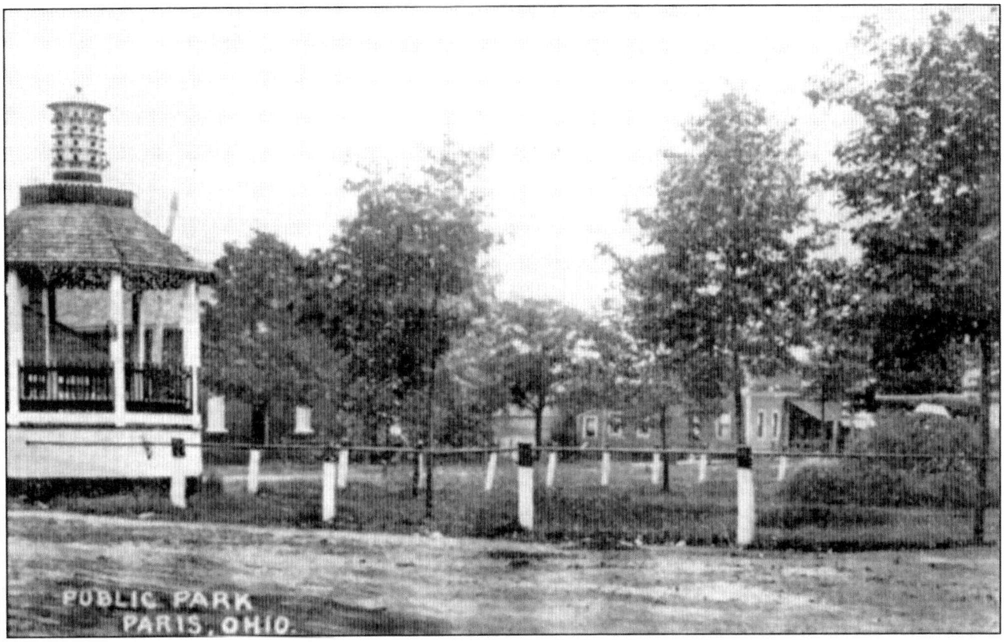

Looking southeast through the square around 1900, one could see the old Emory Chapel before its belfry was added. South of that building was the old post office before it moved to the Kintner Store. Later this post office/store would become Meese's Meat Market where many farmers had their animals slaughtered. The 1985 image below shows the square looking south. Unlike the pavilion that replaced this one, the edifice in this photograph ran east and west. (Courtesy of Daniel Grimminger.)

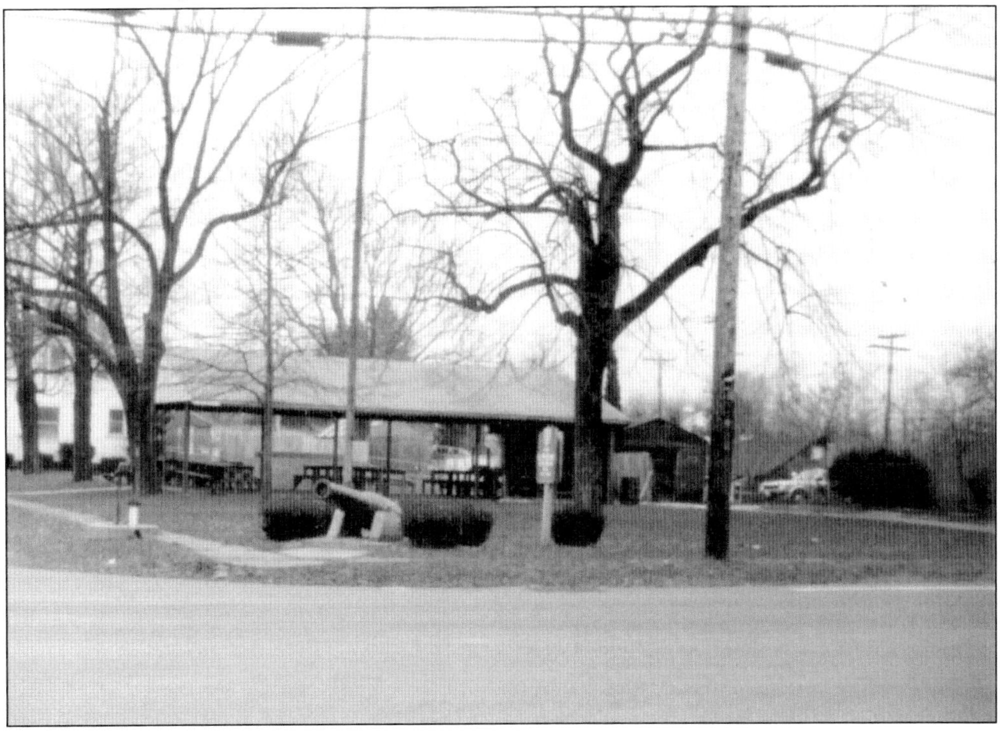

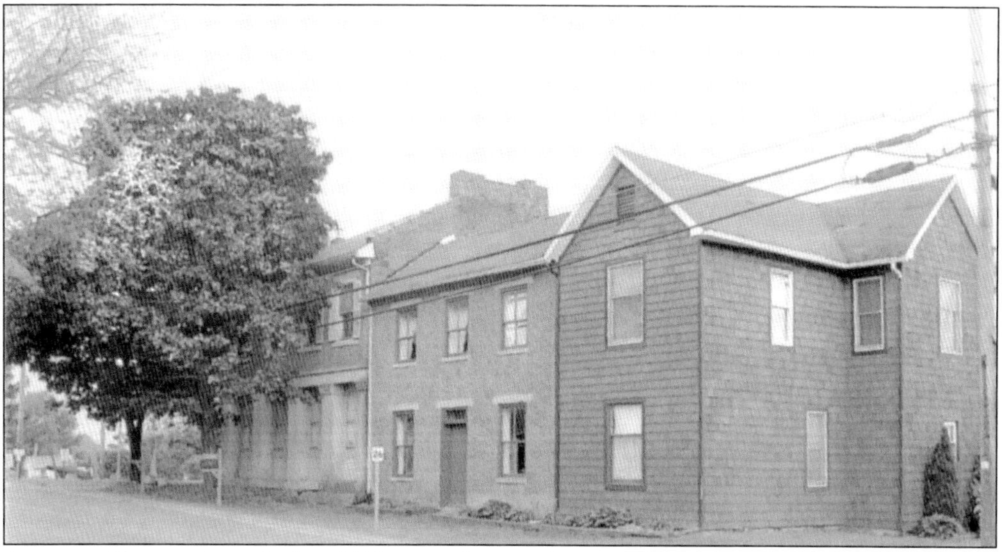

On part of lot no. 1 stands the old Kintner Store and Post Office most recently owned by Betty Onyett. It was in the Kintner Store where people would come to buy dry goods, collect their mail, and learn the latest news. According to Emogene Wartluft, there was a stove that stood along the east wall and customers would huddle around it in the wintertime to stay warm and exchange information. The candy counter was also popular. Connected to Kintner's to the west was the McMacken residence where Hazel McMacken operated an old-folks home. In the back of the Kintner home is the original kitchen with a large fireplace and period wallpaper. The built-in red cupboard is a beautiful example of early Paris craftsmanship. (Courtesy of Daniel Grimminger.)

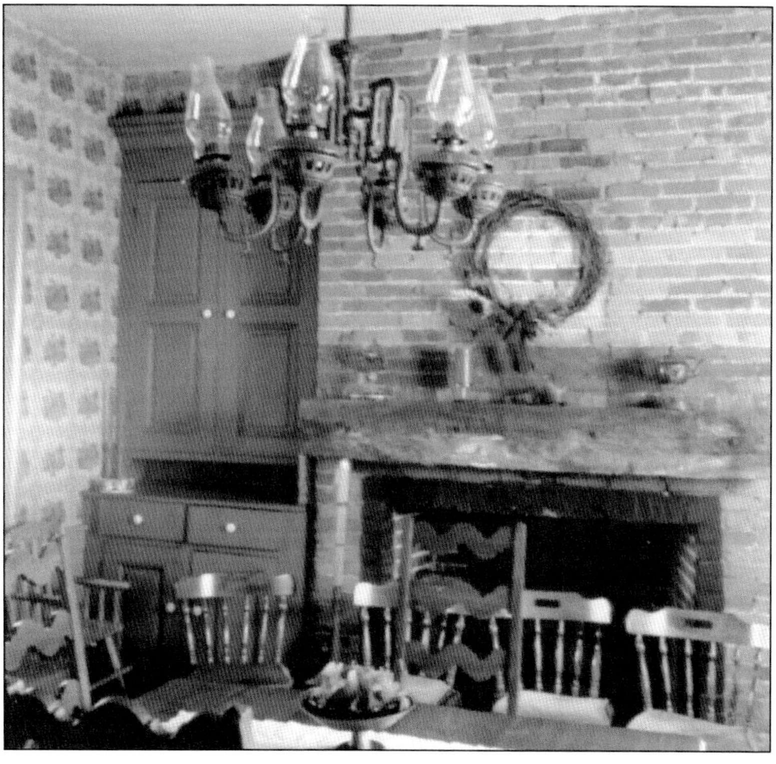

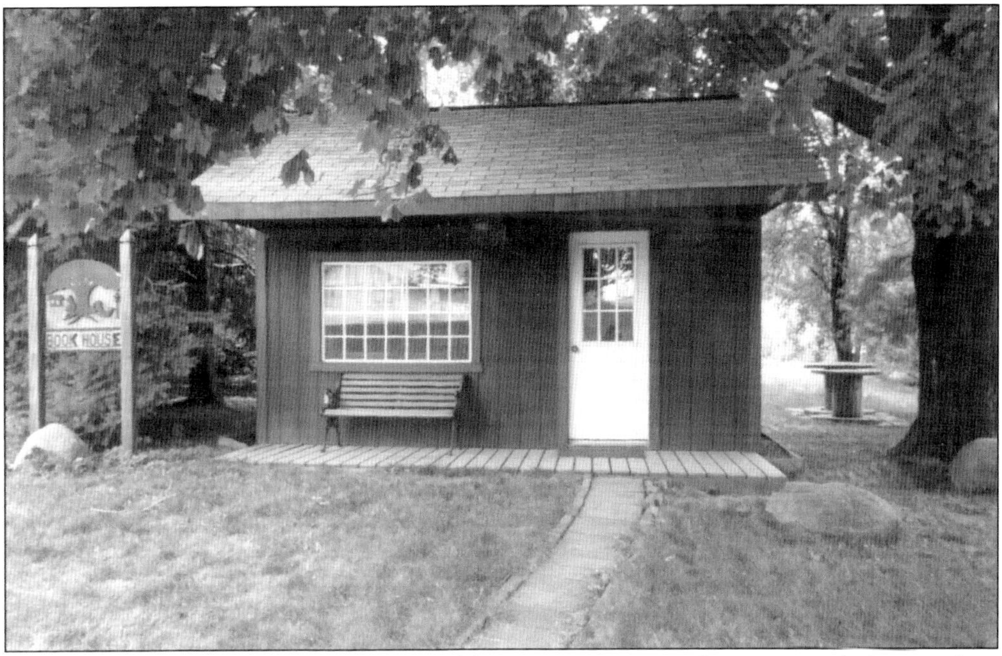

Eloise Wood, who taught in the Paris School for many years, wanted to create a wholesome place for children to learn in the village. In the 1990s, she built the Paris Book House for this purpose and accepted donated books to start a small library there. The local public library book mobile also came regularly to supply the children with books. (Courtesy of Daniel Grimminger.)

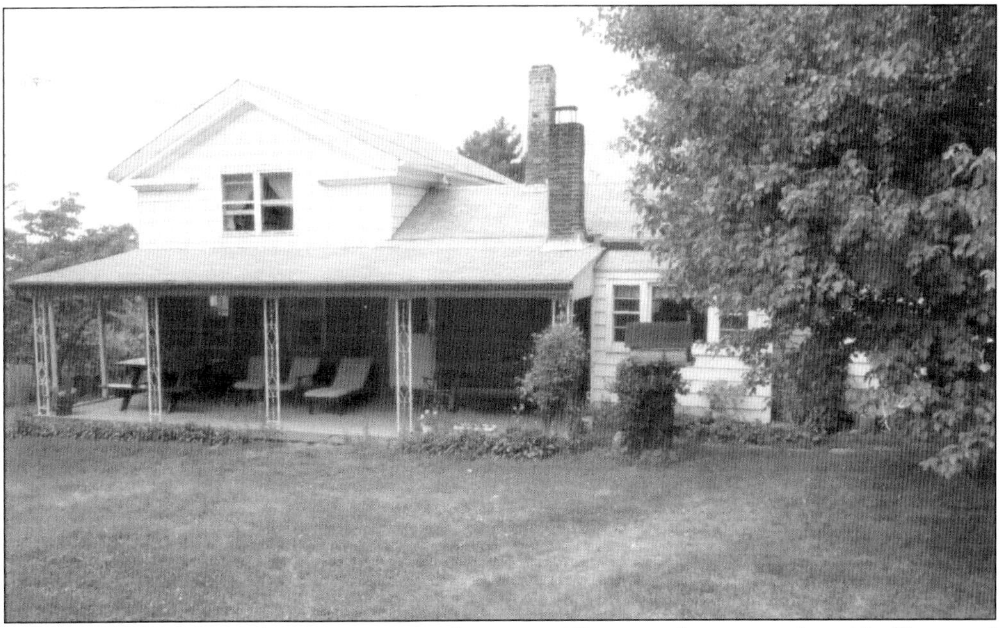

"Woodhaven" was once the Mamie Stimmel property. The grounds were purchased by Eloise and Paul Wood when they came to Paris. One can never leave Woodhaven without Eloise sharing flowers or fruit to nourish the body and soul. Pictured here is the house from the back at Woodhaven. Under the modern siding is a very early structure dating back to the first 30 years of Paris's history. (Courtesy of Daniel Grimminger.)

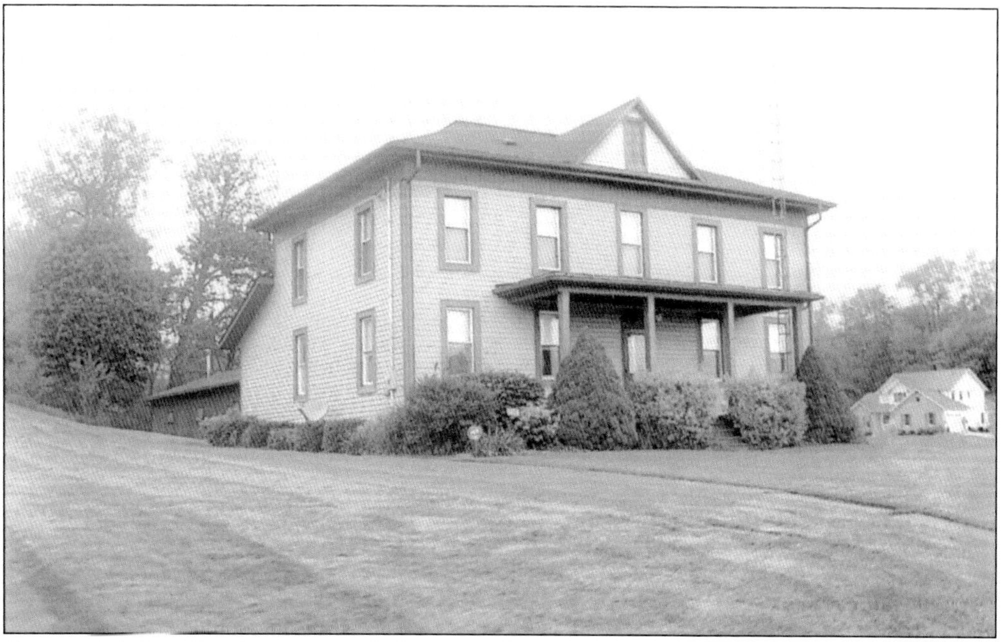

Gene and Arlene Bomberger owned this house for many years. It sits at the corner of Autumn Avenue and Lisbon Street on the Bomberger farm. It is now owned by a son, but the farmland was sold off several years ago. Black Creek runs through the farmland, and the Creek School once sat on this property as well. (Courtesy of Daniel Grimminger.)

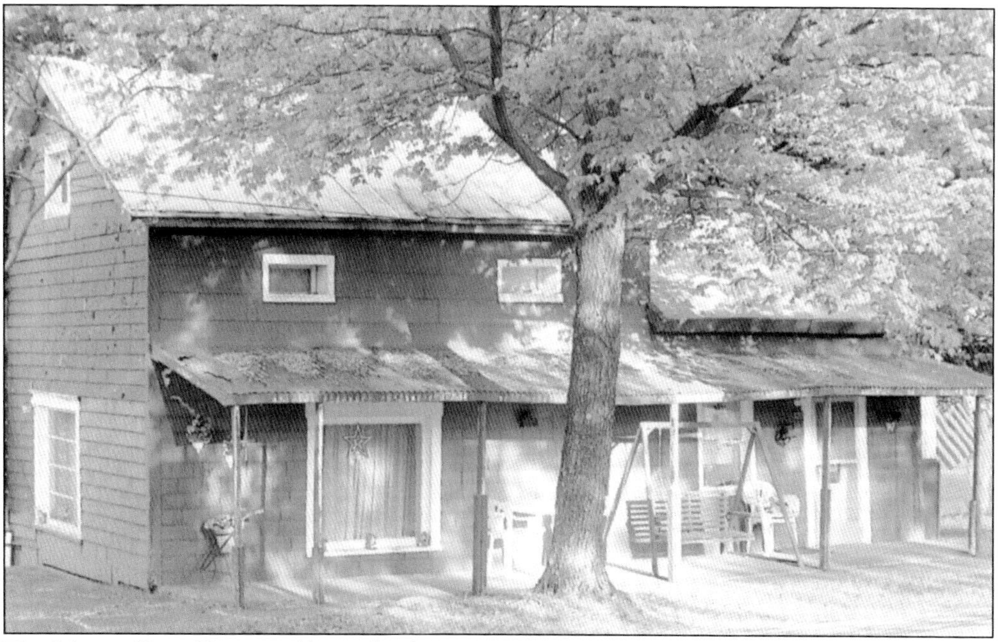

The John and Jane Kinemond house has been in Jane's family well over a century, if not two. There is a barn on the same property that used to be unusually tall for its size until they cut it down a bit. John and Jane's son repairs cars here. Many people remember that John served as the village cemetery sexton since he lived next door to the graveyard. (Courtesy of Daniel Grimminger.)

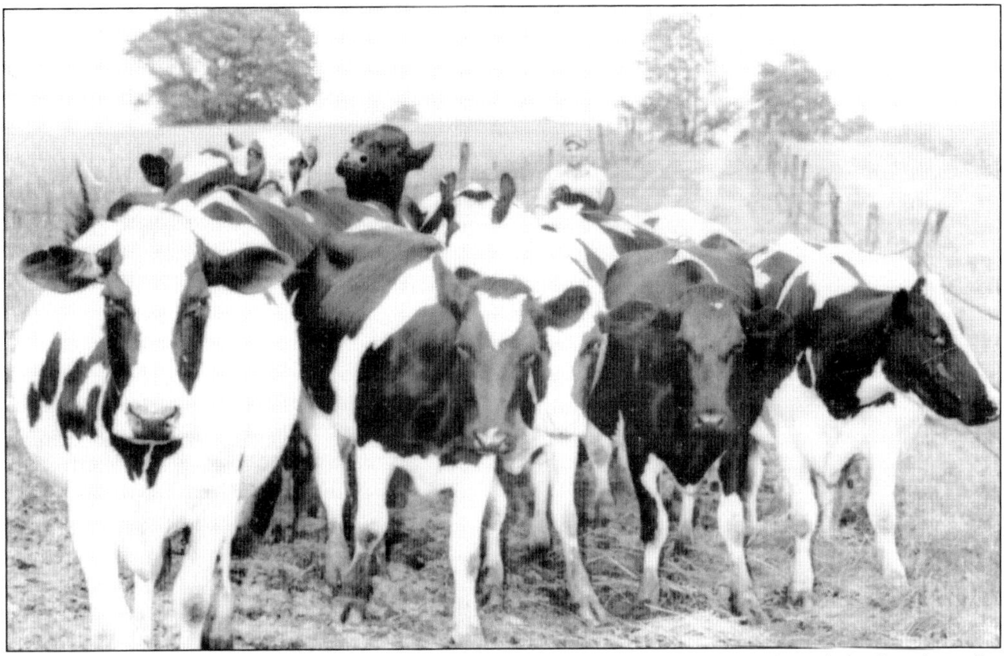

Jay Lutz Sr. was a lifelong member of the Lutheran Church in Paris even though he lived on the family farm in Washington Township, just a few miles away. Here he is shown driving his cattle down the cow lane toward the barn where he milked his small herd. This cow path later became an access road to a new oil well. (Courtesy of Charlene and Junior Grimminger.)

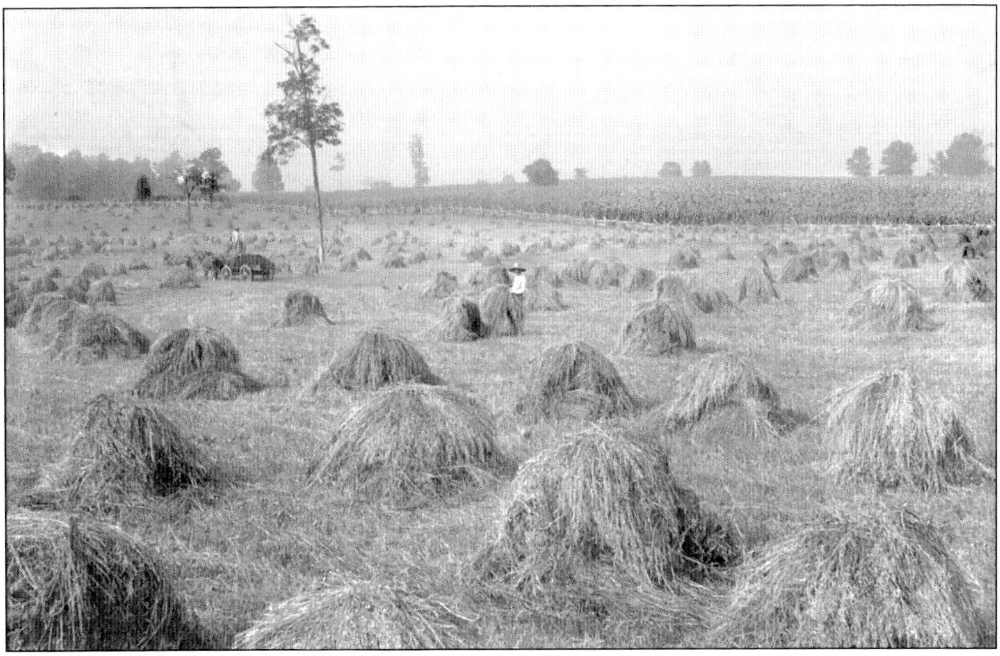

This is another view of Edward Lutz working in the fields of the old Lutz farm on Paris Avenue. The photographer is looking northwest toward Louisville. Notice the man posing on the wagon in the background for the photographer. This picture is undated, but is likely from about 1870. (Courtesy of Charlene and Junior Grimminger.)

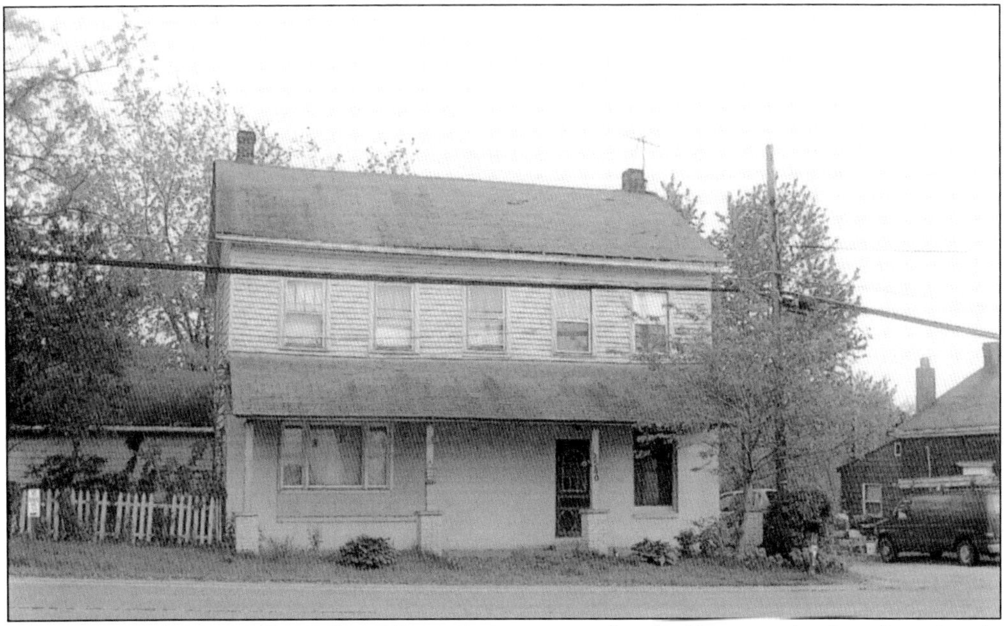

Ebert and Thelma Powell ran Powell's confectionery in this building on the first floor. Linda Lilly and others still recall that they would stroll down to this store to buy ice cream, especially on a hot Sunday afternoon. The Powells lived on Pleasant Valley Road where Thelma, a retired schoolteacher, had built a small one-room schoolhouse in which to tutor students. (Courtesy of Daniel Grimminger.)

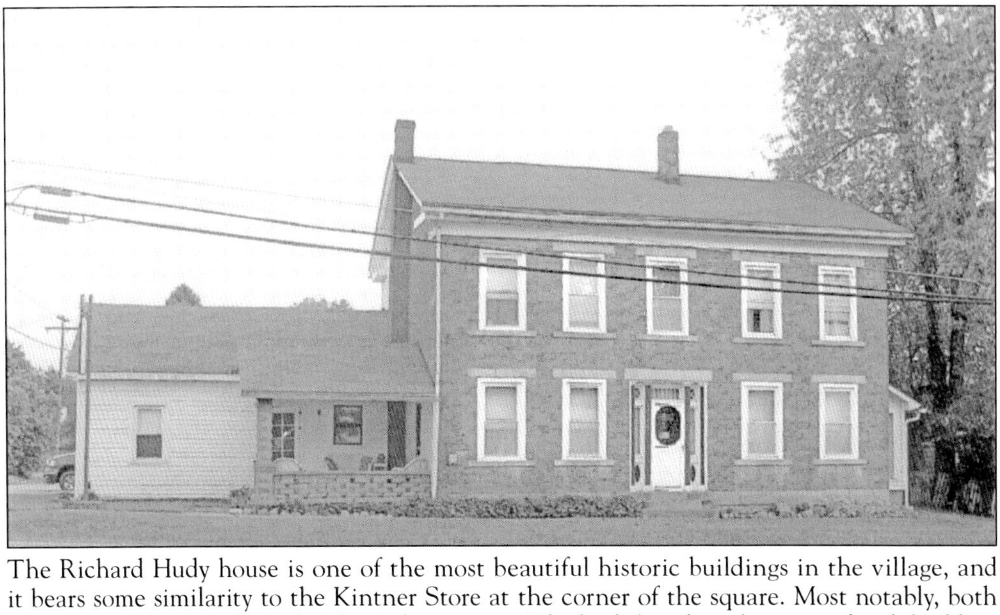

The Richard Hudy house is one of the most beautiful historic buildings in the village, and it bears some similarity to the Kintner Store at the corner of the square. Most notably, both buildings are brick and wooden framed structures. The back (southeast) corner of each building is wooden on the second story. The Hudys have maintained this home beautifully. (Courtesy of Daniel Grimminger.)

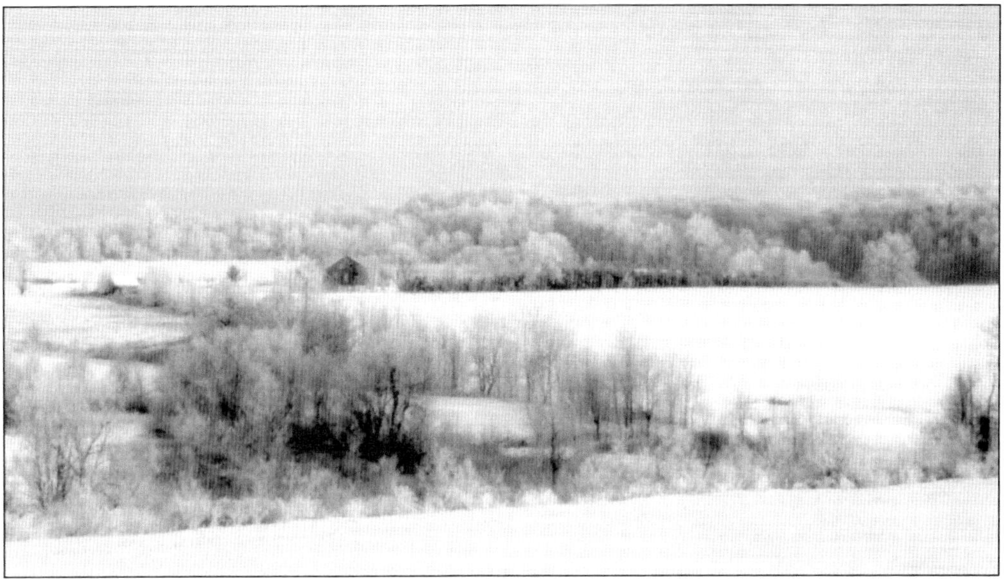

Winter in and around Paris is a glorious experience. This photograph was taken looking northeast from the Junior Grimminger home when there was a lot of ice in the early 1990s. The hilly terrain of Paris makes it an ideal place to sled when the snow is right. (Courtesy of Daniel Grimminger.)

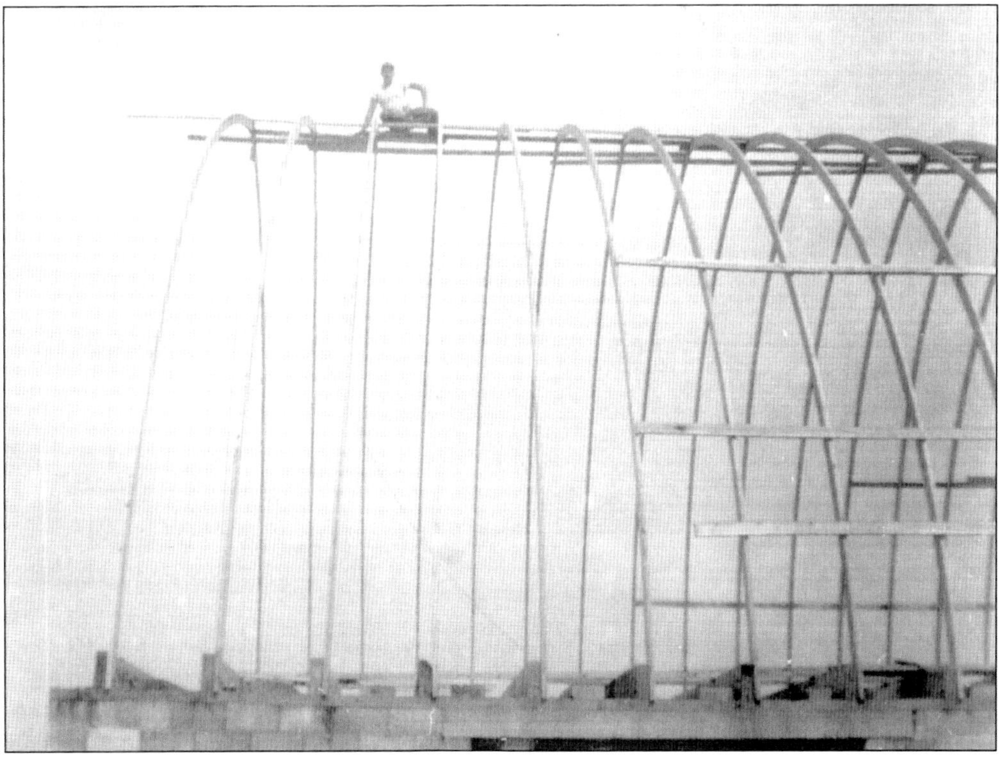

The Grimminger barn (once the Julliard barn) burned down from a spark that came from a tractor on a dry day. Parisians came together to help rebuild the barn and the family's livelihood. Jim Speakman was one such resident who helped. Lerane Grimminger Sr. hired him as a contractor, and he climbed the most terrifying heights without fear. (Courtesy of Charlene and Junior Grimminger.)

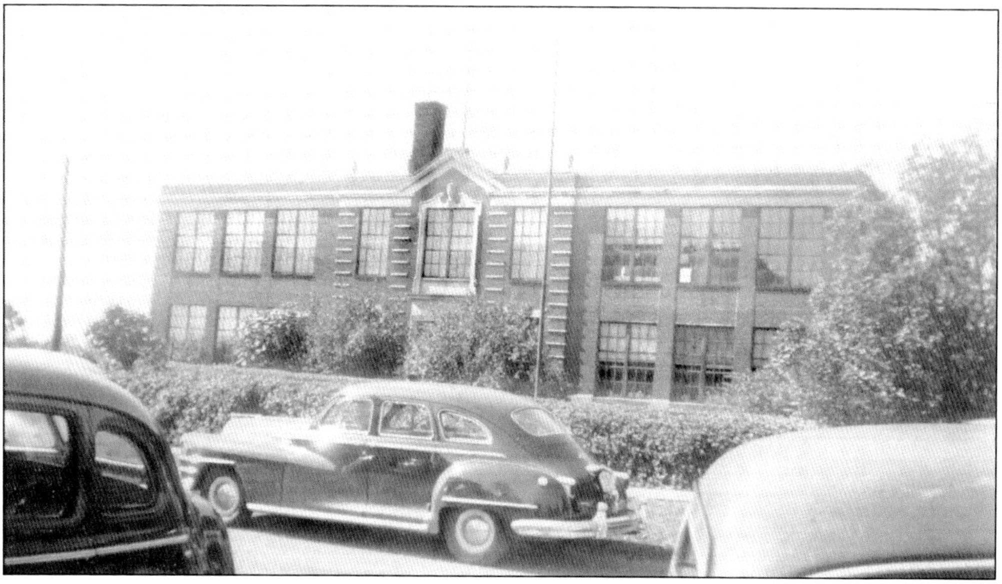

The heart of the Paris community for many years was this school. When the building was demolished, it seems that the last ounce of hope in having a vibrant, active community went elsewhere. Here are two different photographs of the school taken at different angles and times. The earlier of the two reveals that there were originally urn-like finials that decorated the roof to match the finial on the middle, second-floor window frame. By the time these photographs were taken, the modest horse shed that the Lutherans used on Sunday mornings must have been removed for it stood just south of the school edifice. Esther Schoner recalls that her father, Elmer Koontz, bought a "stall" from this building, which he used as the main part of a new machinery shed he built. (Courtesy of Charlene and Junior Grimminger, and Eloise Wood.)

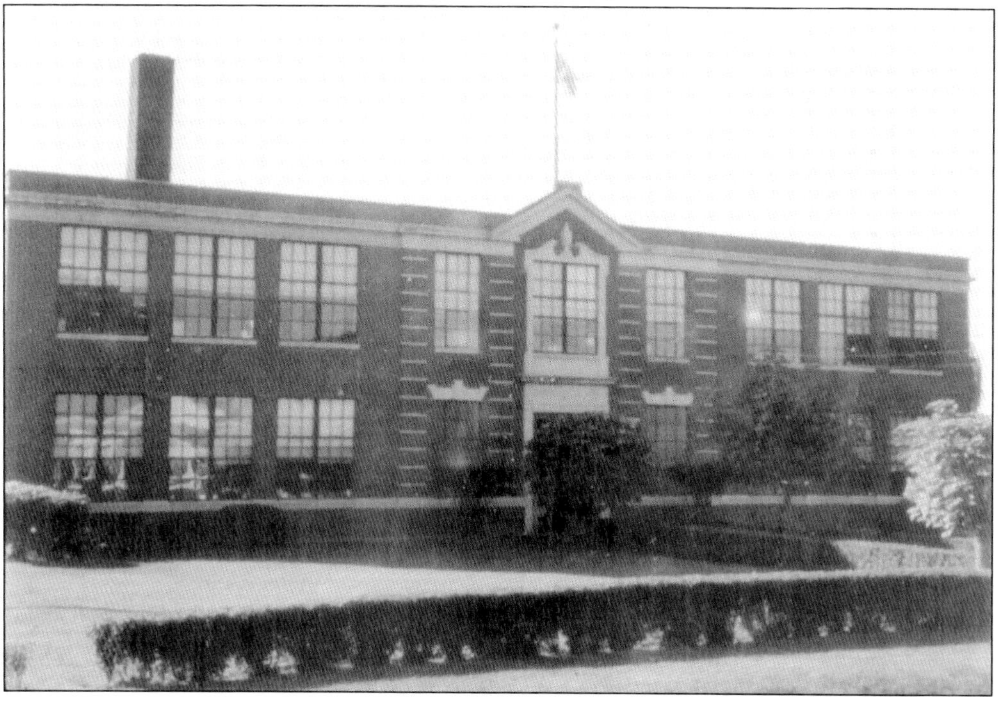

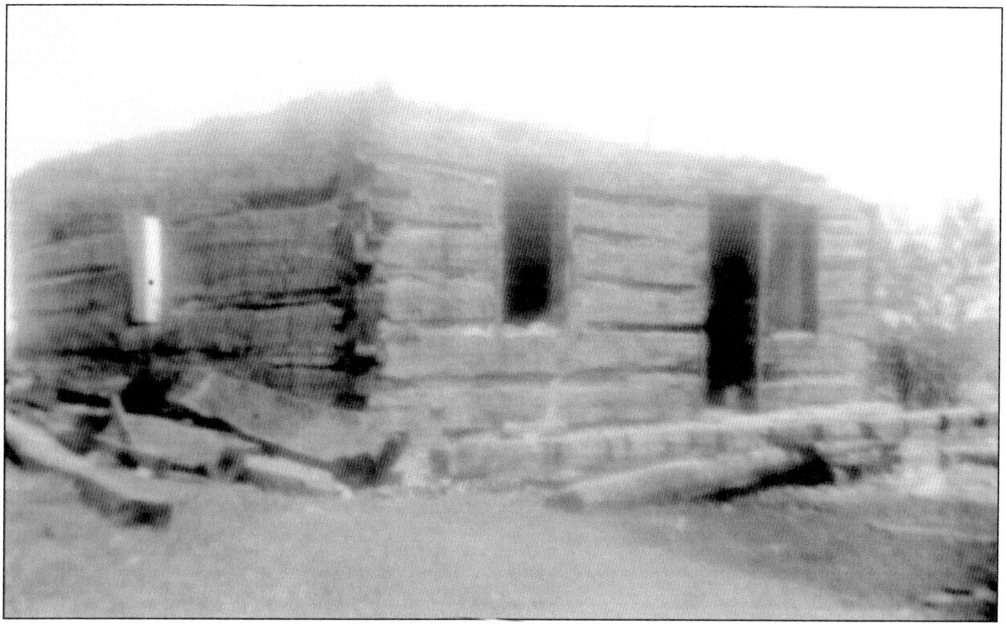

Abraham Lutz settled on the farm later owned by Grant and Pauline Greenwald. His hewn-log home was eventually replaced by a larger house and then became the family's summer kitchen. In October 1961, the Greenwalds sold the original structure to the McFalls, some of Pauline's cousins, but the day after the purchase the McFalls were killed in a car accident. No one knows what happened to the logs. (Courtesy of Daniel Grimminger.)

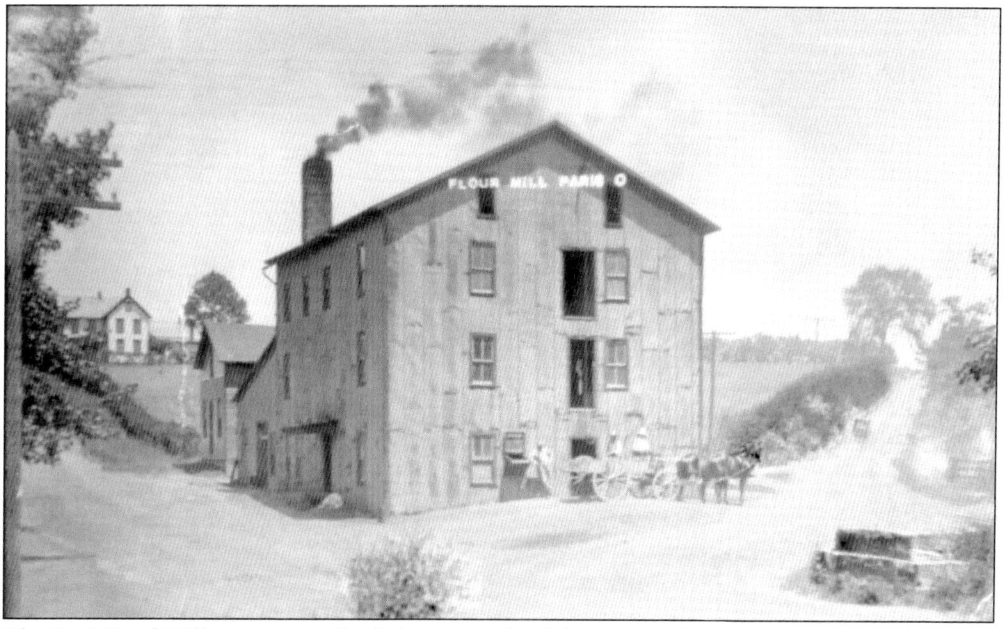

The Paris Feed Mill once sat at the fork just north of the square where a person may either go to Freeburg (right) or on the old dirt road (left). Ruth Kenny, one of Paris's past postmasters, now lives in a modern home on the same lot as the mill was, but it has since been built up with soil. (Courtesy of Daniel Grimminger.)

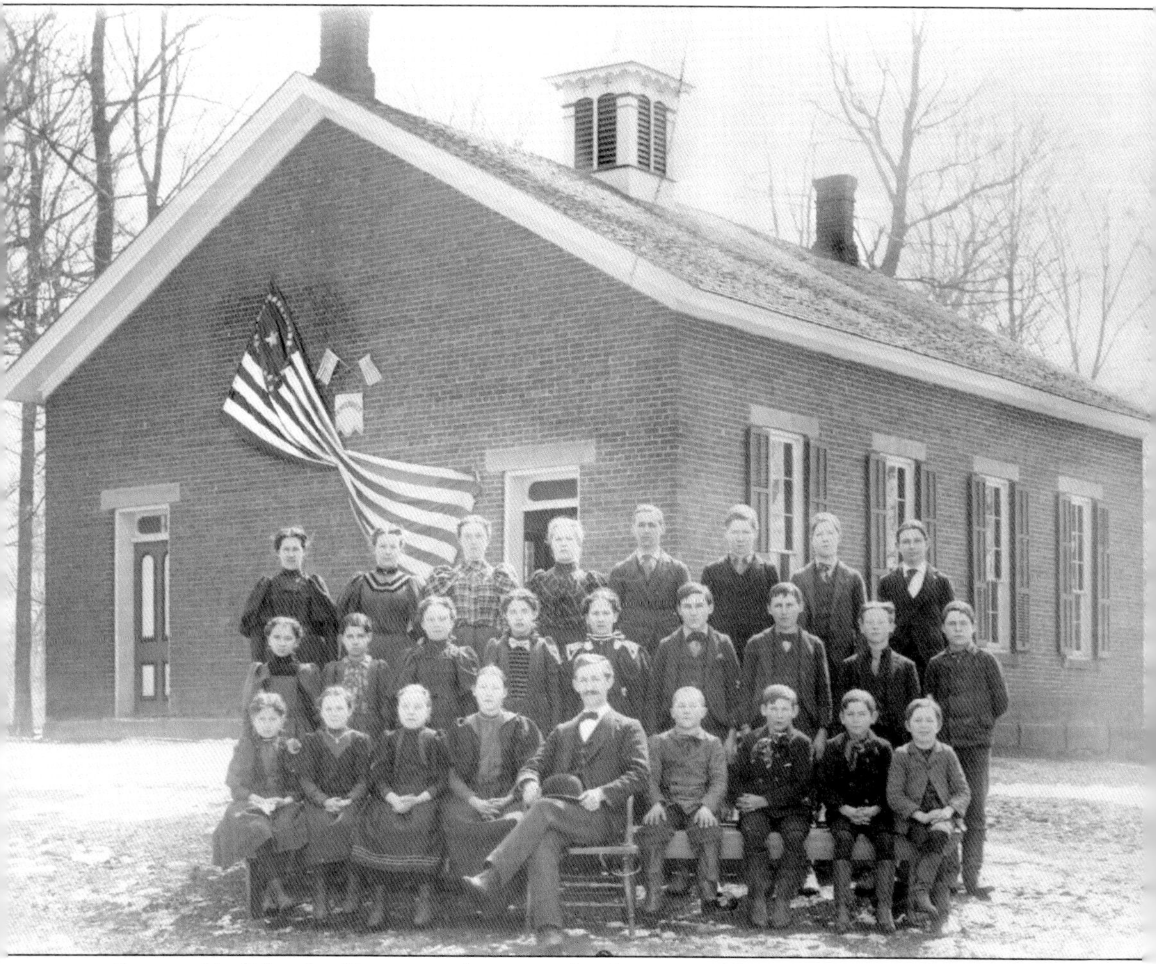

Centerville School still exists today several miles west of Paris. It is painted and serves as a residence, which saved it from demolition—the fate of most of the other township schools like the old Creek School. Notice the nationalistic decoration on the exterior and the distinct copula that likely housed the school bell in this fine period photograph of Centerville School. (Courtesy of Kay Latham.)

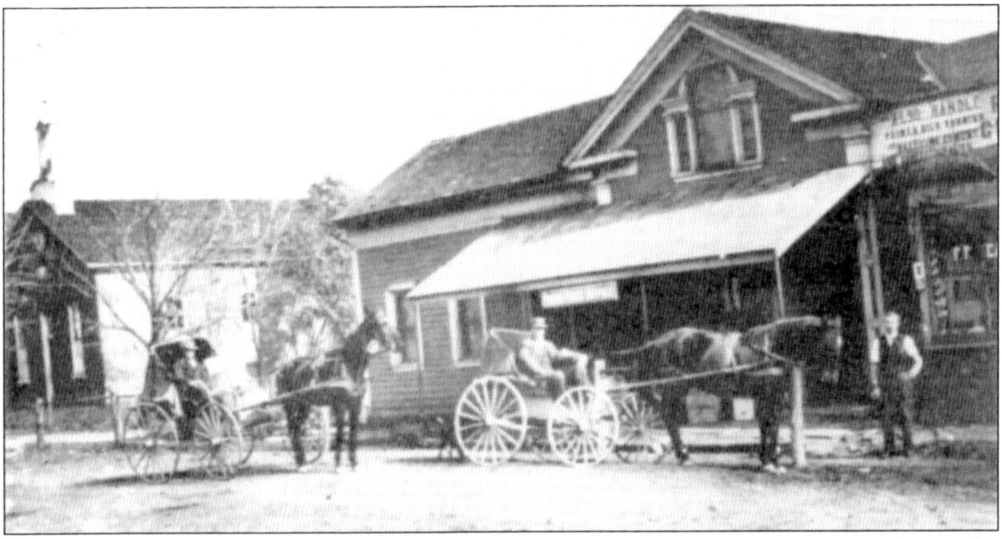

The old post office that was used in the 19th century later became Meese's Meat Market in the later years of the 20th century. This photograph shows the rural mail carriers in front of the building, and the Emory Chapel is clearly present in the background to the left. (Taken from *Paris, Ohio Sesqui-Centennial.*)

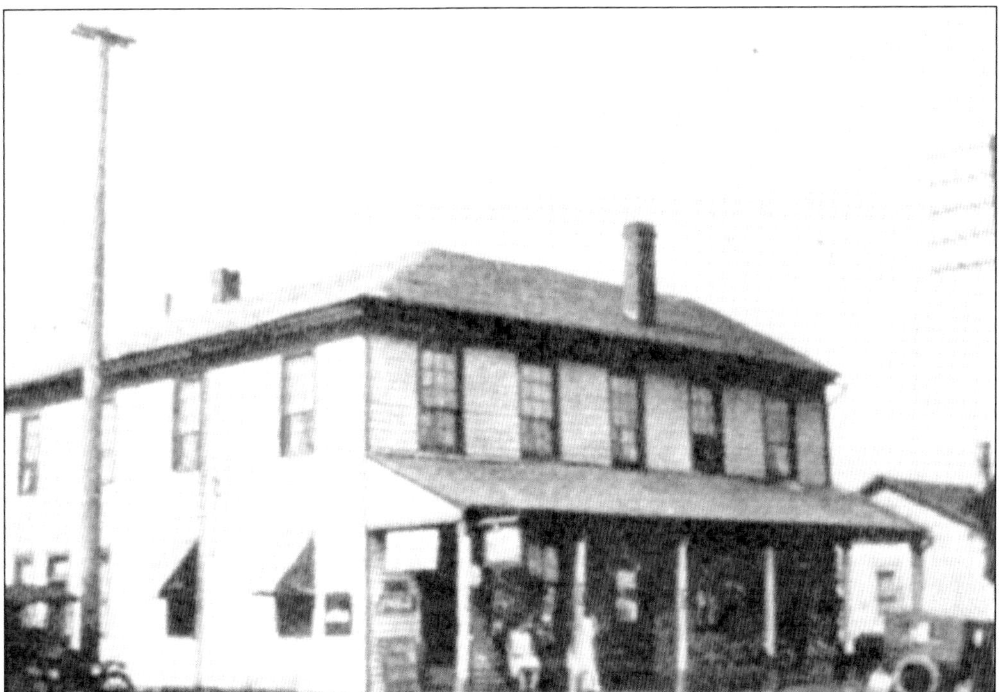

This old tavern was considered by many people to be the downfall of Paris culture. A lot of "carousing" went on there, and there were numerous town drunks. This is one of the few photographs that exist of this building, which was one of the earliest business buildings in the village. (Courtesy of Daniel Grimminger.)

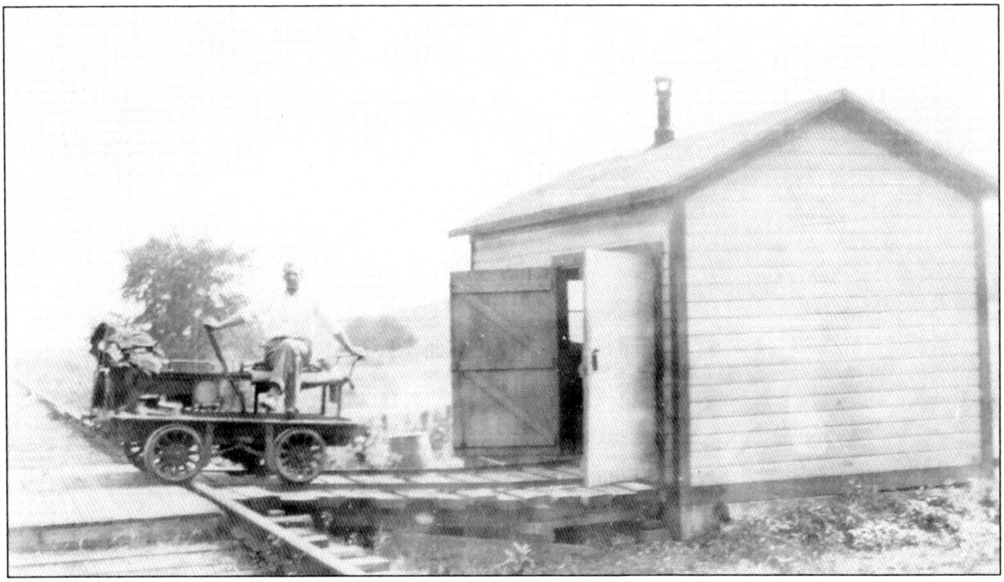

It is a mystery who owned this two-man railroad car or where its house was located. Betty Speakman talks about going to Alliance in a larger "Doodle Bug," and Esther Schoner speaks about a small railroad car like the one pictured that she could see go by from a family farm. What this one might have been used for is uncertain. (Courtesy of Audrey and Les Wade.)

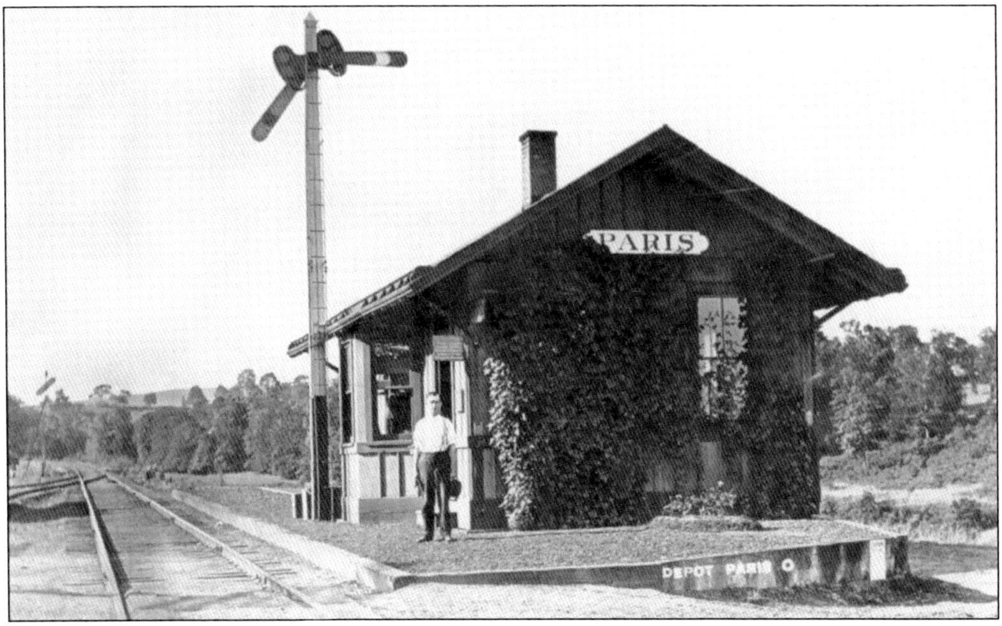

The Paris Depot was a lively place. People got on and off at this stop; farmers would also come here to pick up loads of grain and fertilizer that the train would deliver on the ground. Esther Schoner recalls going with her dad to pick up fertilizer along the tracks. (Courtesy of Vivian Myers Marty, from the Doris Myers Collection.)

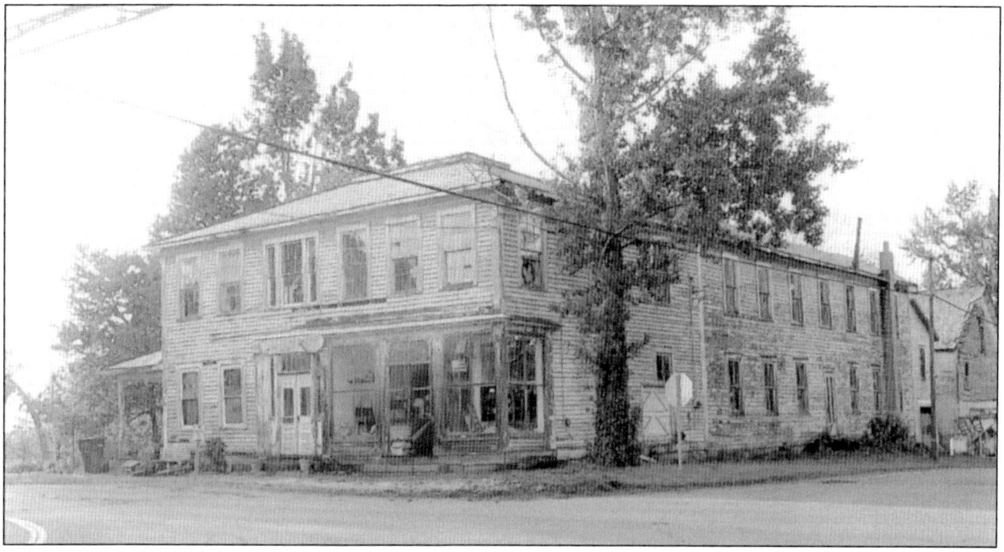

The old Meiser Store has seen better days. This profile of the building shows its hefty size. In the back part of the building (far right) is a stage and dance floor. This may have been what at least one source referred to as Paris's "Opera House." (Courtesy of Daniel Grimminger.)

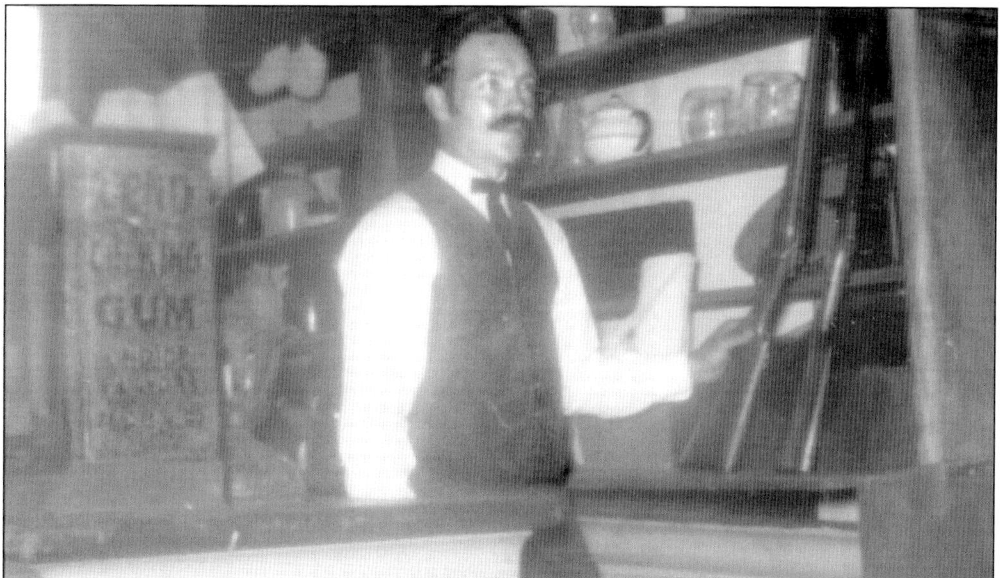

Les Wade poses for this picture inside the front storeroom of the Meiser Store during the festivities of the village sesquicentennial. The dark wood shelf on which he set his guns still exists in the store building. (Courtesy of Daniel Grimminger.)

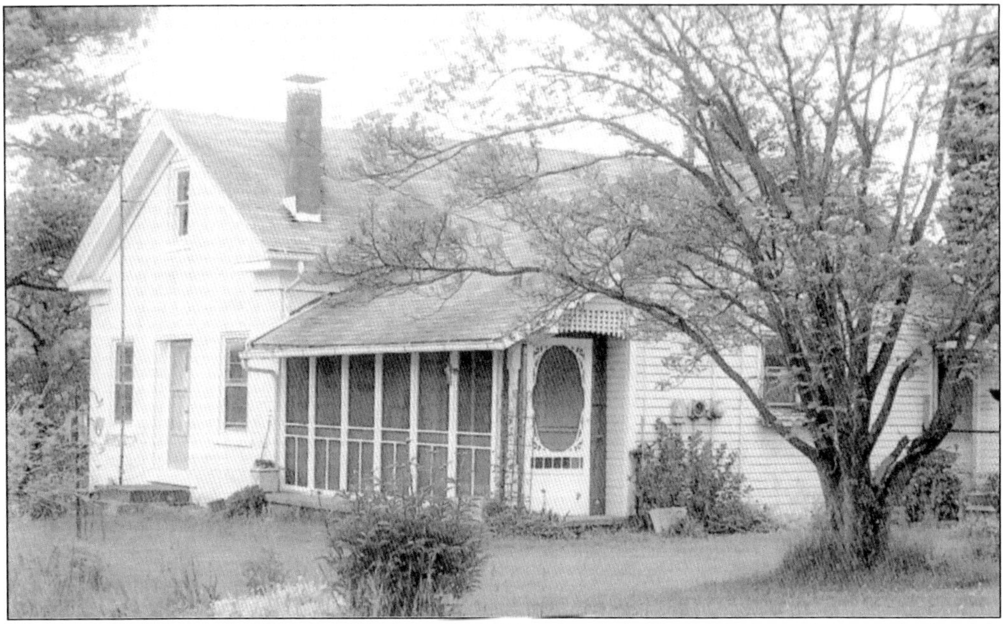

This well-preserved brick home was once owned by the Gugelman family and was a blacksmith shop. It likely was a typical redbrick Pennsylvania Dutch-style edifice in the 19th century. Now it is adorned with light yellow paint. A screened-in porch was recently added by the current owners. (Courtesy of Daniel Grimminger.)

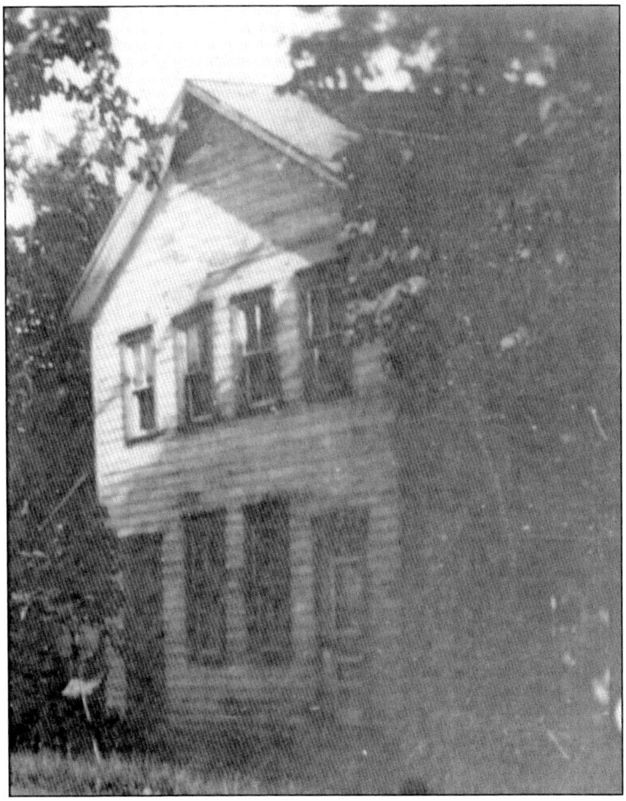

No one still living is able to remember this building, which means that it disappeared sometime before 1910. It appears in the background of the Livelsberger family portrait and sat somewhere between the Meese's Meat Market building and the Kinemond residence on the east side of Paris Avenue across from the Lutheran parsonage. (Courtesy of Linda K. Lilly.)

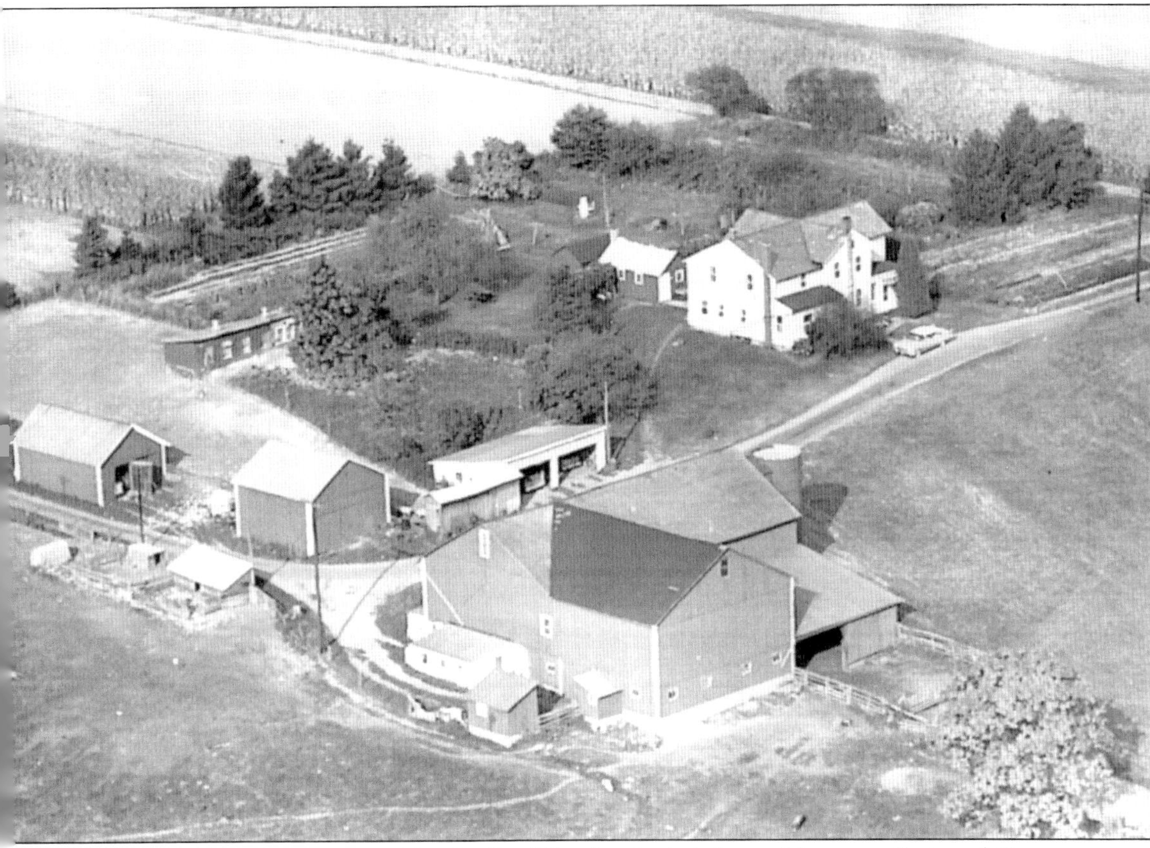

The old Mong farm is now owned by the Jim Kiko family. It is located between Paris and New Franklin on Lisbon Street. Recently the original house on the property burned and the Kikos built a new one. (Courtesy of Steven Tibrea.)

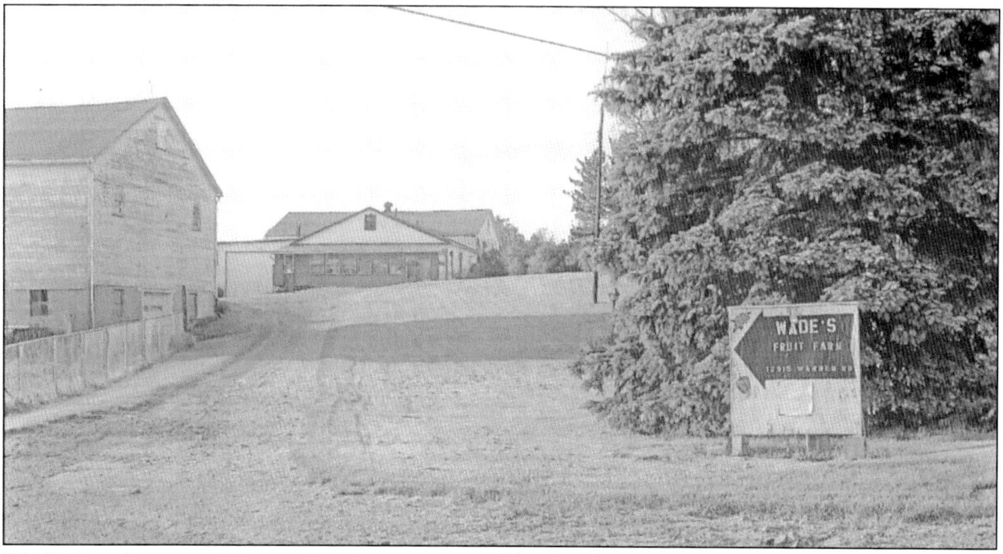

Wade Fruit Farm on Warren Road grows several kinds of fruit, but most recently its main cash crop has been blueberries. Not too long ago, Charlene and Junior Grimminger would pick a couple hundred pounds for freezing because the price was so amazing and the taste of the berries excellent. Other fruit farms like Waltz's Strawberry Patch are wonderful places to visit with friends while picking. (Courtesy of Daniel Grimminger.)

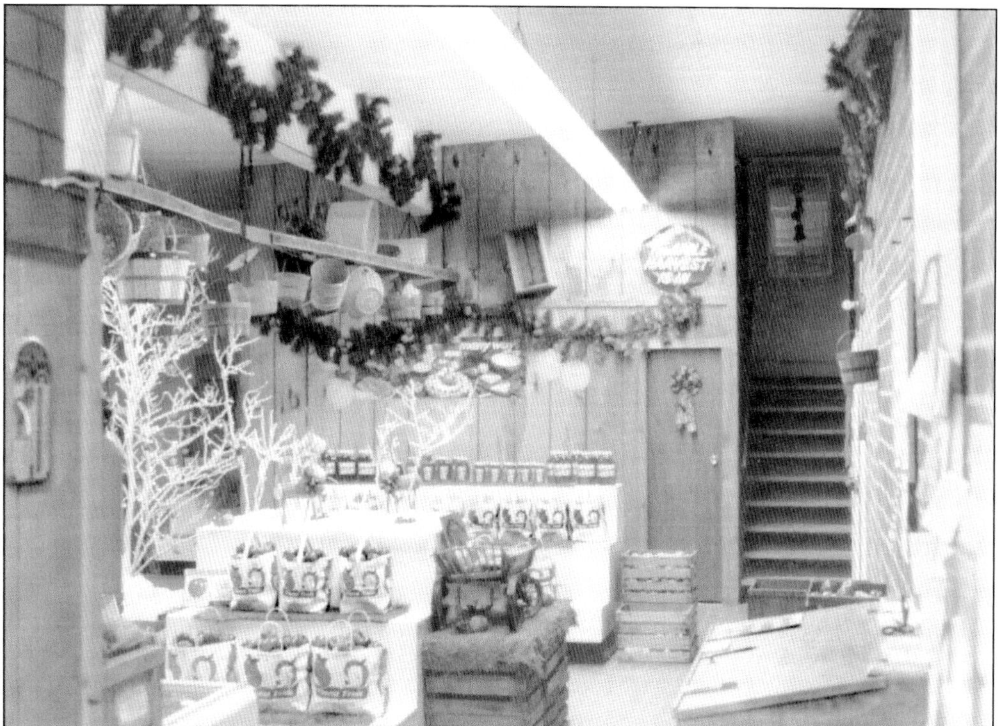

Arrowhead Apple Orchard has a small showroom off of the sorting and cooler rooms that is always full of apples and other tasty products. Shown here is the store as it was decorated for the Christmas season by Fred and Truus Monhemius. (Courtesy of Fred and Truus Monhemius.)

In the Parisian countryside, children would learn how to drive on the seat of a tractor. By the time they would get to driving age, shifting a car's gears was familiar. Junior and Clarabelle Grimminger are on the tractor at harvest time with an unnamed farmhand. (Courtesy of Charlene and Junior Grimminger.)

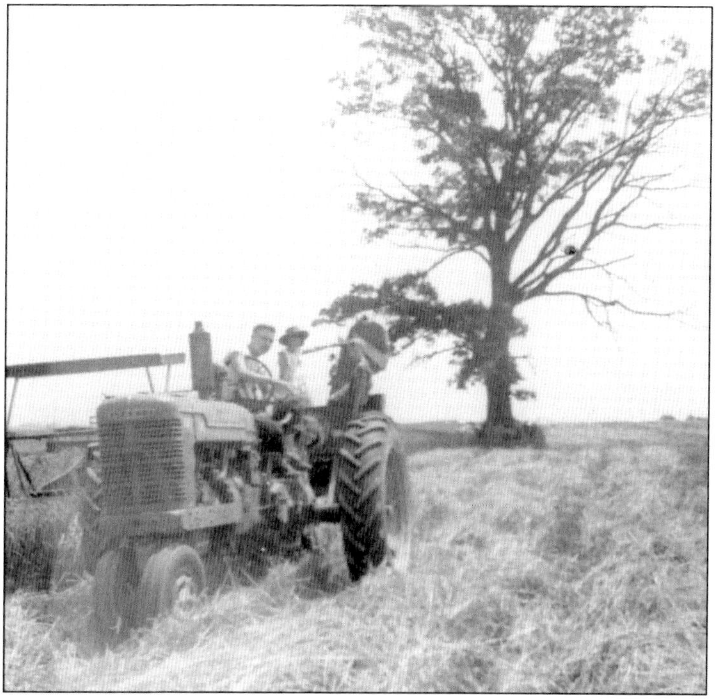

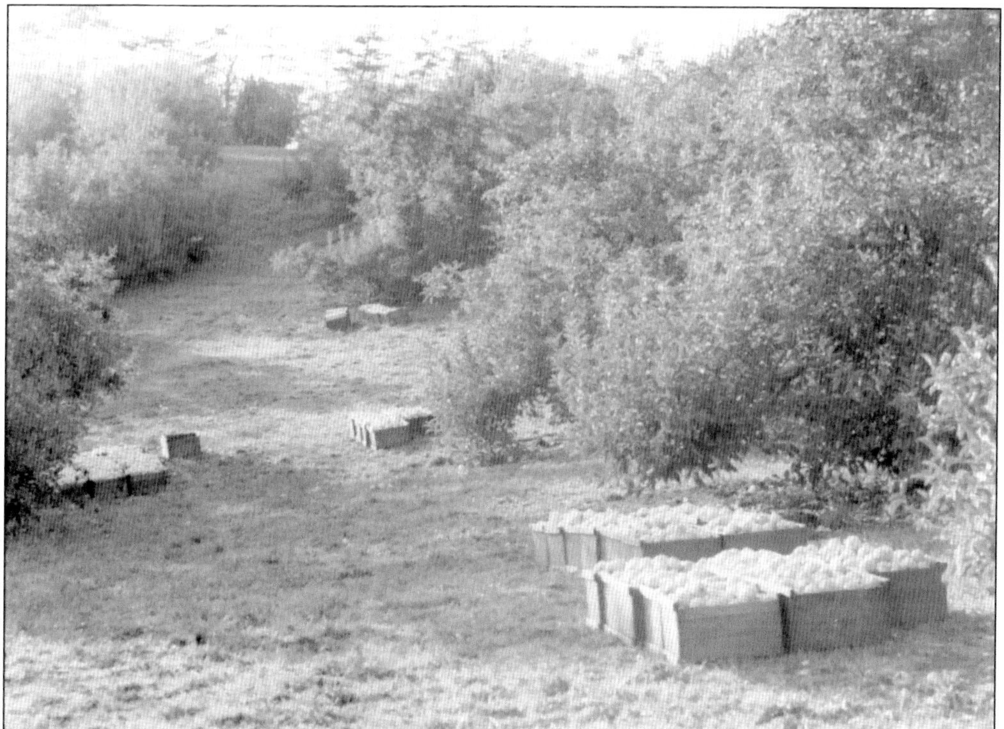

After the fruit is picked from the trees and placed in these crates, the tractor brings them to the sorting area where they are graded and packaged for storage. This beautiful orchard landscape is in the Arrowhead Apple Orchard west of Paris. (Courtesy of Fred and Truus Monhemius.)

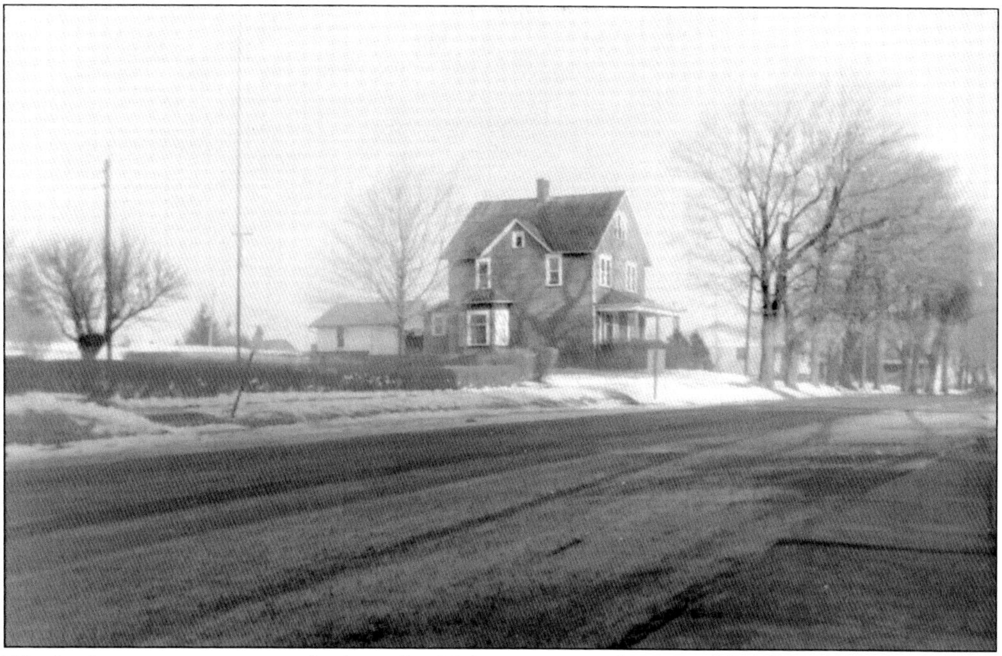

The Lutheran parsonage was built in the 20th century, and it resembles the farmhouses on the Charles Lutz farm (where the author lives) and the Shearer farm. This picture was taken in 1970, and the house is the same today except the congregation had it painted white since. (Courtesy of Betty Speakman.)

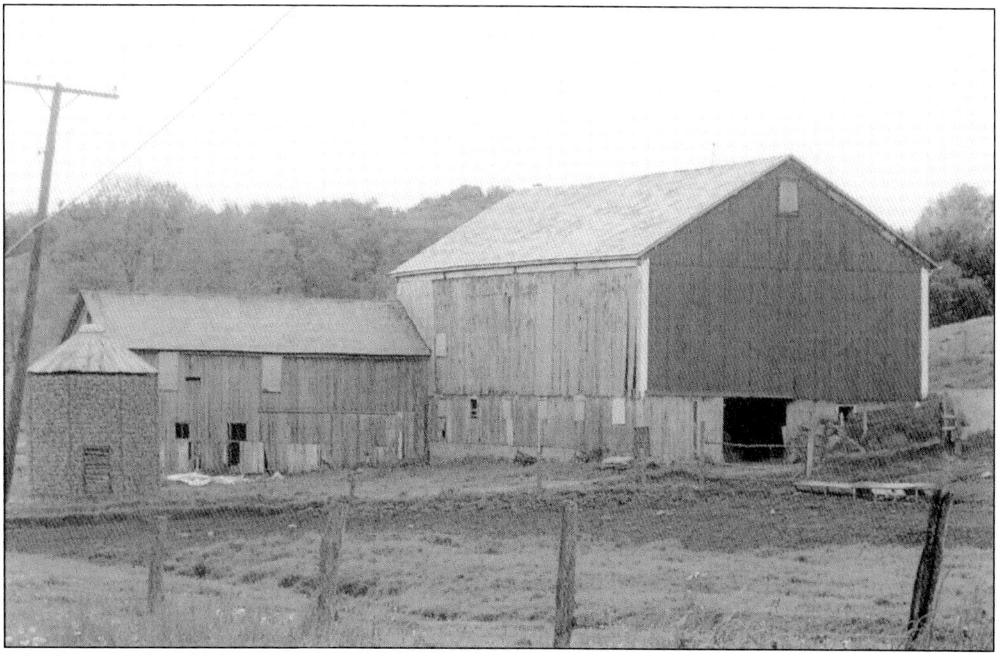

This barn on the old dirt road, now owned by the Snyder family, once housed a harness shop in the small wing of the building. Such a shop would have been of use to everyone in the 19th century. The barn is now painted on several sides but shows its age on the unpainted sides. (Courtesy of Daniel Grimminger.)

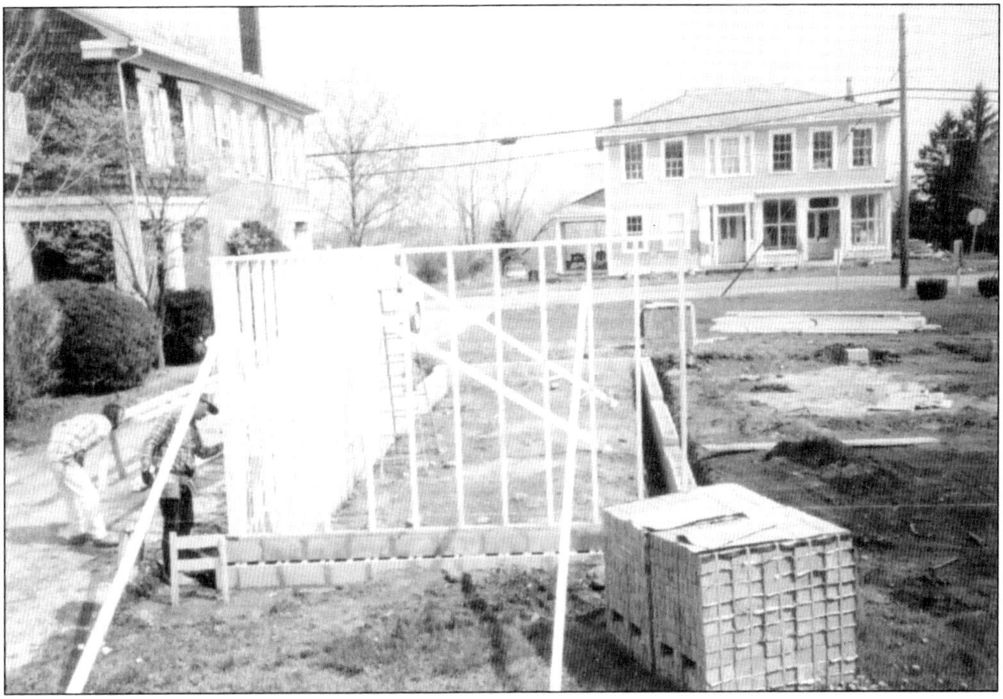

In May 1992, the community received a court settlement from a company that dumped waste in the community along the old railroad. With that settlement, the community decided in part to build a new pavilion with a kitchen and bathrooms. The project has just begun in this picture with the Kintner Store building (left) and Meiser Store building (across the street) observing patiently. (Courtesy of Audrey and Les Wade.)

One of the longest farm lanes is on the Julliard-Grimminger farm. This photograph shows just how high the snow would drift without a snow fence in the Paris area. The long lane was terrific for sledding; Lerane Grimminger Sr. and Junior Grimminger loved to hop on the family's fleet of Radial Flyers, especially with grandchildren, and fly down the icy lane. (Courtesy of Charlene and Junior Grimminger.)

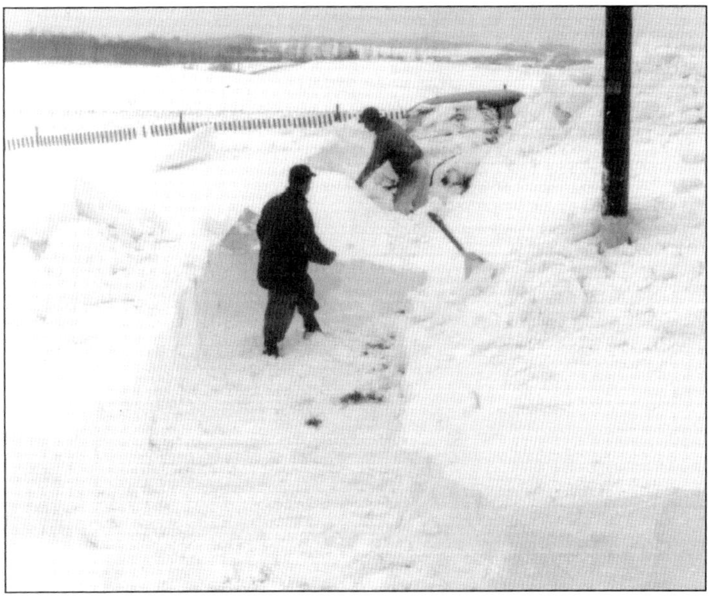

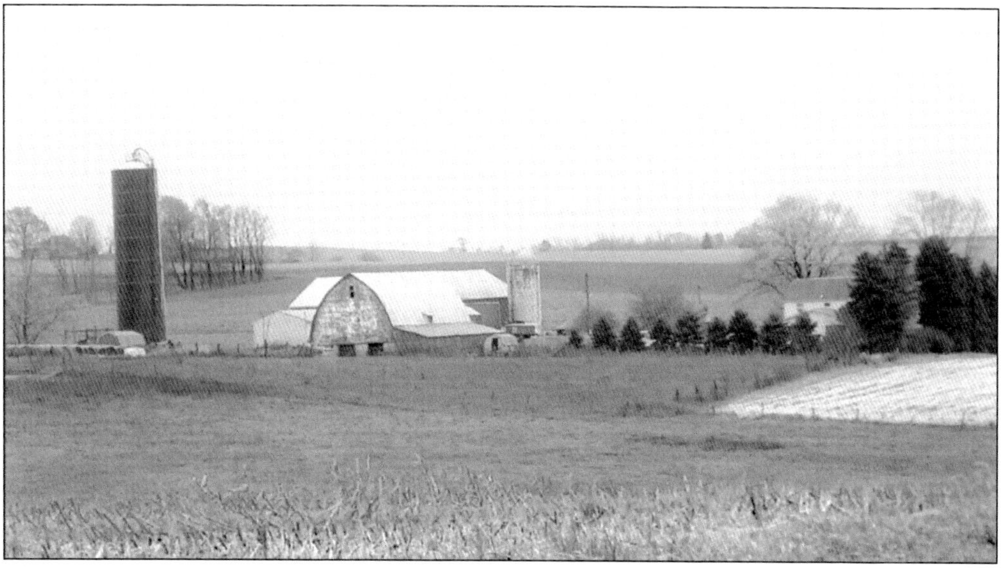

The David Sponseller farm, located on Parks Avenue, was once farmed by David's father, Lloyd. It borders several other farms, and its land lays nice and flat. The Sponsellers have been active in the Paris community for many years. (Courtesy of Daniel Grimminger.)

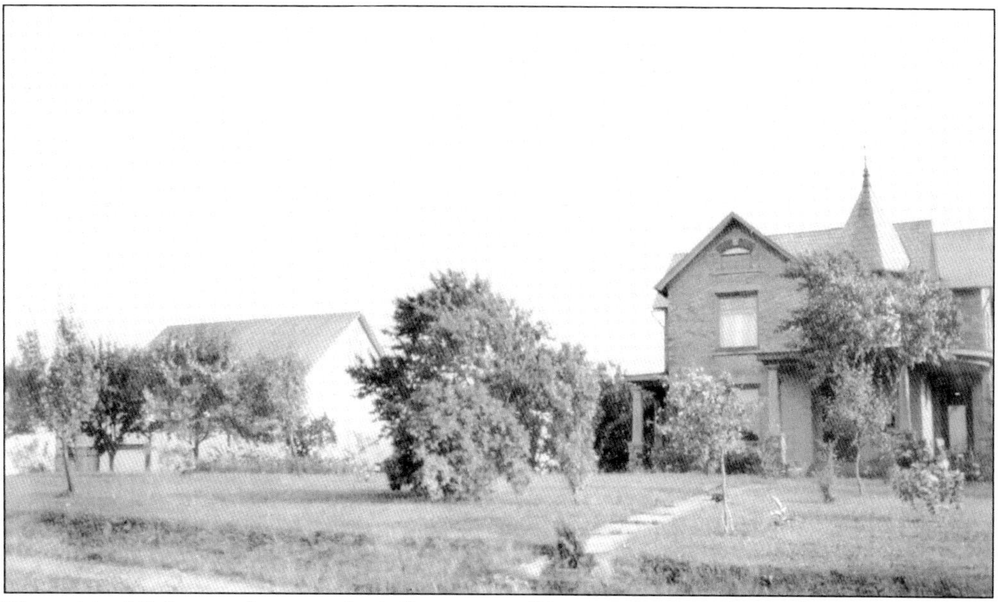

The original Sefert residence on the hill just east of Paris is where Audrey Gill Wade was raised. This picture was taken sometime between 1927 and 1935. The property seems to have changed its looks little since then. (Courtesy of Audrey and Les Wade.)

Three

Paris Churches

Religious institutions have been at the center of Paris's existence even before it became a village (1814). Rudolph Bair gave land for the establishment of a schoolhouse and "Union Church" (German Lutheran and Reformed) in 1813. In 1816, the congregations built a log edifice on the east side of the "Pekin Road" (Paris Avenue). This union was typical of such Pennsylvania-Dutch churches because the two groups would share a building and circuit-riding preachers. As the congregation grew due to the influx of Pennsylvania-Dutch migrants, the union congregation had to build a larger brick structure in 1848.

Eventually the two churches could not coexist in the same building due to disagreements and the need for more space. This led to the split of the union; the Reformed church, recently called Israel United Church of Christ, built a new building across town in 1891. From 1876 to 1962, this congregation shared a pastor with the Reformed church in Robertsville. The Lutheran pastor had duties to preach at Christ Lutheran Church in Mapleton in the same way. This was not always a happy arrangement. Pastor Carl Duwe told the author that he was not aware that taking the call with the Lutherans would mean preaching in more than one church until after he accepted the call and arrived in Paris. It was under Pastor Rice that the Lutheran arrangement with Mapleton was dissolved in the 1970s.

Revivalism took root later in Paris (1873), manifesting itself in the Emory (Methodist) Chapel (now owned by the Community Association) and in the dealings of Rev. Maas, a Wesleyan Methodist who bought the Meiser Store in the 1970s to start a Bible college. The nucleus of the Methodist congregation was five families: the Blanchards, Hennings, Sponsellers, Fairbanks, and Baughmans. When the church closed, the parishioners were absorbed into either the Lutheran or Reformed Churches of the village.

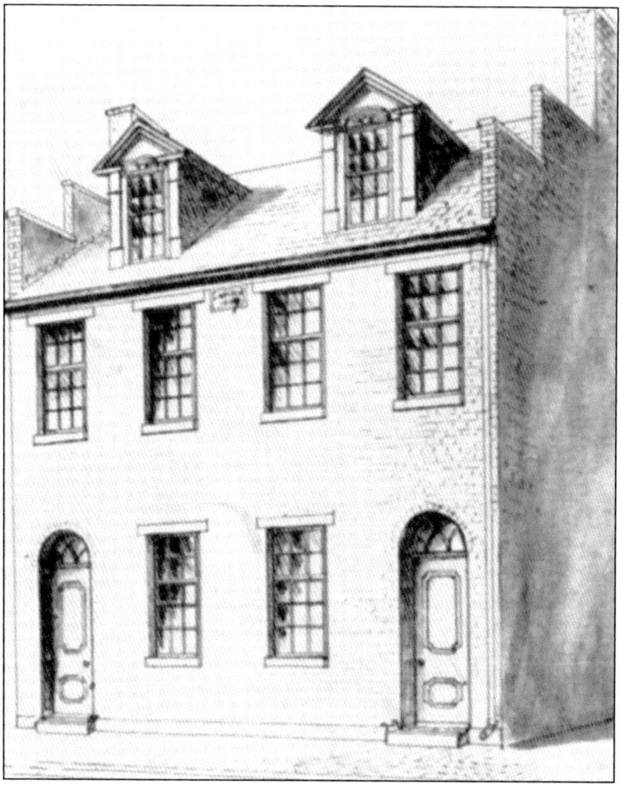

Early in the life of Paris, the union congregation (Lutheran and Reformed Churches) was served by clergy who preached at numerous churches in their charge. These circuit riders included Wilhelm Schmidt (1803–1839), who rode out to Paris from Canton where his primary duty was to preach at "Jerusalem's Church" (now First Lutheran Church on Tuscarawas Street). While he was serving Paris, he started a Lutheran seminary in his home in Canton and then used the building in this sketch (1830) just before moving his newly formed institution to Columbus. This building is on East Tuscarawas Street not far from First Lutheran Church and is currently being restored. (Taken from C. V. Sheatsley's *History of the First Lutheran Seminary of the West, 1830–1930.*)

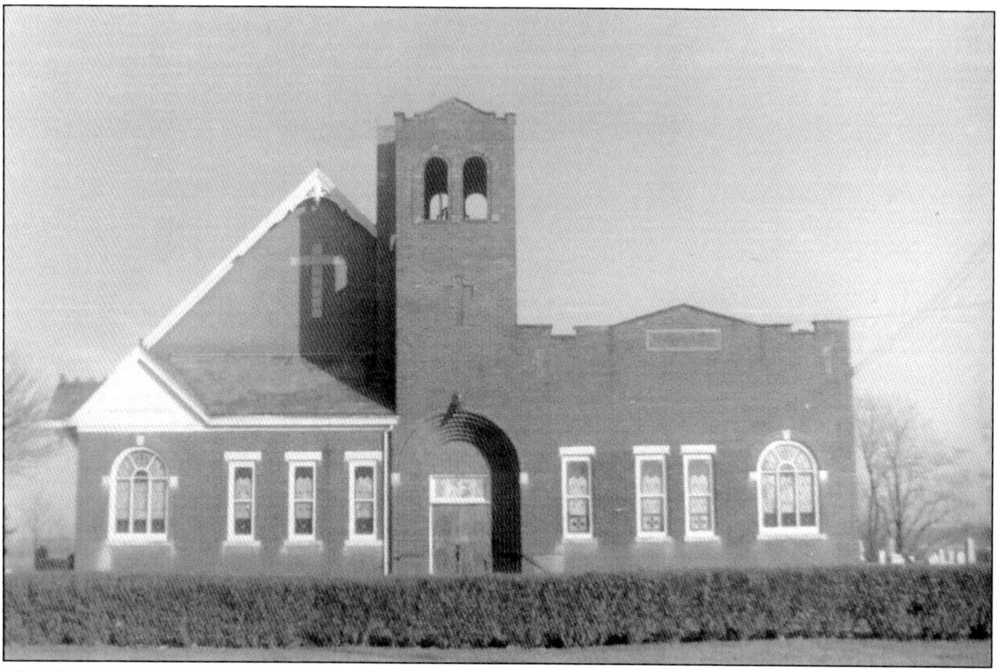

This fairly recent photograph of Israel's Evangelical Lutheran Church was taken in 1970. The hedge along the sidewalk was left over from the school property that once stood where the photographer was standing to take the picture. (Courtesy of Betty Speakman.)

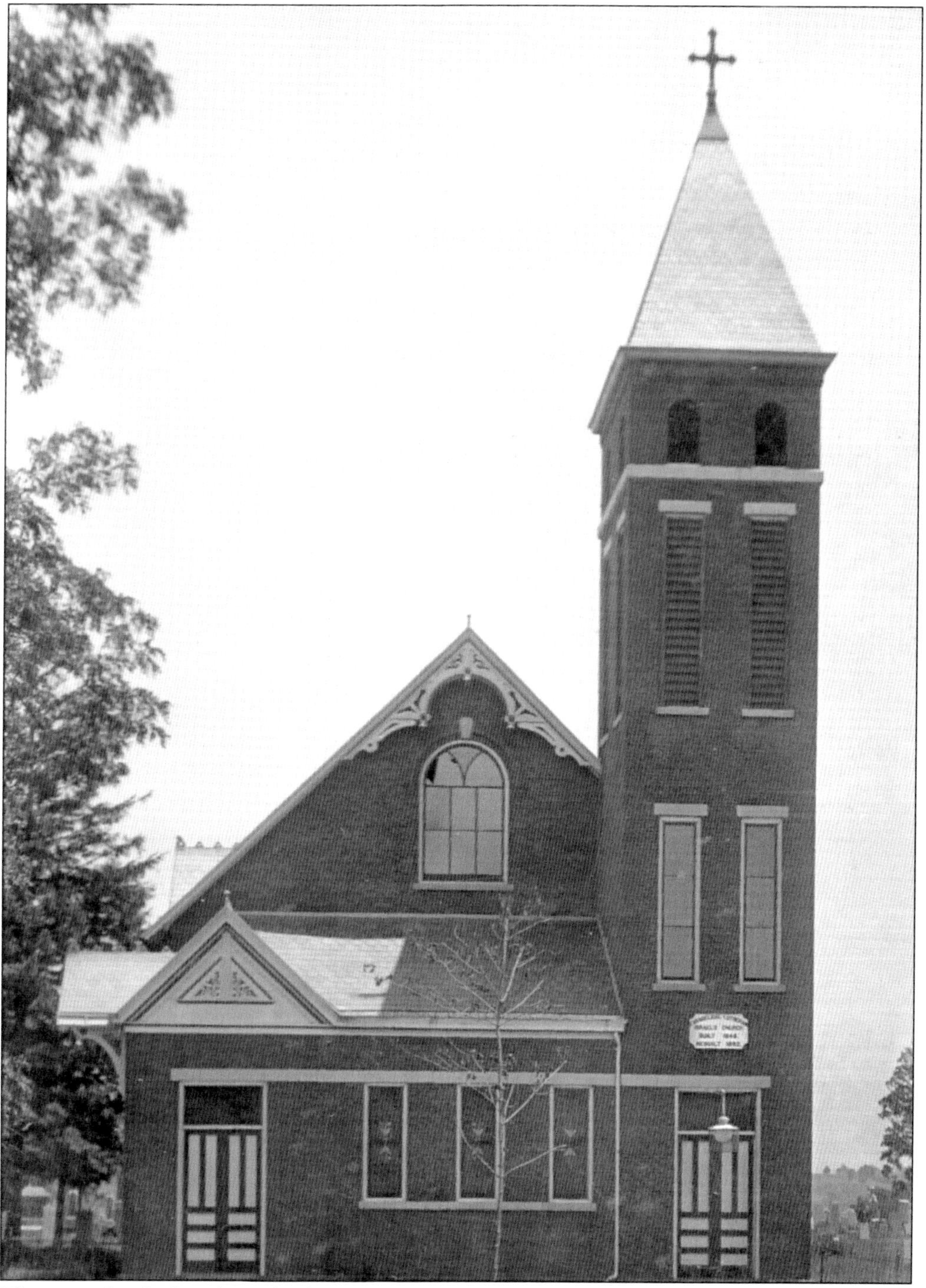

The union brick church was built in 1848, as there was a great migration of Pennsylvania Dutch people at that time. This image, taken from a picture postcard from around 1908, shows the church as it looked before renovations and a huge addition in 1927. The belfry's original character and the Victorian charm of the building's trim were lost in 1927, never to be regained. (Courtesy of Daniel Grimminger.)

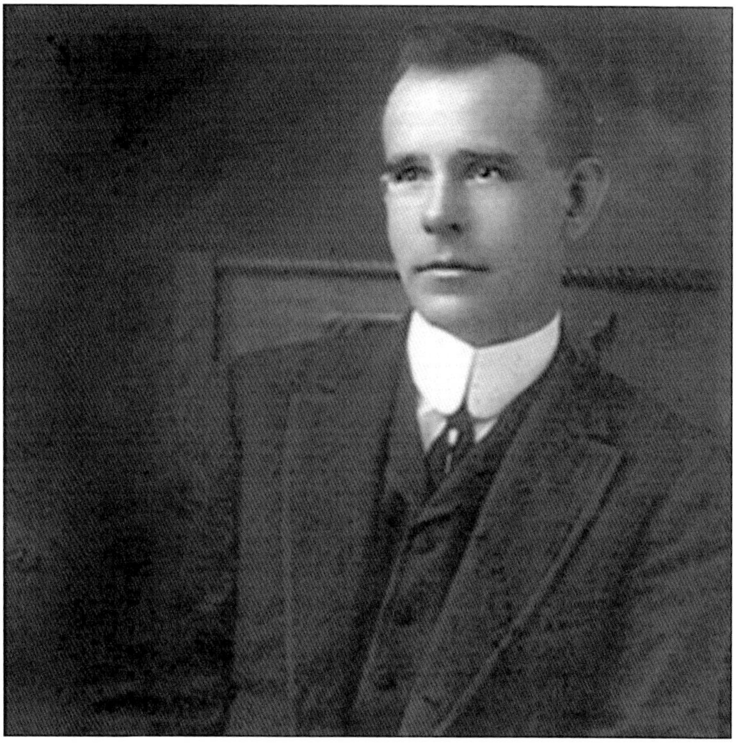

Rev. C. V. Sheatsley was a son of Israel's Lutheran Church. He was born in Paris and spent a good deal of his life in Columbus, where he went to seminary and followed Jacob Sheatsley as pastor at Christ Lutheran Church, Bexley. In this picture, the young scholar is evident. (Courtesy of the Evangelical Lutheran Church in America Archives, Chicago.)

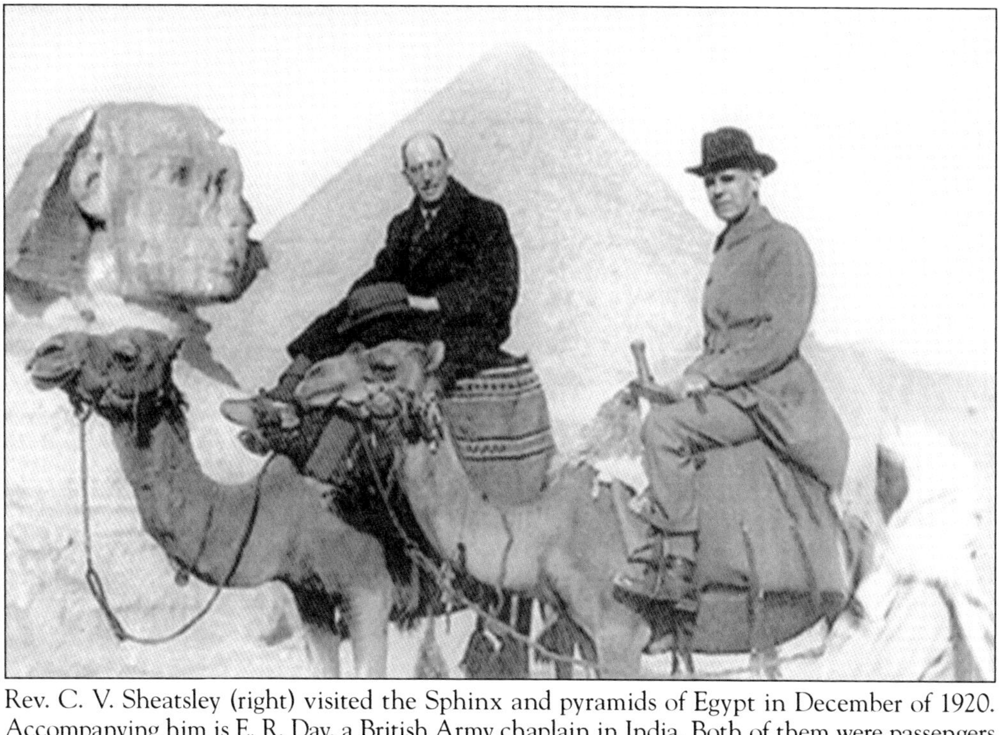

Rev. C. V. Sheatsley (right) visited the Sphinx and pyramids of Egypt in December of 1920. Accompanying him is E. R. Day, a British Army chaplain in India. Both of them were passengers aboard the SS *Narkunda*. Sheatsley was the head of foreign missions for the American Lutheran Church (ALC). (Courtesy of the Evangelical Lutheran Church in America Archives, Chicago.)

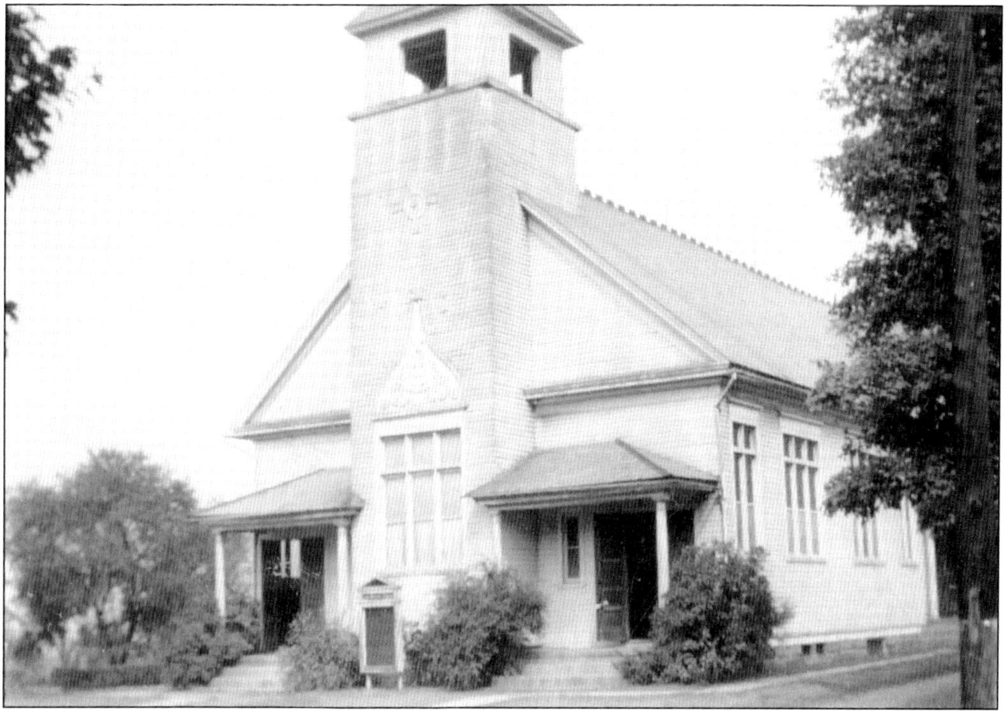

This picture was taken October 1, 1939 on Rally Day. It shows the Reformed Church, then just less than 50 years old. The ornamentation on the wood of the front of the edifice had by this point been painted white. Later the church would become plainer and this decoration would be removed or covered entirely. (Courtesy of Don and Barb Gram.)

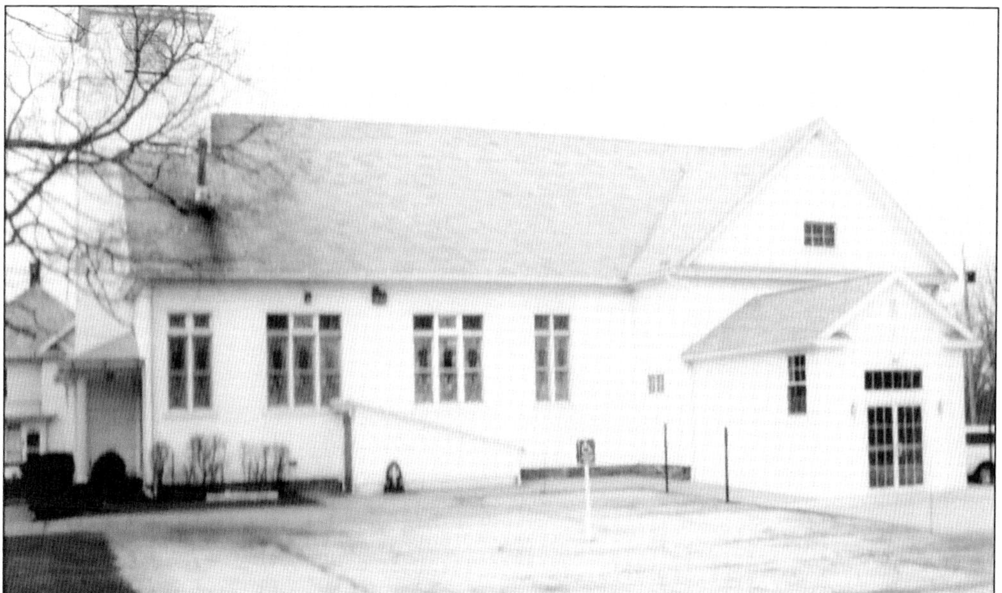

In order to facilitate those in the Reformed congregation who have special physical needs, the United Church of Christ added on to the east side of their church in 2009 to accommodate such members; this includes an elevator. (Courtesy of Israel United Church of Christ.)

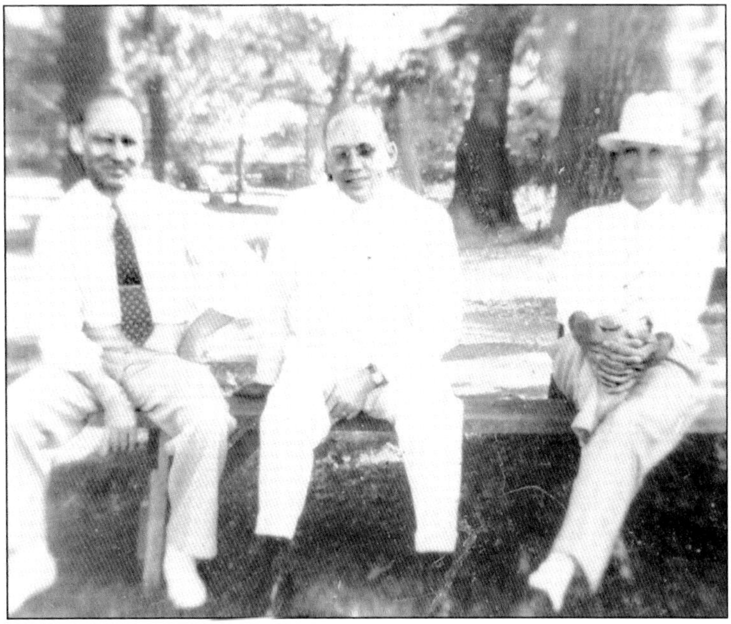

In this rare fingernail-sized photograph, Pastor John Wannamaker (left) and parishioner Elmer Koontz (right), flank Pastor Carl Duwe. This picture was probably taken at a Sunday School Picnic in Alliance judging from the pavilion in the background. The two pastors served the Lutherans at different times and would have had little opportunity to return let alone at the same time. (Courtesy of Daniel Grimminger.)

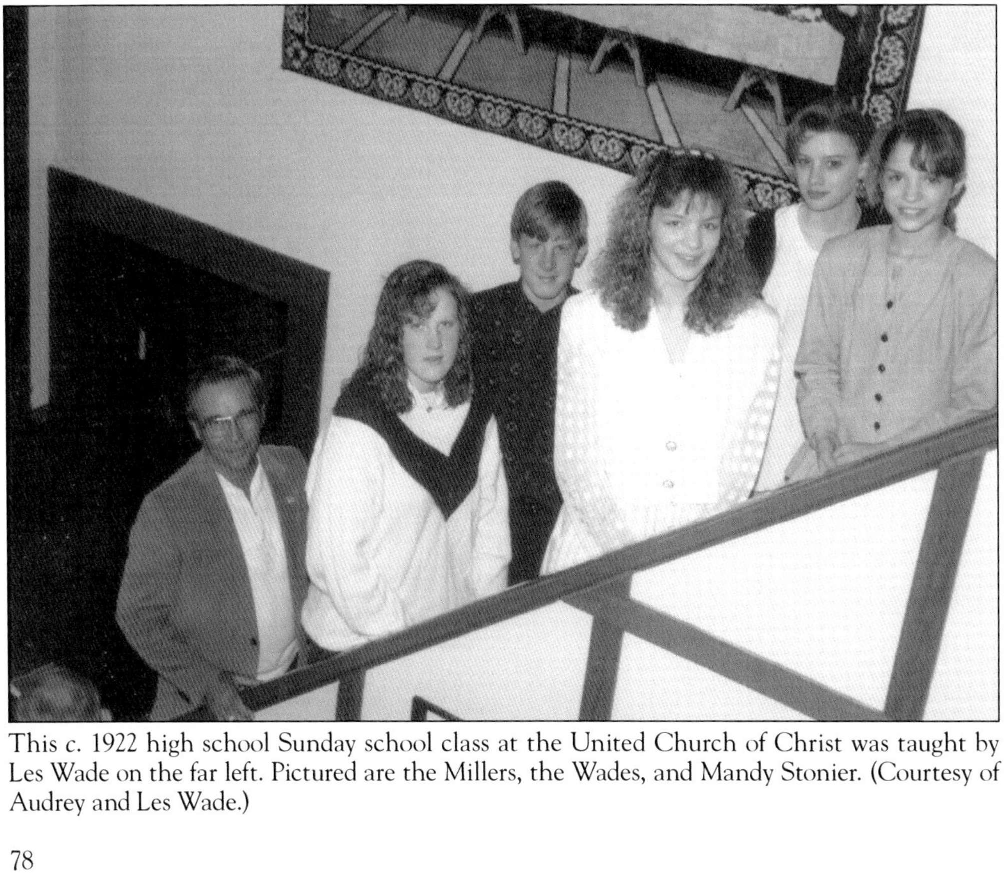

This c. 1922 high school Sunday school class at the United Church of Christ was taught by Les Wade on the far left. Pictured are the Millers, the Wades, and Mandy Stonier. (Courtesy of Audrey and Les Wade.)

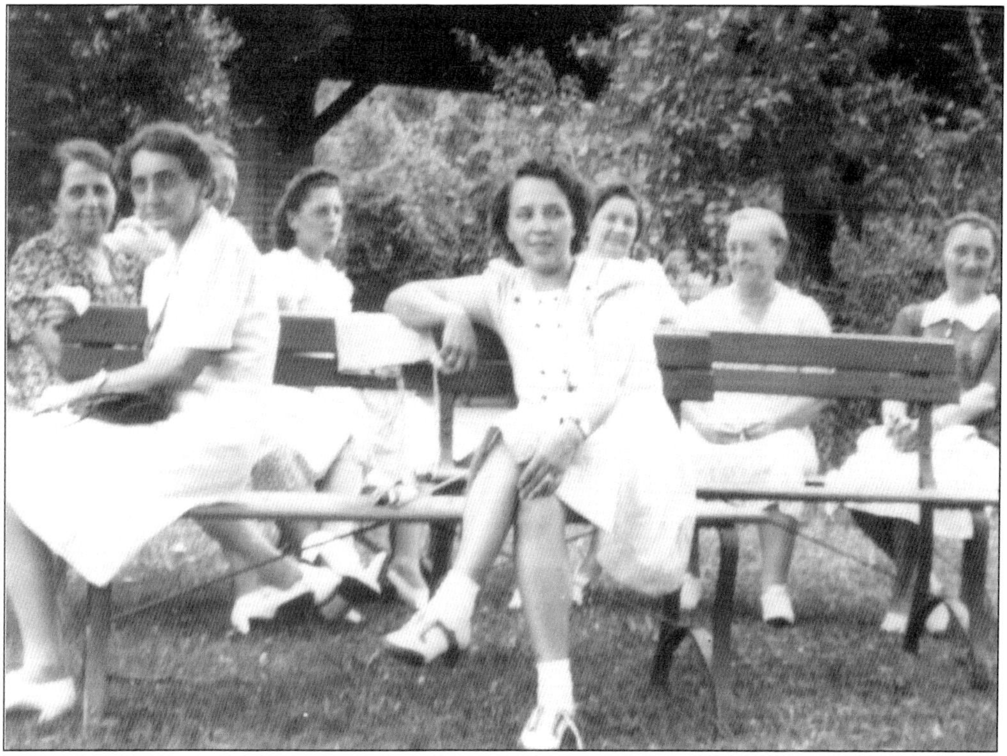

The Lutherans had an annual Sunday School Picnic every summer. At times it was at Coy's Grove, a cow pasture on the Coy farm between Paris and Mapleton, and at others in the pavilions at Silver Park in Alliance. These two pictures, taken in August 1942 at Silver Park, tell of a leisurely afternoon when the women of the Lutheran Church rested as they visited with each other. The names as they appear on the back of the first photograph, from left to right, are Anna Starkey, Mrs. Art Mong, the Starkey Girl, Fern Lutz, Ethel Crowl, Mrs. M. Mong, and Bertha Augustine. The second photograph has captured, from left to right, Amanda Lutz, Mary Lutz, Julia Wartman, Grace Wartman, Elva Lutz, and Pauline Greenwald (in the distance). (Courtesy of Charlene and Junior Grimminger.)

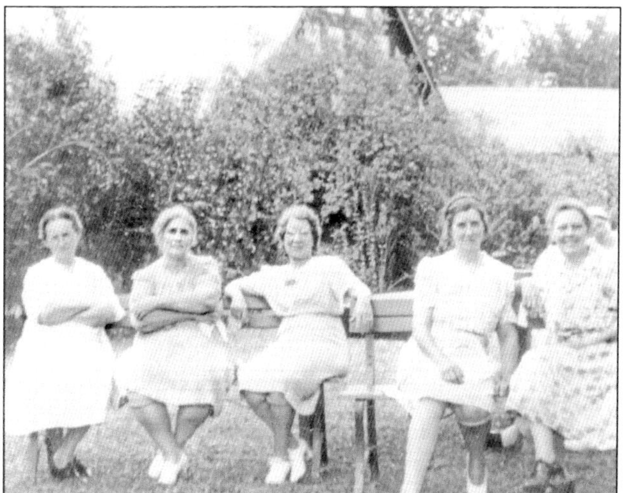

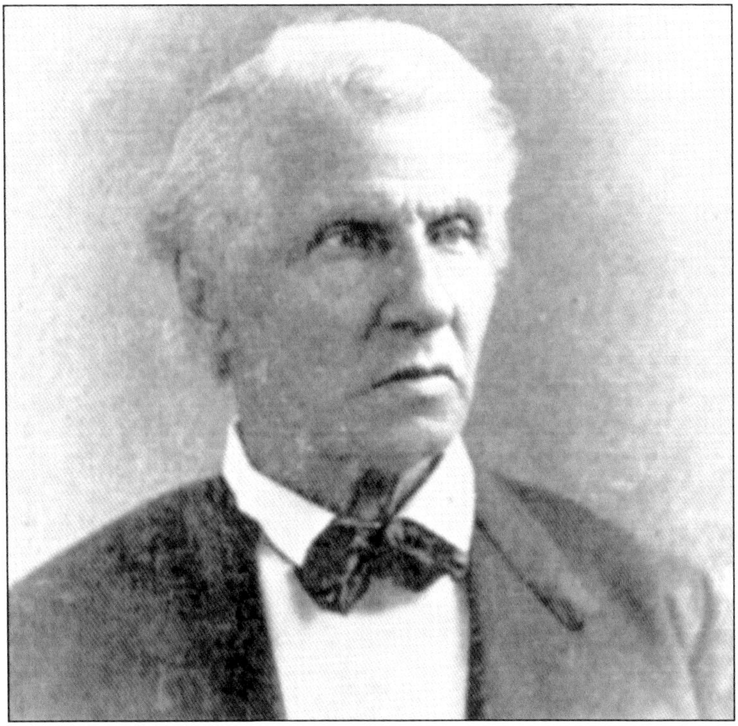

Peter Herbruck (1813–1895) was the most influential Reformed minister to serve Paris. He was born in Bavaria, Germany, and died in Canton. From 1831 to 1886, he served the Canton charge of Reformed Congregations that included Paris. During his ministry, he performed 2,611 marriages, conducted 2,560 funerals, baptized 5,938 people, and confirmed 2,717. Two of his 13 children became prominent Reformed pastors. (Taken from Bollinger's *History of Saint John's Classis.*)

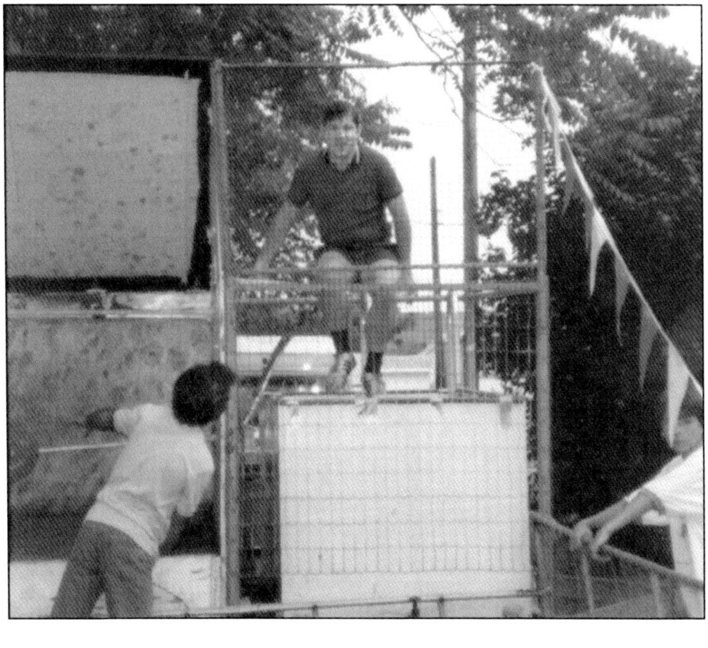

Pastor Alfred Nelson Krebs came to Paris in 1988 from the Lutheran mission fields of Peru. His down-to-earth style, fine preaching, and singing voice made him a hit with Parisians. He sat in a dunking booth to help raise money for a summer community youth program, which was funded in part by a bequeathal from the Pearl Zuber estate. Krebs is still missed in the community. (Courtesy of Daniel Grimminger.)

Because many people had Victorian tastes in American churches during the late 19th century up through the mid-1900s, many churches were painted various colors within their nave and chancel areas. The Lutheran Church in Paris is no exception. Shown here is the church interior at the time of the Lutz-Rupprecht wedding in 1964. (Courtesy of Charlene and Junior Grimminger.)

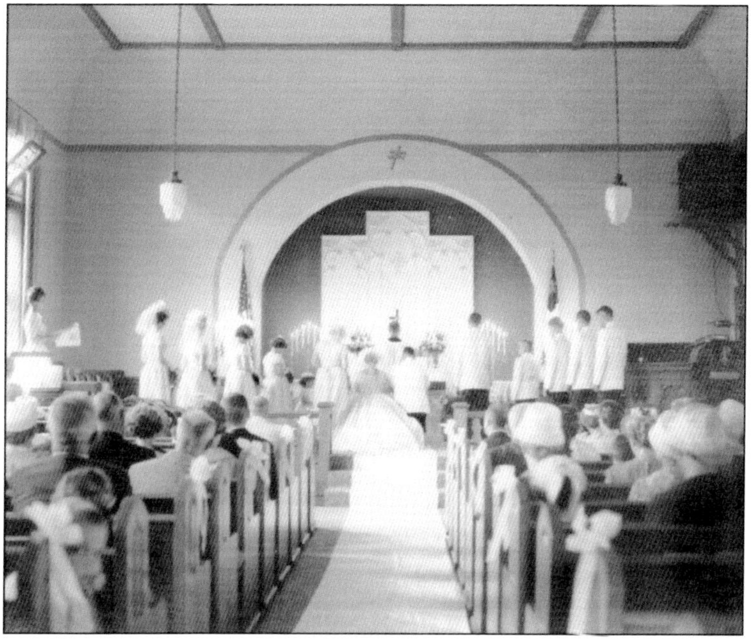

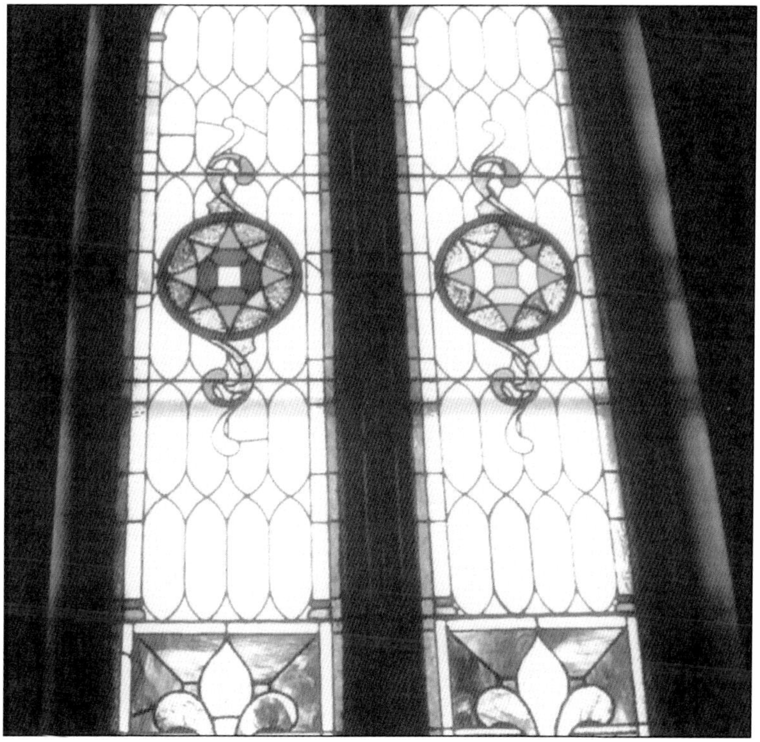

These Lutheran Church stained-glass windows are original to the first brick church structure of 1848. The basic geometric shape of the glass design has not explicit religious imagery, but Pastor Fred Krebs always interpreted the star-like medallion in the center of these windows as the Star of David. In the 1990s, all of the Lutheran windows were re-leaded by Studio Arts and Glass. (Courtesy of Esther and Wayne Schoner.)

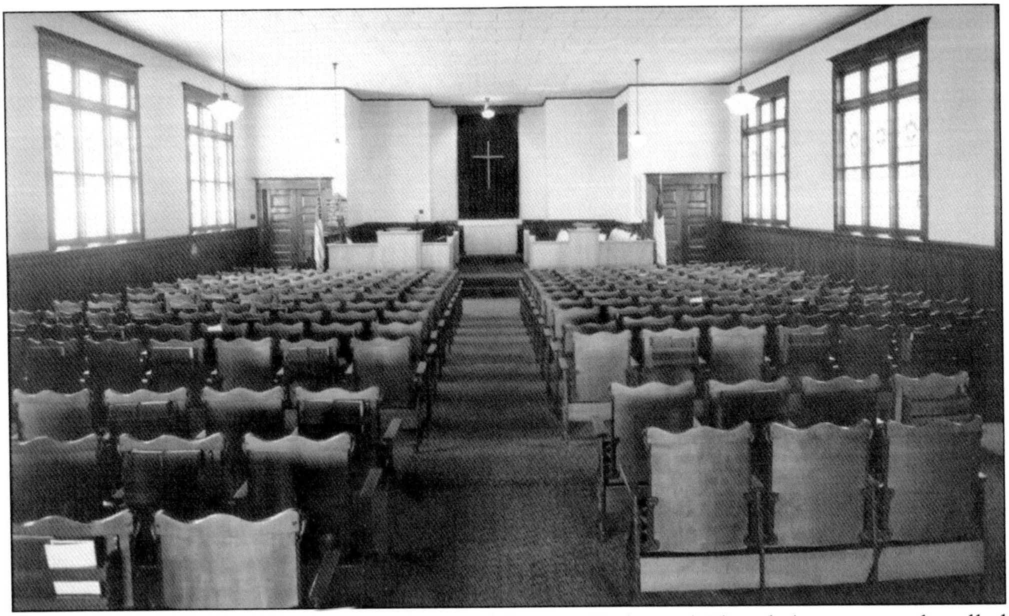

Few changes have been made to the interior of the Paris Reformed Church (more recently called Israel United Church of Christ). In this picture, one can see the auditorium-type seating that the church had before 1960. Later the congregation would replace these seats with pews in a blond finish. (Courtesy of Israel United Church of Christ.)

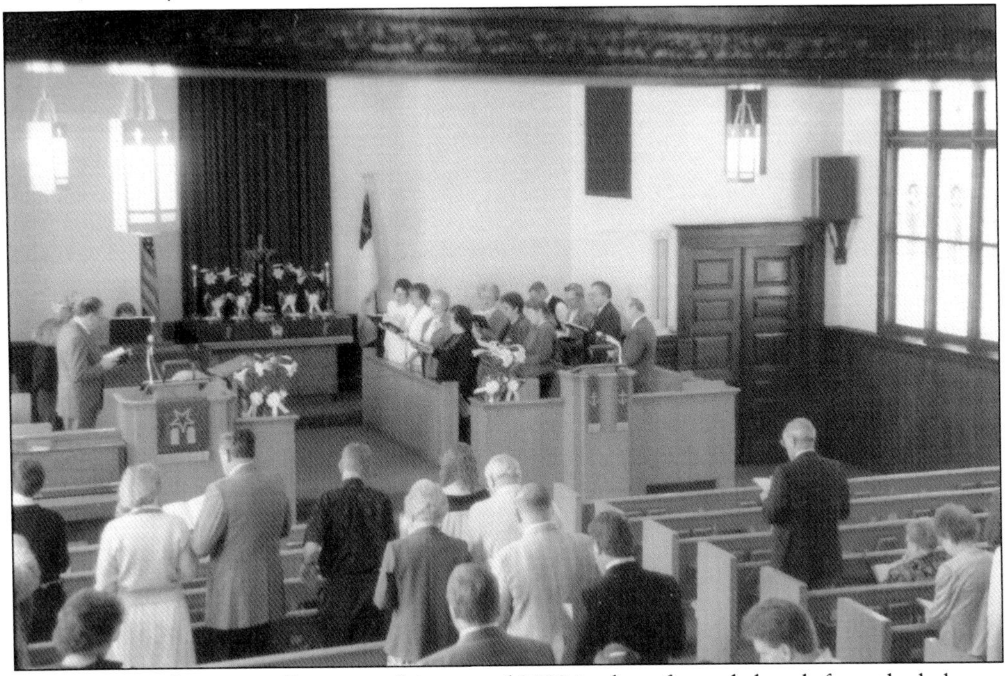

This photograph captures Easter worship around 1992 in the reformed church from the balcony. The choir and Easter lilies signal a special occasion in the liturgical calendar. Faintly noticeable is the pressed wood design in the upper part of the photograph. Originally a door came down at this place to separate the nave of the church from the Sunday school classrooms in the rear and balcony. (Courtesy of Audrey and Les Wade.)

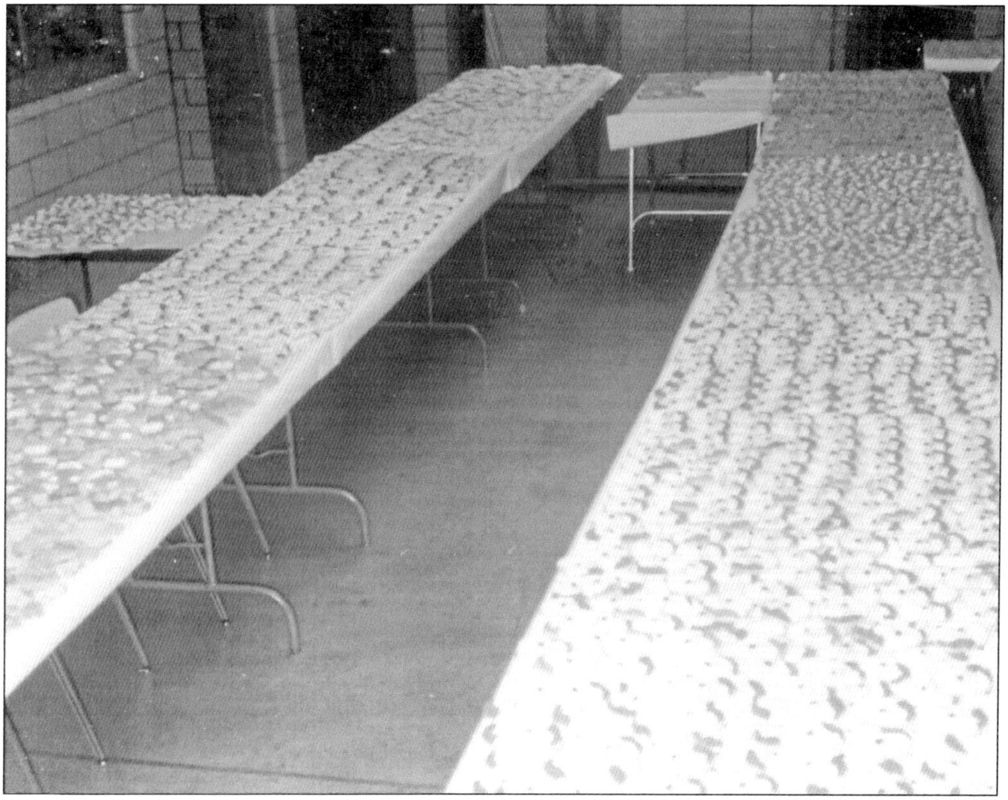

Under the valuable sponsorship of Richard and Carol Mong, the Luther League was an active auxiliary group of the Lutheran congregation. Among its annual activities was a two-week Christmas cookie bake-off that raised money for the organization. Thousands of cookies were baked at Espresso Pizza shop (East Canton) before the youth decorated them at Paris. This photograph shows a small fraction of one weekend's work. (Courtesy of Daniel Grimminger.)

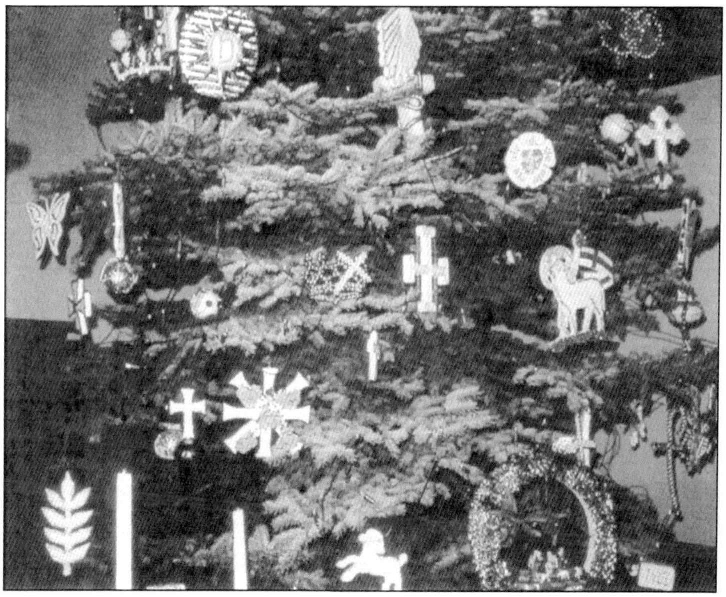

Israel's Lutheran congregation has a Christmas tradition that stretches back into the middle years of the 20th century involving the hanging of "Christmons" on their tree. These decorations, depicting religious symbols in white and gold, were made by the women of the church. Every year the Luther League would decorate the church on a Saturday. (Courtesy of Esther and Wayne Schoner.)

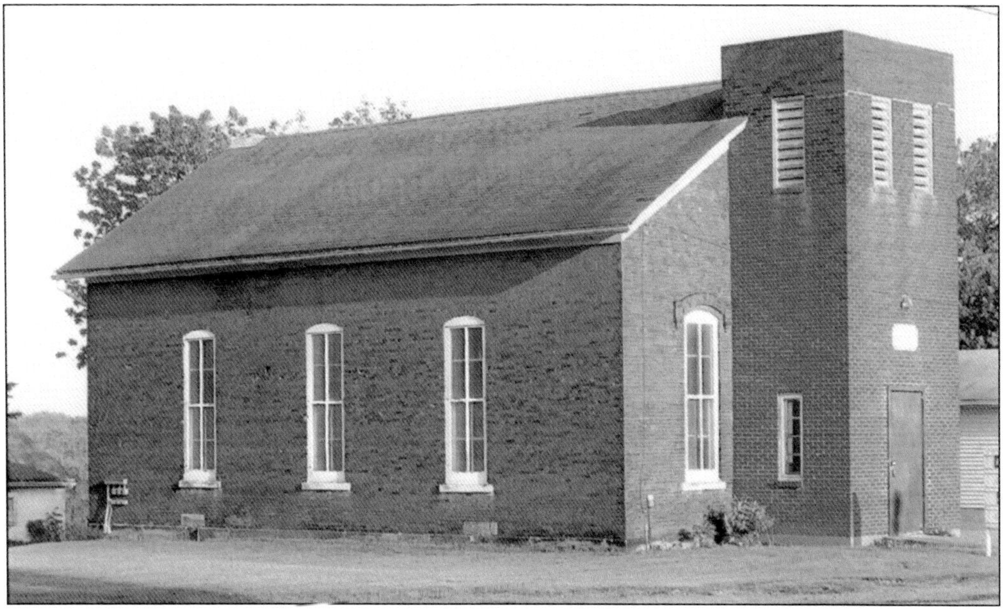

While it was always a small congregation, the Emory Chapel was at the center of the village. It may be because the German congregations in town discouraged revivalism for many years that Methodism did not take hold earlier in Paris as it did in Minerva, Osnaburg, and New Franklin. Andrew Carnegie gave money to the congregation to help them buy a piano. (Courtesy of Daniel Grimminger.)

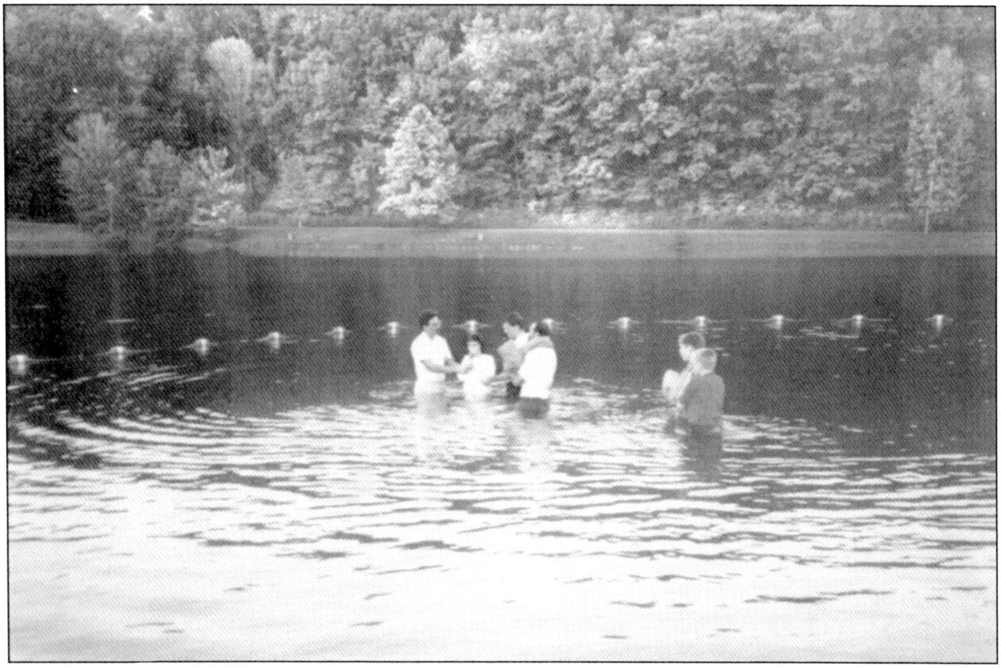

Not only are the churches in Paris active, but there are other religious groups at play in the life of the area. Bob and Ruth Fisher, owners of Hidden Valley Lake, allow outside religious groups to come use their lake for Baptisms. Here Ruth Fisher receives the Sacrament shortly after moving to Paris. (Courtesy of Bob and Ruth Fisher.)

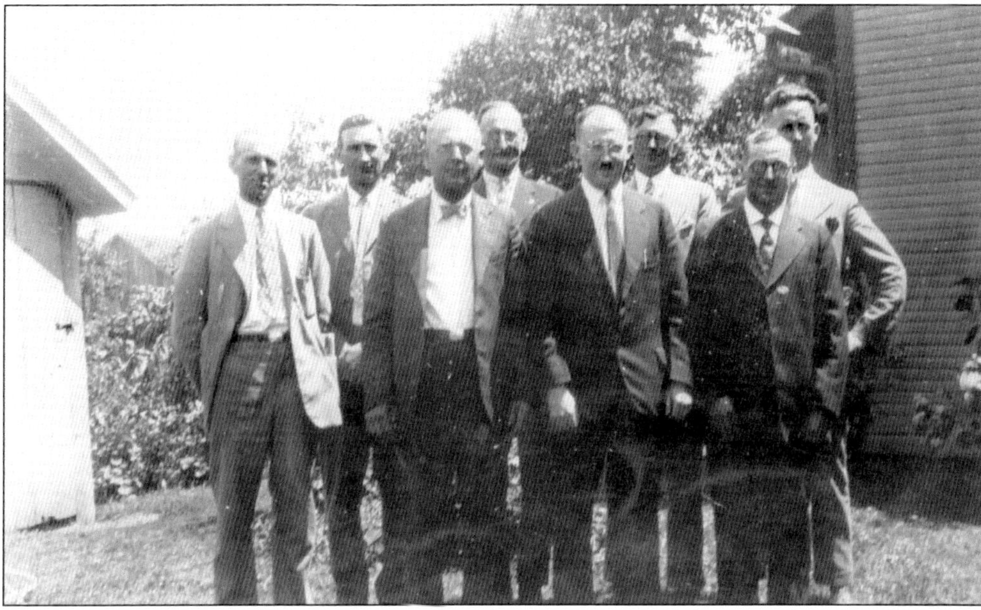

The Reformed Church called its governing board a "Consistory," while the Lutherans called theirs a "Church Council." The members of the 1926 Reformed Consistory appear in this photograph. They are, from left to right, Tom Motts, Homer Foltz, Amos Ramsayer, G. L. Starkey, Rev. Elliker, Bert Sprankle, Roscoe Skelley, and Ed Waltz. (Courtesy of Israel United Church of Christ.)

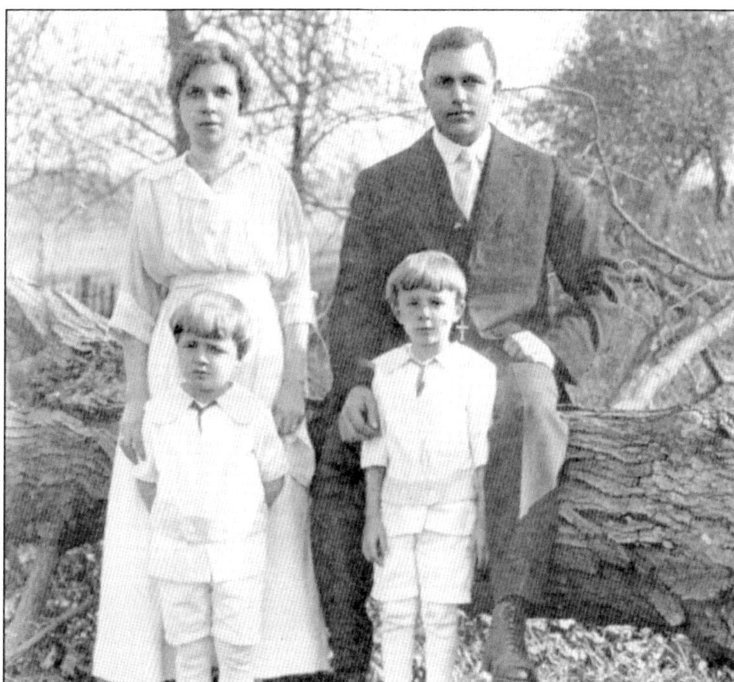

Rev. C. L. Cooperider and his family pose at a fallen tree for this picture. He was the Lutheran pastor responsible for the establishment of a high school in the Paris School. However, it only lasted about four years. Like many of the other Lutheran clergy to come to Paris, the Cooperiders were also involved at Columbus with Lutheran higher education and parish work. (Courtesy of Daniel Grimminger.)

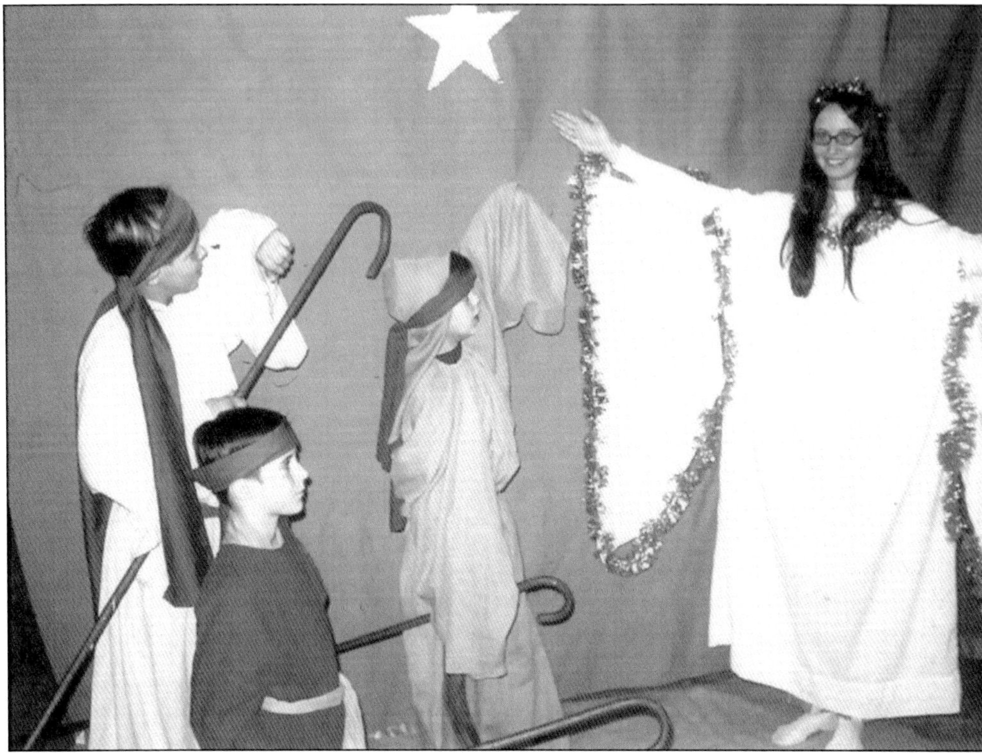

Members of the Lutheran Church remark about two monumental Christmas Pageants in the last 100 years that are memorable. The first happened possibly in the 1930s or 1940s. The hooks that they used for the curtains were permanently put into the walls of the chancel and are still present. This picture is a scene from the second one in 1972. Diana Monhemius served as the Angel, while the shepherds are unknowns. (Courtesy of Esther and Wayne Schoner.)

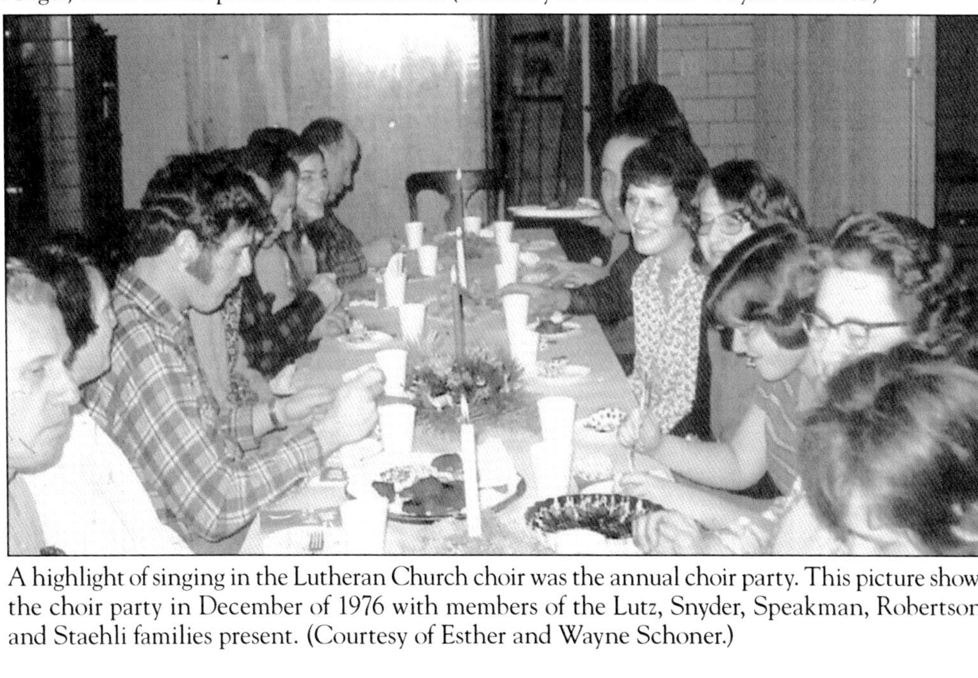

A highlight of singing in the Lutheran Church choir was the annual choir party. This picture shows the choir party in December of 1976 with members of the Lutz, Snyder, Speakman, Robertson, and Staehli families present. (Courtesy of Esther and Wayne Schoner.)

Wilhelm Schmidt, one of the most important clergy to serve the village, is memorialized in this bronze tablet at Trinity Lutheran Seminary in Columbus. He lived a very short life (1803–1839) because of his strenuous labors as a pastor, seminary founder, and teacher of young seminarians. After he established his seminary in Canton, the Lutheran synod moved it to Columbus. (Courtesy of Daniel Grimminger.)

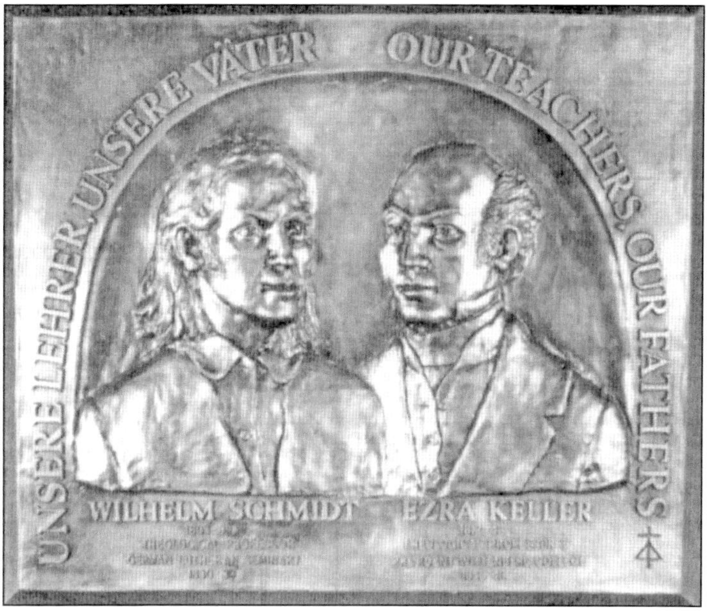

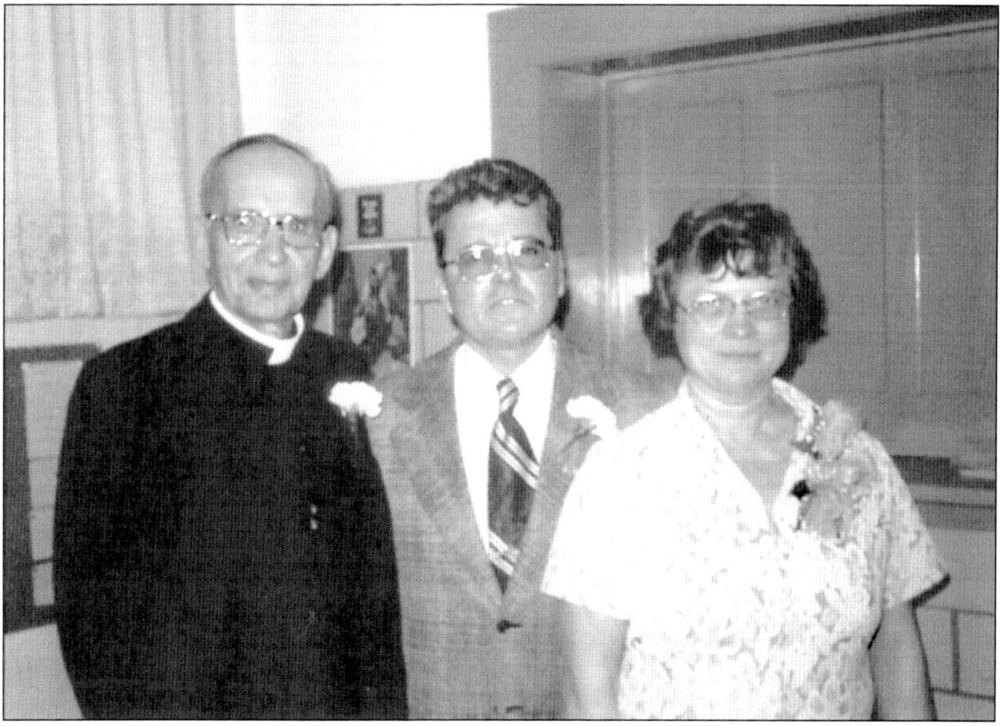

Many people came to Paris for Pastor Donald Rice's 25th anniversary of ordination. He served Paris Lutherans from 1969 to 1987. Pictured from left to right are Pastor Carl Duwe (1903–1996), who served the Paris Lutherans in the first half of the century, and Pastor and Miriam Rice. Under his pastorate, the church grew numerically and the congregation was healthy. (Courtesy of Esther and Wayne Schoner.)

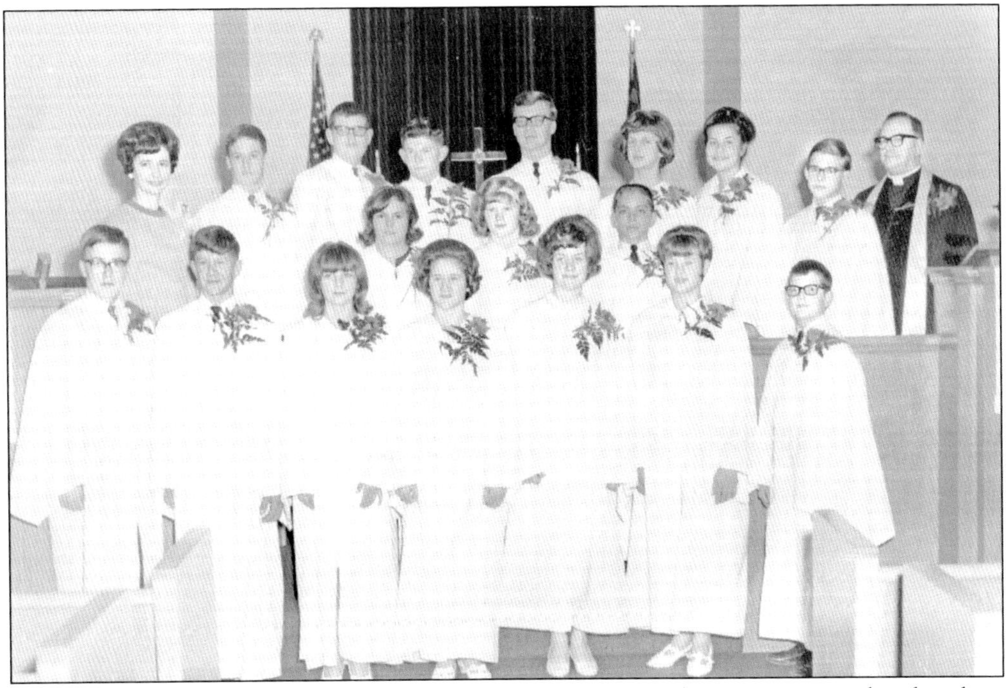

Rev. Dr. Denver Springer, possibly the most educated Reformed pastor to serve the church in Paris, confirmed this large confirmation class in 1967. The lay catechist, Marion Wilson is also pictured on the far left of the back row. (Courtesy of Israel United Church of Christ.)

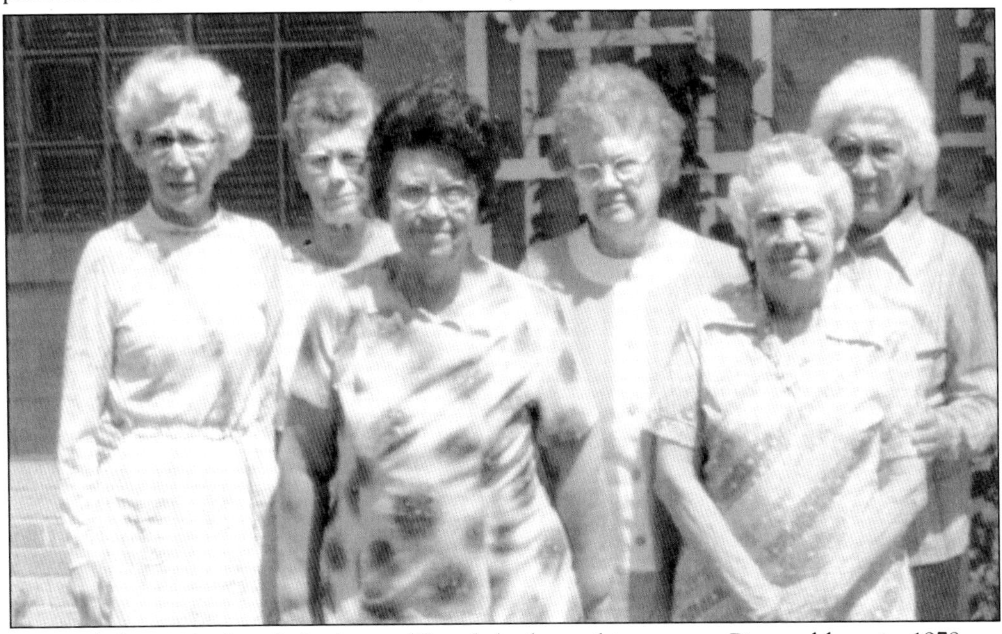

Up until the 1990s, Israel's Lutheran Church had a quilting group. Pictured here in 1978 are the remaining quilting ladies. From left to right they are (front row) Verda Myers Erb and an unidentified woman (who may have been Alice Lautzenheiser even though she was not a Lutheran); (back row) Lois Lutz, Pauline Greenwald, Pauline Thomlinson, and Hilda Wilson. (Courtesy of Daniel Grimminger.)

Four

EVENTS

Early Paris was lively. One account, which gives clues as to the happenings around the town, claimed, "We've had some mighty big celebrations here. . . . One time the republicans put up a flag pole and the democrats put up a bigger one, just to get ahead of the republicans. The republicans then put up a pole 200 feet high and when that was up we had a big celebration" (Howells).

The most prominent and stable event of modern Paris has been the annual Memorial Day festivities. This involves a parade with color guard, the East Canton Band, fire engines, historic cars and tractors, and children either riding bikes or marching. Years ago, these kids would often hold irises, but now small American flags are usually given to the children for them to carry. The Lutheran Church and United Church of Christ (Reformed) rotate every other year to run the "eat stand," which raises money for a project or operating expenses of either church. After the parade, a service follows in the cemetery.

Square dances are held twice a year. The street is closed off, and young and old alike come out to swing their partners. These dances happen on Memorial Day and Labor Day weekends. The Paris Lions Club has a chicken barbeque every year, and folks from all around come to eat at the square of Paris and to take out food.

Out of all of the recent private celebrations of the village, the Jedel-Graf wedding might have drawn the largest crowd. Rosemary Jedel, whose father, Ulrich, is a German immigrant and who grew up next to the current post office, married an outsider. Both of them had international connections that brought people from several continents to the wedding. The celebration started with the rehearsal dinner, which consisted of a roasted pig and homemade apple wine (made by the bride's brother Ricky) and a square dance in the street. Another Jedel brother provided other entertainment with juggling and fire tricks.

Beyond Memorial Day, the two existing churches have celebrated milestones in recent years as has the village (1964 and 1989).

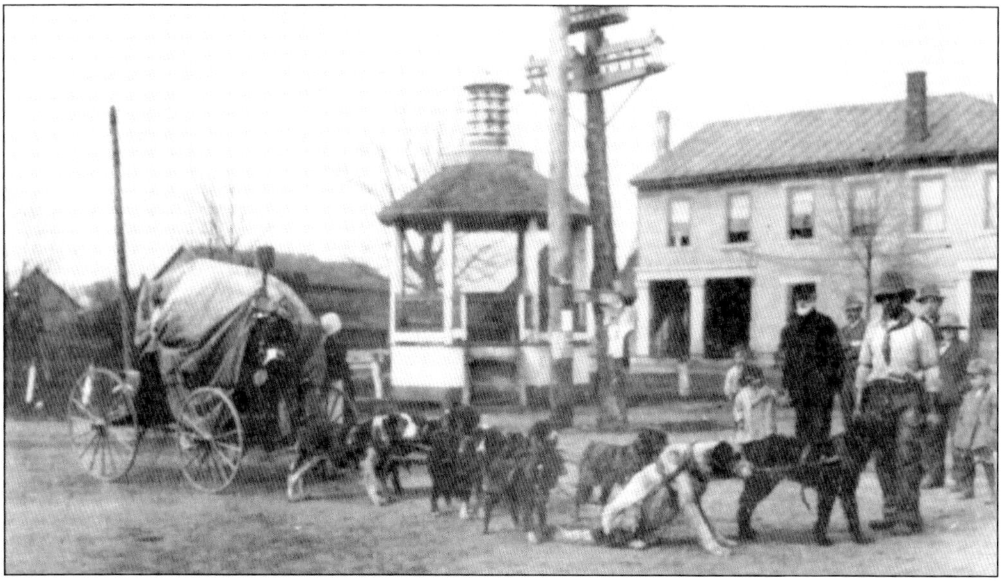

At the center of the village, laid out in the shape of a cross, is the square, where socializing and festivities always took place. Pictured here around 1900 is a traveler who stopped through Paris with his dog team. The bandstand and the martin houses overlooking the square are clear here as is the Kintner Store. (Taken from *Paris, Ohio Sesqui-centennial.*)

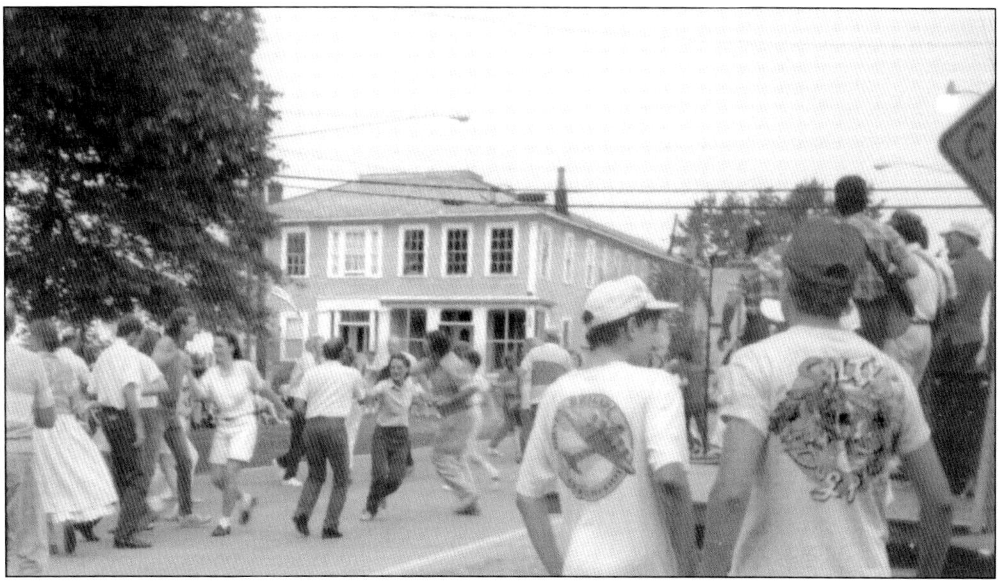

Square dances still happen twice a year in the village. The street is blocked, the hay wagon is parked to the side of the Methodist Church building for the caller and band, and the people come to dance or watch. Few places have regular square dancing in this area anymore, which says something about Paris. (Courtesy of Daniel Grimminger.)

Mamie Stimmel, the village schoolteacher, would bring people in the community together and give them parts in plays. Here John Stimmel, the town's talented mechanic, is shown in his costume for one such play that happened at the old Creek School just west of the village. Betty (Stimmel) Speakman, his daughter, tells the story that this play was taken on the road to such places as Washington Township to the Fox School. (Courtesy of Betty Speakman.)

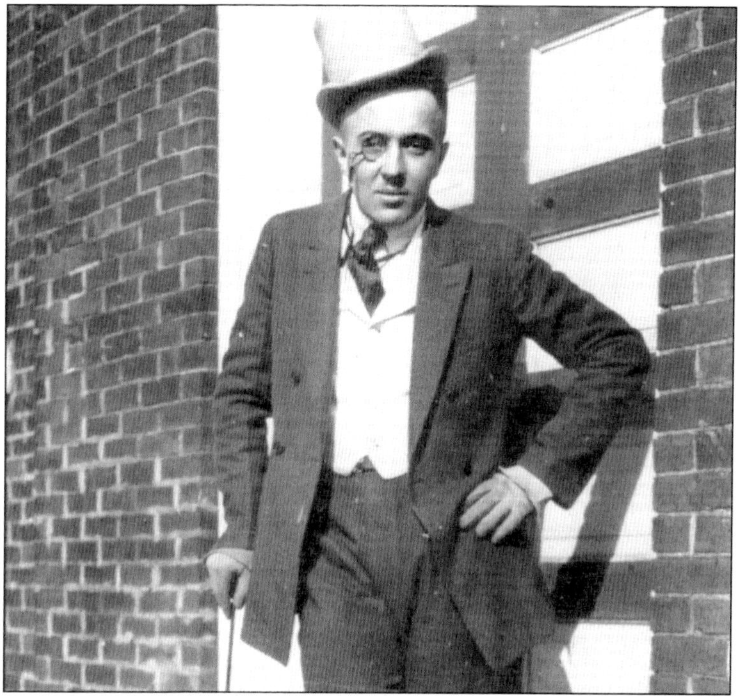

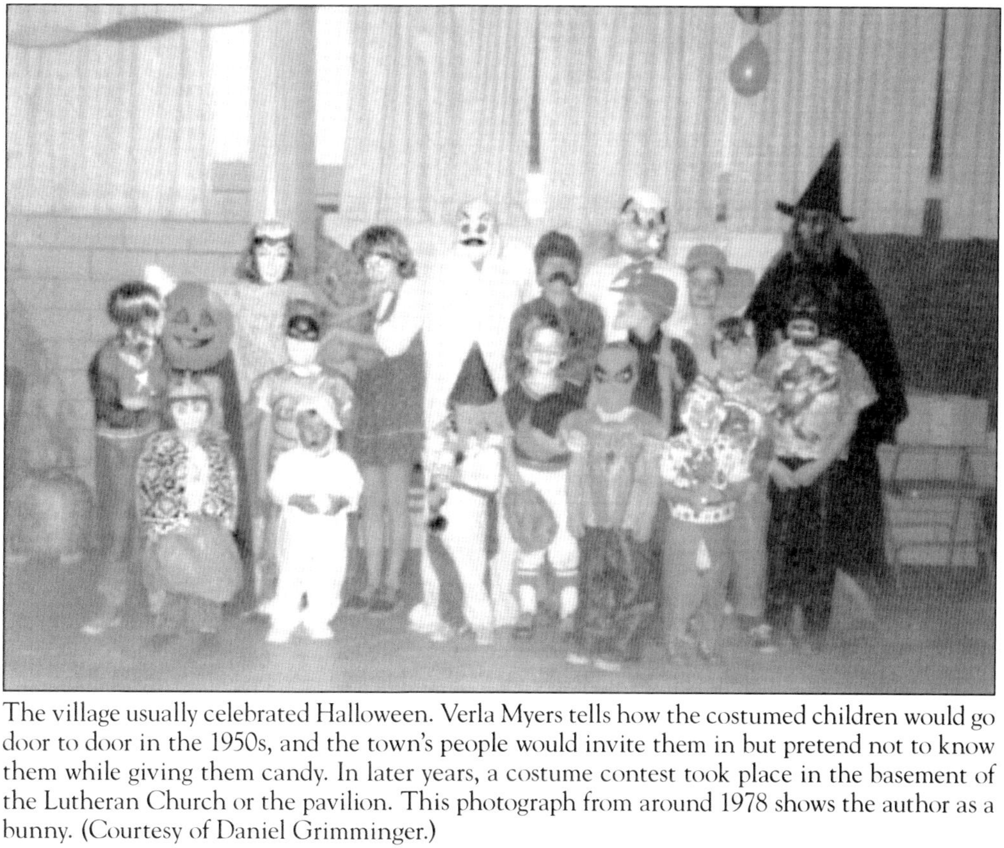

The village usually celebrated Halloween. Verla Myers tells how the costumed children would go door to door in the 1950s, and the town's people would invite them in but pretend not to know them while giving them candy. In later years, a costume contest took place in the basement of the Lutheran Church or the pavilion. This photograph from around 1978 shows the author as a bunny. (Courtesy of Daniel Grimminger.)

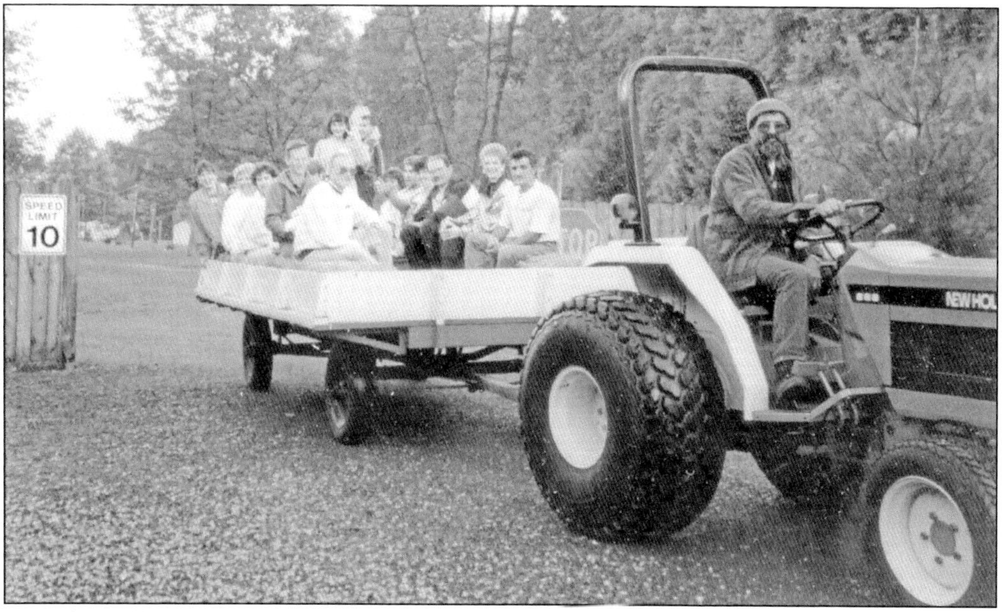

Hayrides and bonfires are common in farm country at harvest time. Bob Fisher, owner of Hidden Valley Lake, is shown here on the tractor giving rides to a church group. This ritual is usually accompanied by a wiener roast and fresh apple cider. (Courtesy of Bob and Ruth Fisher.)

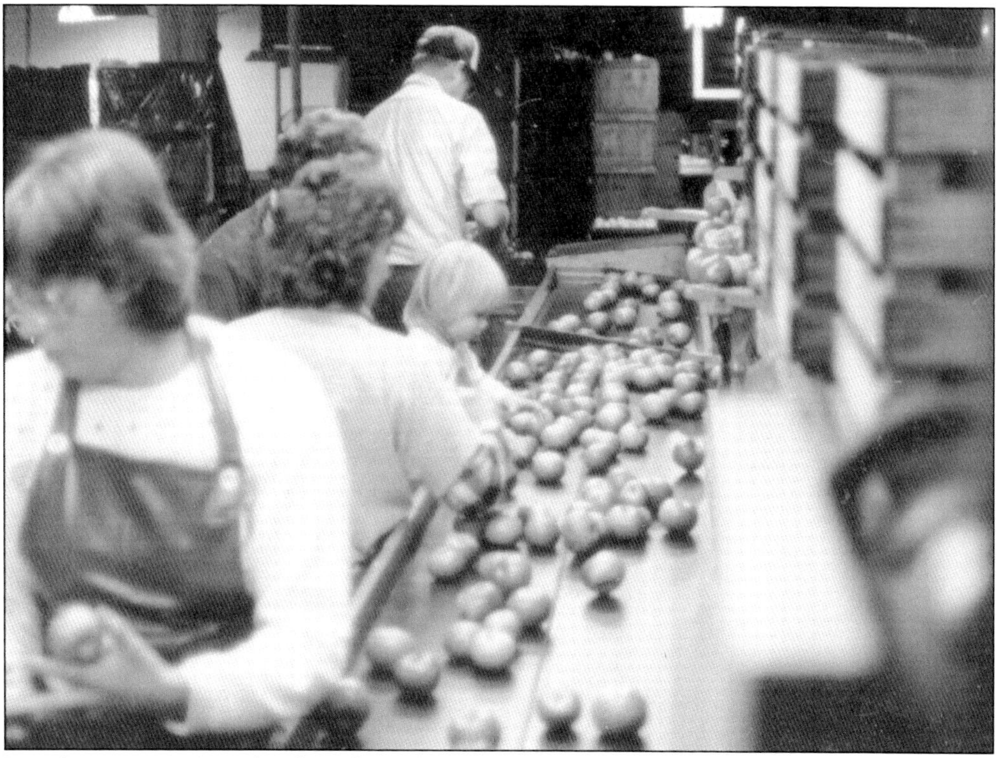

It is a busy time at Arrowhead Apple Orchard in the fall. Sorting thousands of apples is a constant process as they are brought in via large crates after being picked. The sorters grade them on size and condition. (Courtesy of Fred and Truus Monhemius.)

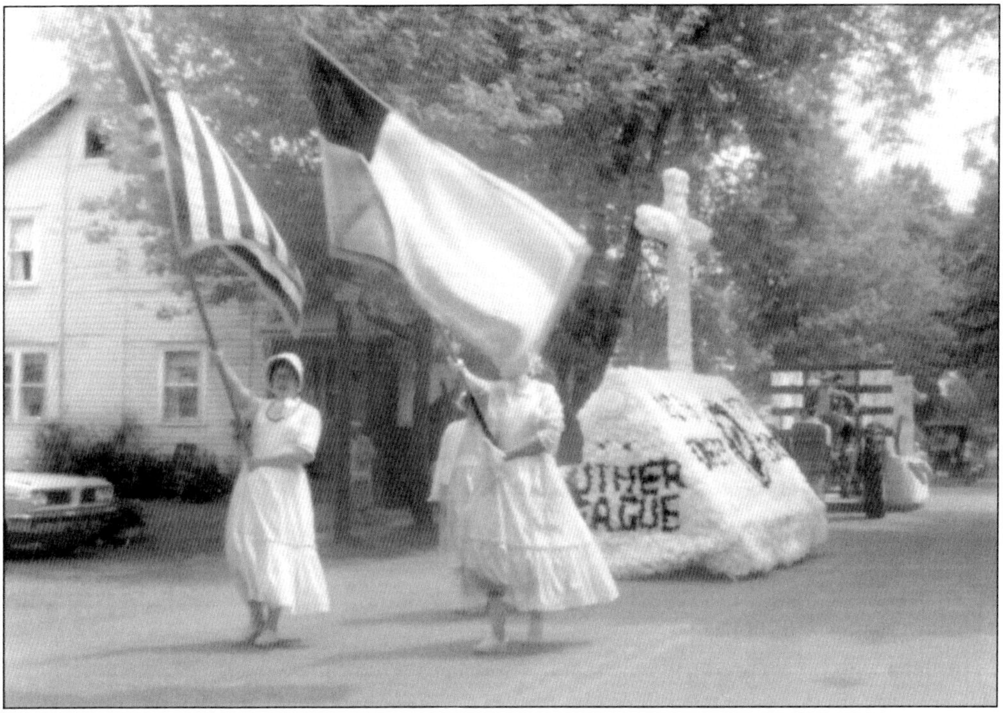

One of the most celebrated events in Paris history was the sesquicentennial (1964). Men grew beards, a community picnic was held at Hidden Valley Lake, and a parade topped the celebration. Lutheran youth (the "Luther League") built a float and decorated it for the parade. Pictured in front of it are Joy (Lutz) Armstrong on the left and Charlene (Lutz) Grimminger on the right. (Courtesy of Charlene and Junior Grimminger.)

Part of the yearly Paris ritual involved erecting snow fencing. Pictured from left to right, Louis Beutler from Paris, Elmer Garner of Robertsville, and George Gill from Paris were part of 13 Stark County crews to remove approximately 30,000 feet of fence that year. This photograph shows them working 1 mile north of Paris toward Freeburg. (Courtesy of Audrey and Les Wade.)

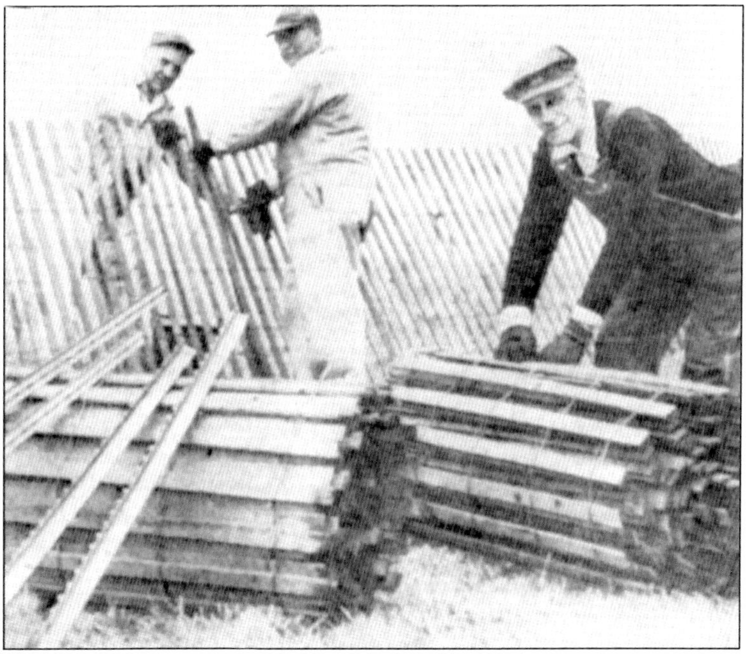

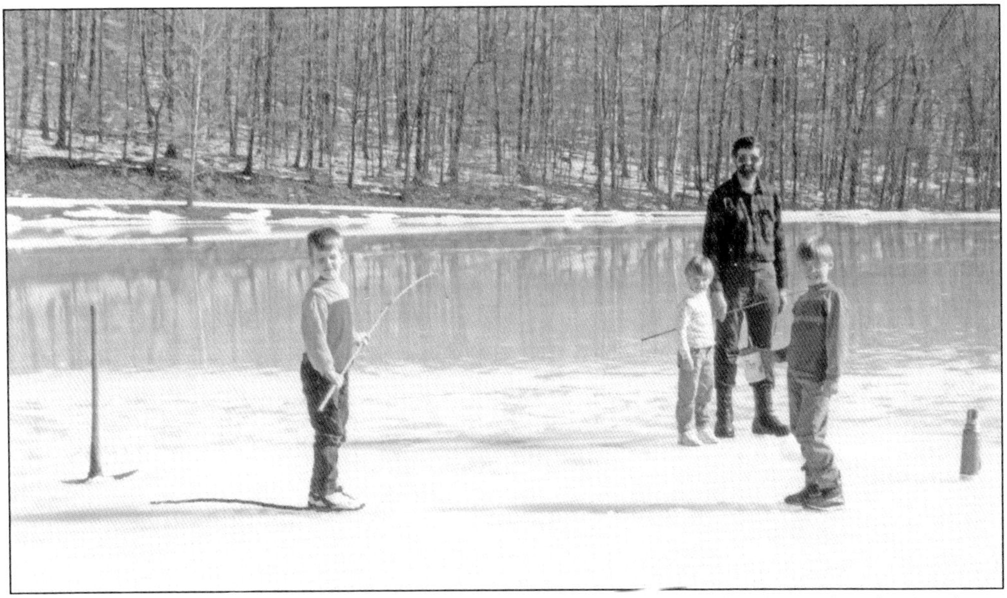

It is not very often in the Paris area that one hears about ice fishing today, but Bob Fisher has been known to take his grandchildren out on the ice at Hidden Valley Lake for the rare opportunity. Pictured here on the ice in March 1993 are Bob and his grandchildren, from left to right, Michael, Holly, and David. (Courtesy of Bob and Ruth Fisher.)

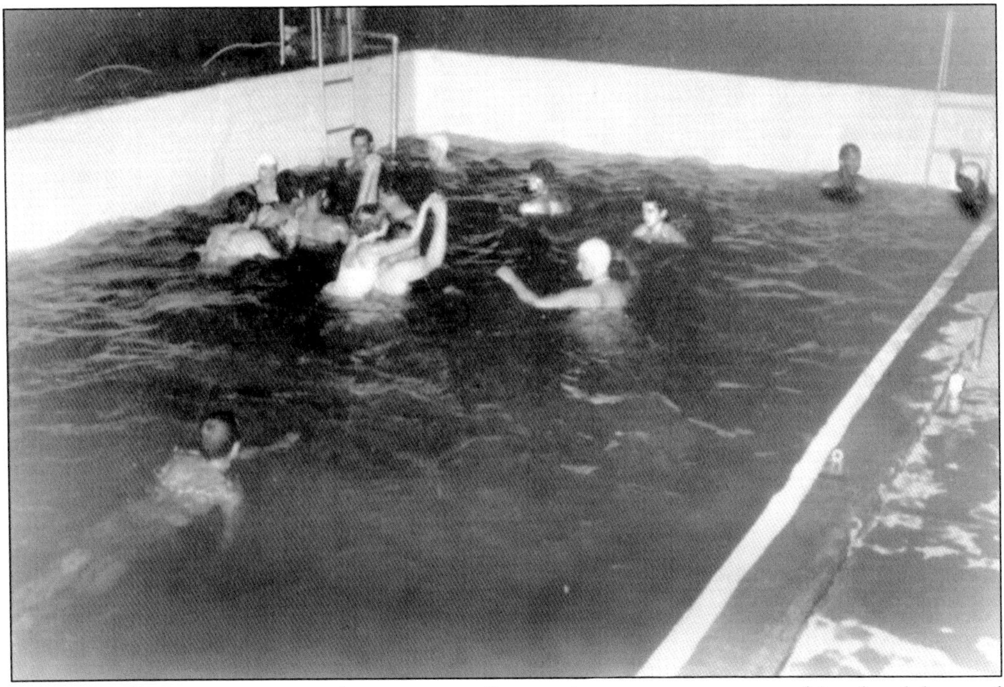

In a time where swimming pools were a city fixture, it was rare to see anything but lakes and swimming holes in the country. Many people in the area recall swimming in the Sponseller lake (on Parks and Georgetown Roads). In 1961, the Grimmingers poured the cement by hand on their farm to make their own swimming pool and held a pool party in October. (Courtesy of Charlene and Junior Grimminger.)

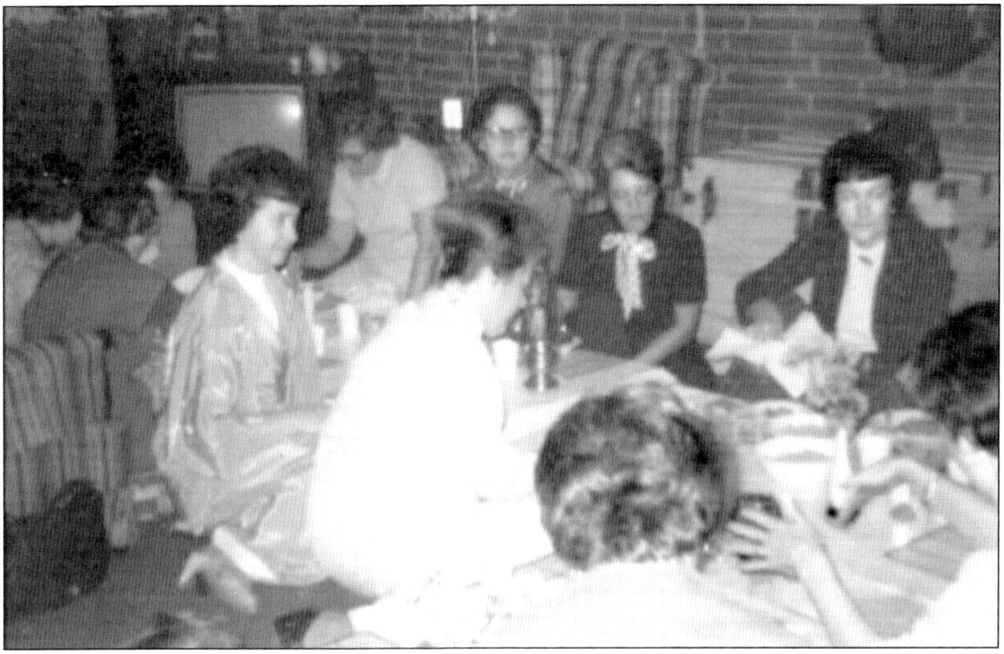

The Paris Junior Civic League has been an active force in the Paris area for the better part of a century. At this event, held in December 1974, the woman gather at the home of Charlene Grimminger for an Asian meal served on the floor; some of them even came in Asian attire. (Courtesy of Charlene and Junior Grimminger.)

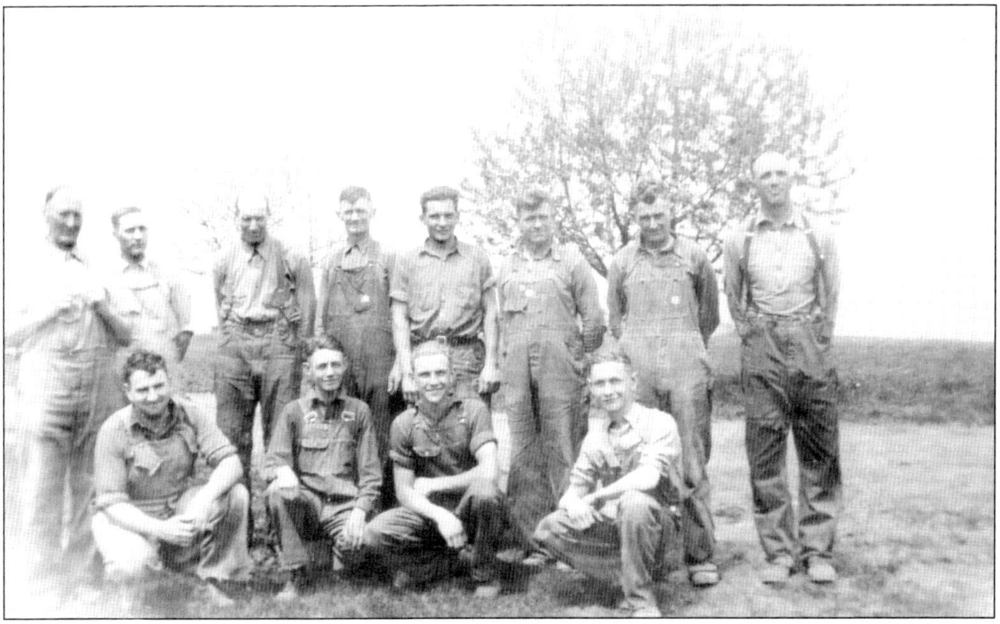

At harvest time, the farmers would share a threshing machine and each other's labor. They would migrate to each farmer's land until they had all of their work done. At lunch and supper, the wives would pull out their best china for the crew. Pictured here is a thrashing crew around 1935 that included Jay Lutz Sr. (far left, front row), Charles Lutz (second from right, back row), and Abe Comfort (fourth from left, back row). (Courtesy of Charlene and Junior Grimminger.)

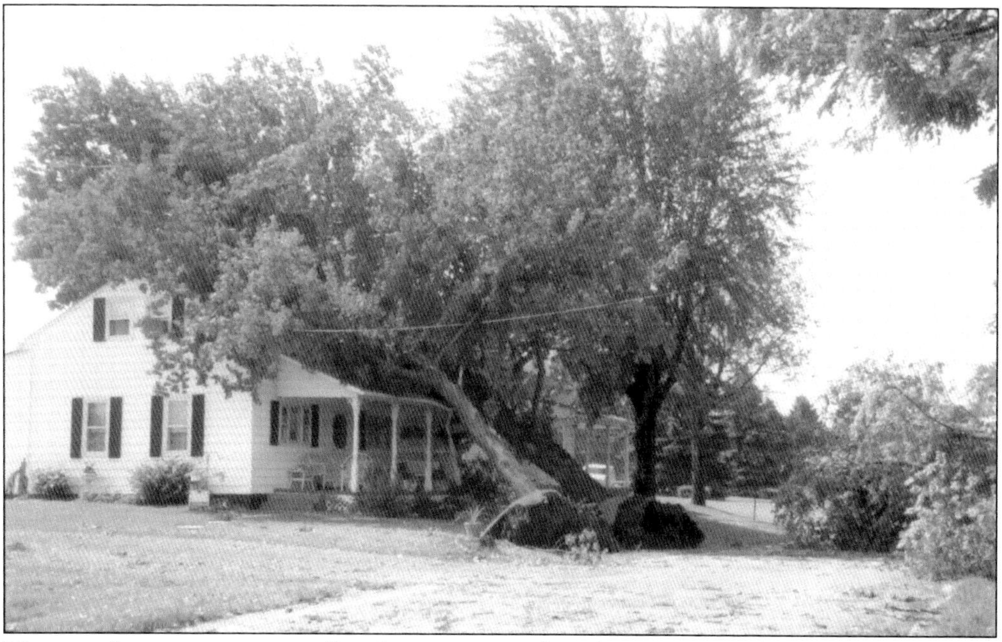

The most devastating events in Paris history seem to have been two tornados in the 20th century. While there were no fatalities in either incident, thousands of dollars of damage was done to local properties. In the 1998 tornado, Barbara (Kenny) Wise's house served as a pillow for the tall, aged trees in front of her house just south of the cemetery. The 1998 tornado was extreme. Normally Paris is immune to tornadic activity because of its place high on a hill. As a result of this "Microburst," as the local papers and newscasters called it, all ways in and out of the village were blocked for several days with trees and debris, and electric service was cut off for over a week for some residents. The photograph below was taken by the author looking south from the Methodist Church building. (Courtesy of Daniel Grimminger.)

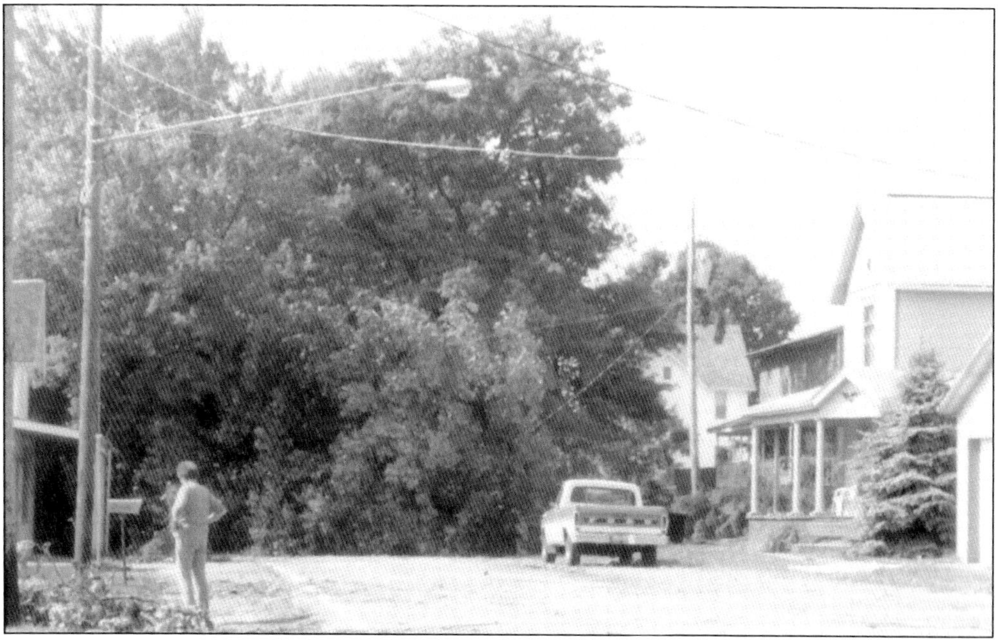

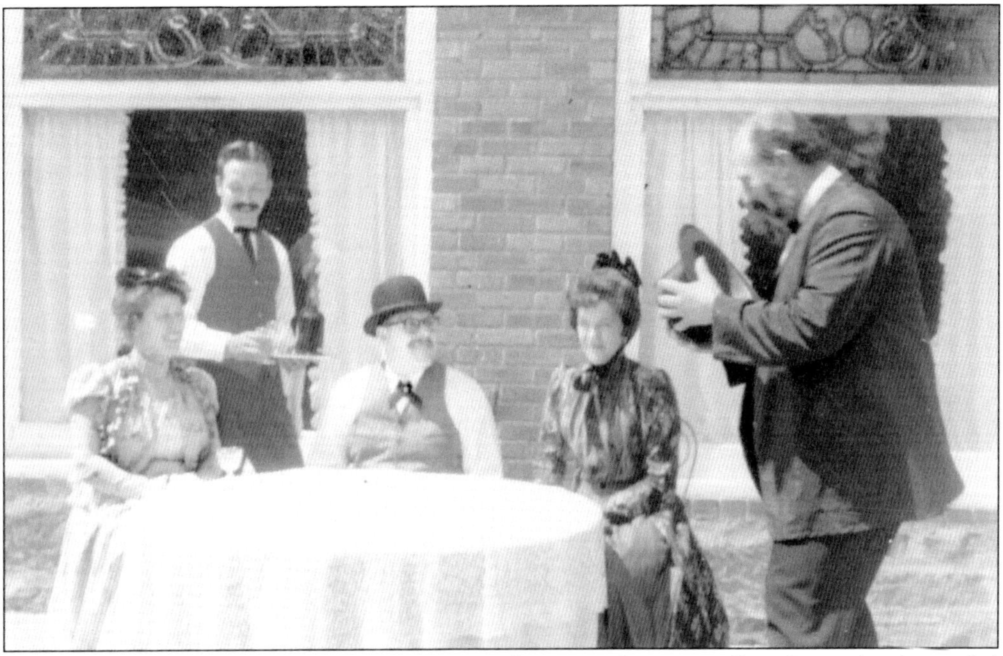

The sesquicentennial was a huge homecoming of Paris residents as well as those who descended from Paris families. Many people dressed up in 19th-century attire as part of their observance of the village's birthday. Pictured here from left to right are Donna Monnot, Les Wade, Herm Monnot, Audrey Wade, and Millard Speakman.

The Paris Cub Scout troop was led in the mid-1980s by Sue Miller. She often held the meetings in her farmhouse just south of Paris on Paris Avenue. Here the scouts pose on Memorial Day before marching in the parade. Pictured from left to right are Daniel Grimminger, David Goodge, Dan Riggle, and an unidentified boy with troop leader Sue Miller. (Courtesy of Daniel Grimminger.)

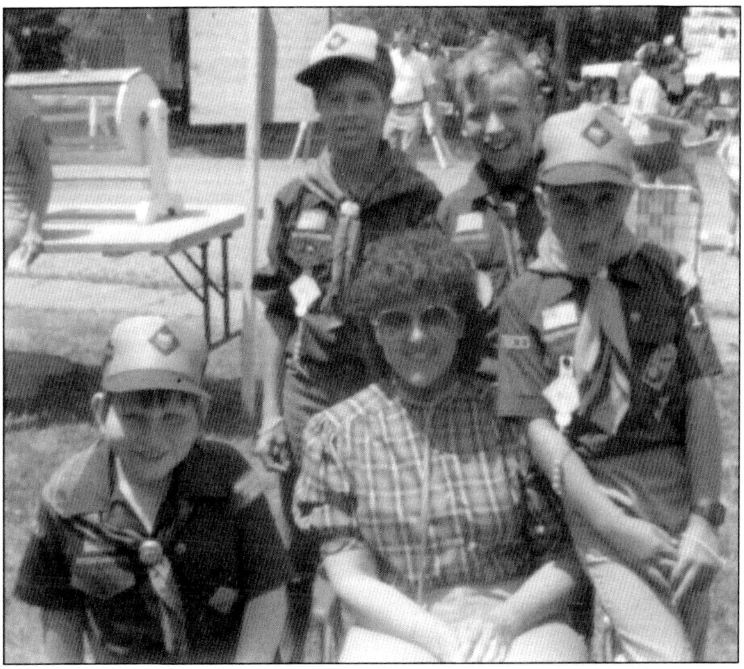

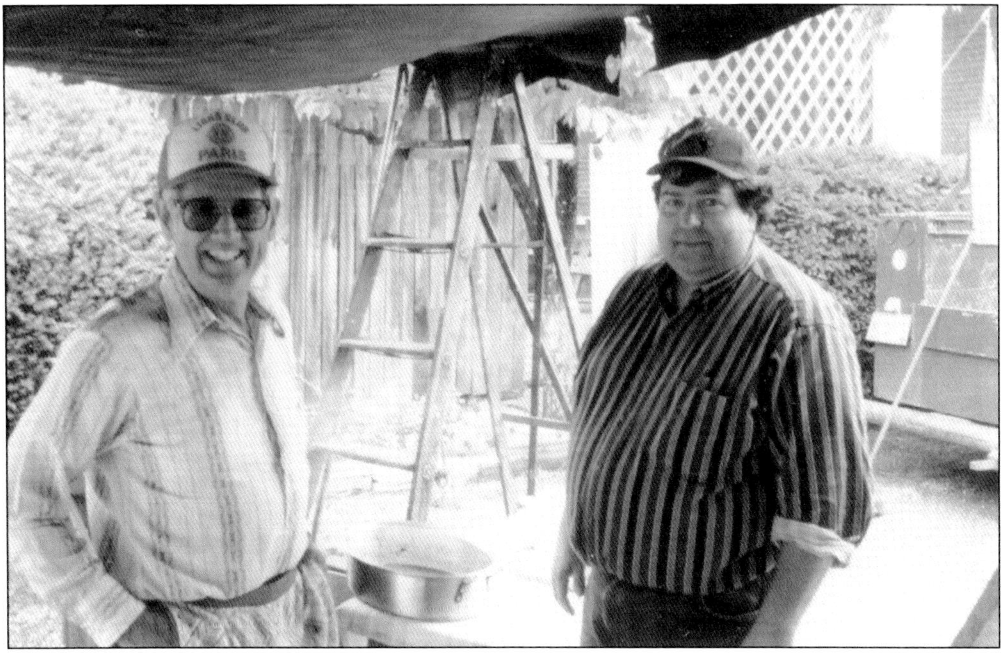

The village Lutheran and Reformed people take turns every other year with the "eat stand" on Memorial Day. Behind the building, the men generally grill and prepare other food items, and inside the pavilion the final preparations go into each order. Pictured here are Austin Snyder (left) and Jay Lutz. (Courtesy of Daniel Grimminger.)

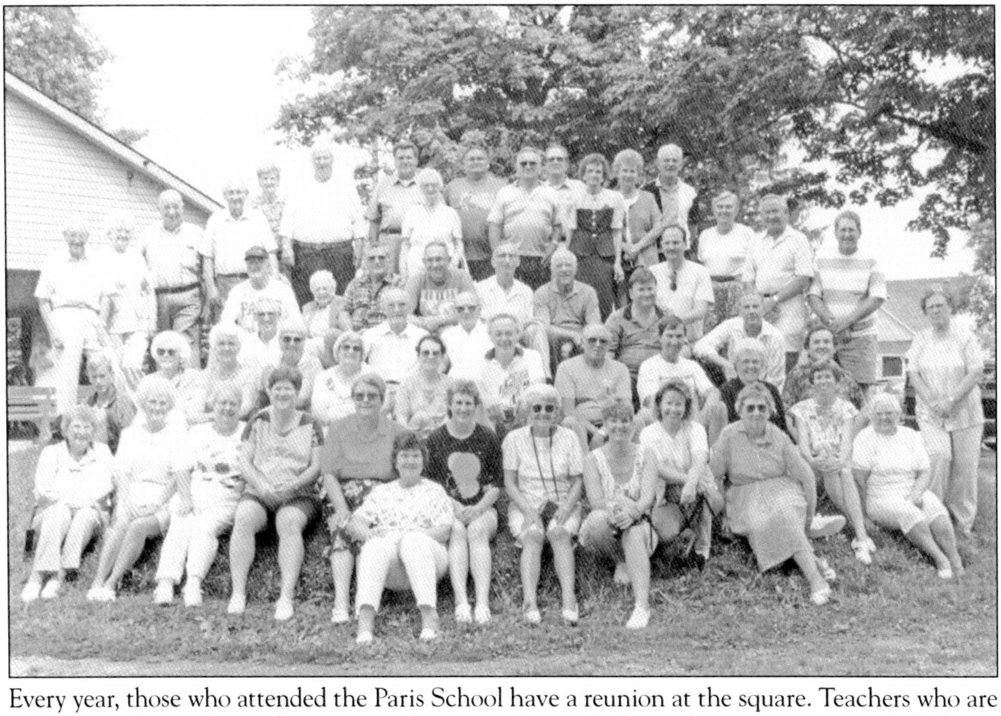

Every year, those who attended the Paris School have a reunion at the square. Teachers who are still living also traditionally come to the event. In 1995, the gathering was particularly large. (Courtesy of Audrey and Les Wade.)

Five

Music

The arts have flourished in the village for many years. Early on, Paris had its own "military company," complete with a drummer, Peter Myers, and a fifer, Samuel Unkefer (Danner, 67). Most of the residents, being of Pennsylvania-Dutch stock, used their private hymnals and likely followed the Pennsylvania tradition of holding singing schools to help folks learn how to read music and provide another means of socializing. A "Paris Coronet Band" photograph proves that by the end of the 19th century, Paris seems to have reached a high level of musical proficiency just as their Pennsylvania relatives had by this time.

The next century, however, saw two influential music teachers. Edna Burget, a spinster who lived on a family farm just outside of Paris with her single sisters and brother, taught hundreds if not thousands of students, as did Betty Keith. Keith, a transplant from Canton, had an organ and piano studio on the Keith farm south of Paris and taught for the Hammond Organ Studio in Alliance. The author also taught lessons in his home.

Pipe organs in Paris are copious. Fred Monhemius, who came from the Netherlands after World War II, played for many years in the Lutheran Church, which has a Hillgreen and Lane Organ. Early in 1966 he purchased a mechanical-action organ from the Lutheran Church in Hartville and installed it in his basement at the Arrowhead Apple Orchard. Likewise, the author, a student of Keith's, purchased the 1970 Wicks organ from Kountze Memorial Lutheran Church (Louisville) for his home to practice on and concertize guests.

It is significant that the Juilliard family, endowers of the Juilliard School of Music, lived just west of town. Their cultural influence is not certain, but they probably brought music to Paris.

Betty Onyett made her mark on the village. Originally from Alliance, she bought the Kintner Store in the 1980s and held "music parties" of baroque and later folk music. She was a trained cellist and her sister Louise Love, an opera singer, trained at the Curtis Institute of Music. Sometimes three or four rooms would be full of simultaneous music-making.

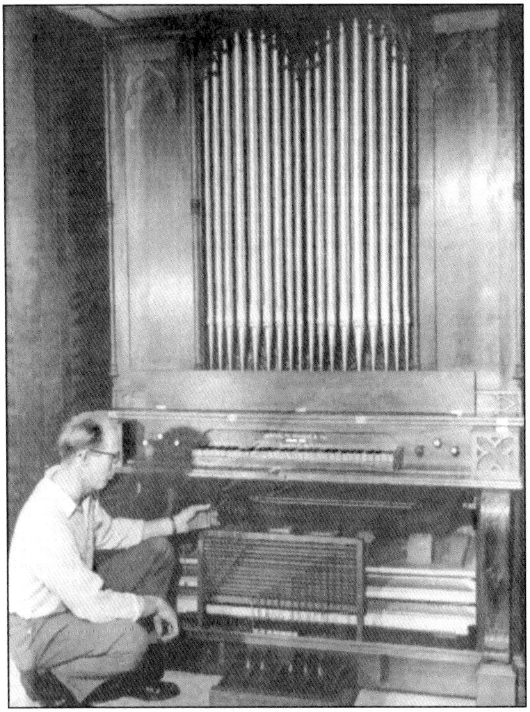

Fred Monhemius purchased this historic mechanical-action organ from the Lutheran Church of New Baltimore, which sold their building to an Anabaptist church that had no need for an organ. The 200 wood and lead pipes and its electrified air chest made this Derrick, Felgemaker Company organ a conversation piece. (Courtesy of Fred and Truus Monhemius.)

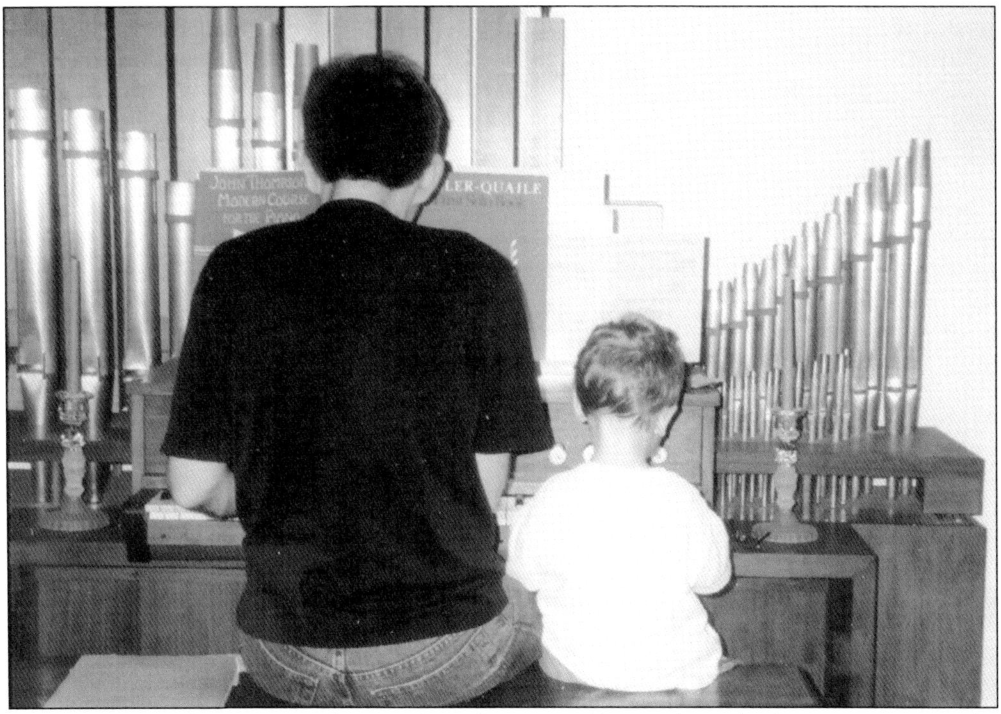

Having gained early inspiration from Fred Monhemius and his mother, Charlene Grimminger, who would hold him on her lap to play her Allen organ in the home, the author became an organist. He eventually bought this 1970 Wicks organ with a divided keyboard and full pedal board for his Paris home. Seated with him on the bench is his little nephew Brandon Grimminger.

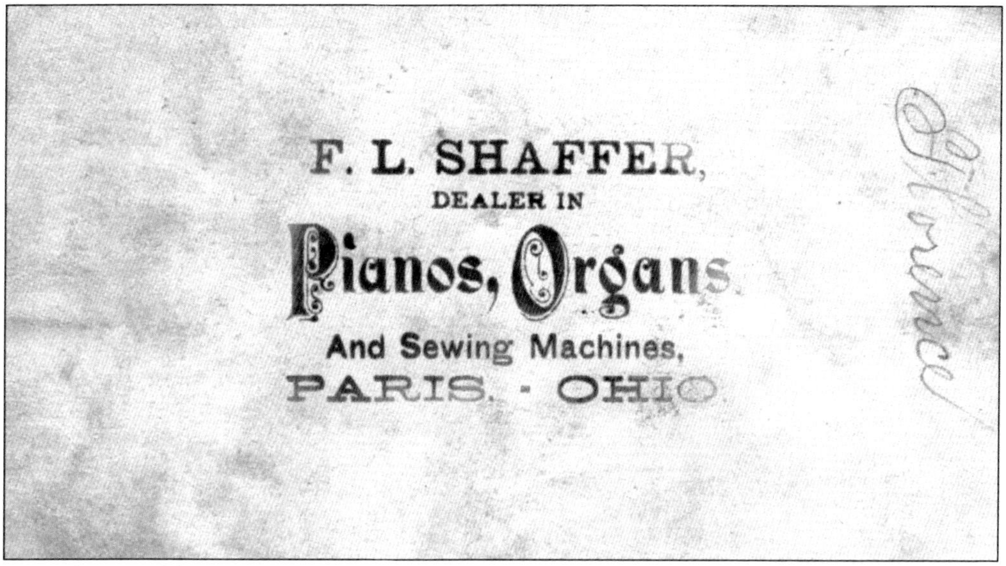

According to older Parisians, pianos and organs were sold in the Meiser Store building on the north side of Lisbon Street across from the square. The colorful illustration on the front of the card would have been a draw to little kids whose parents wanted them to learn how to play an instrument. In Europe and America, by the mid-1800s, the piano was a sign of social status. Not only was it practical as most families and friends would gather in the parlor room to make music together, it also showed that the owner had reached a level of social status that surpassed their ancestors, making it popular even in Paris. The author remembers such pianos in the homes of Doris Myers and Doris Rice, where the owners were not able to play much, but they retained the instruments nevertheless. (Courtesy of Daniel Grimminger.)

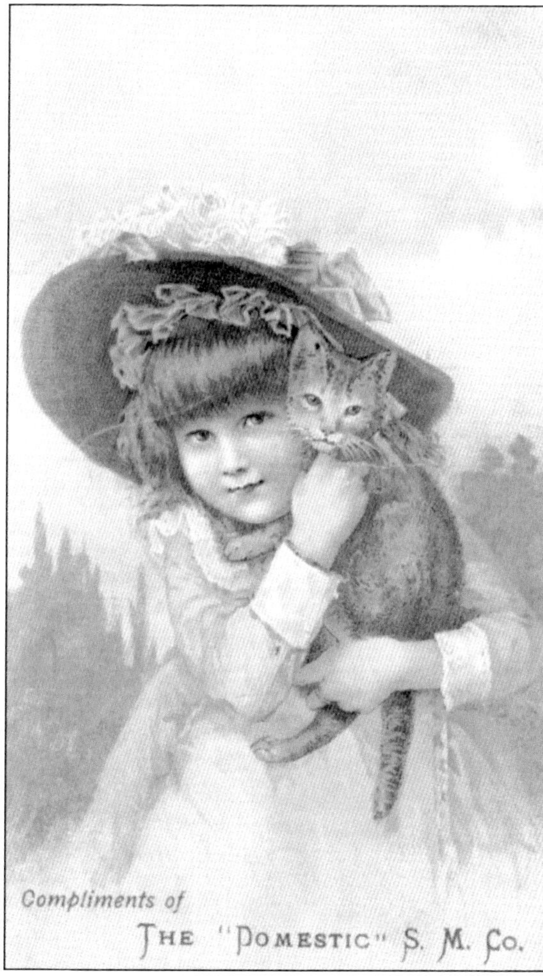

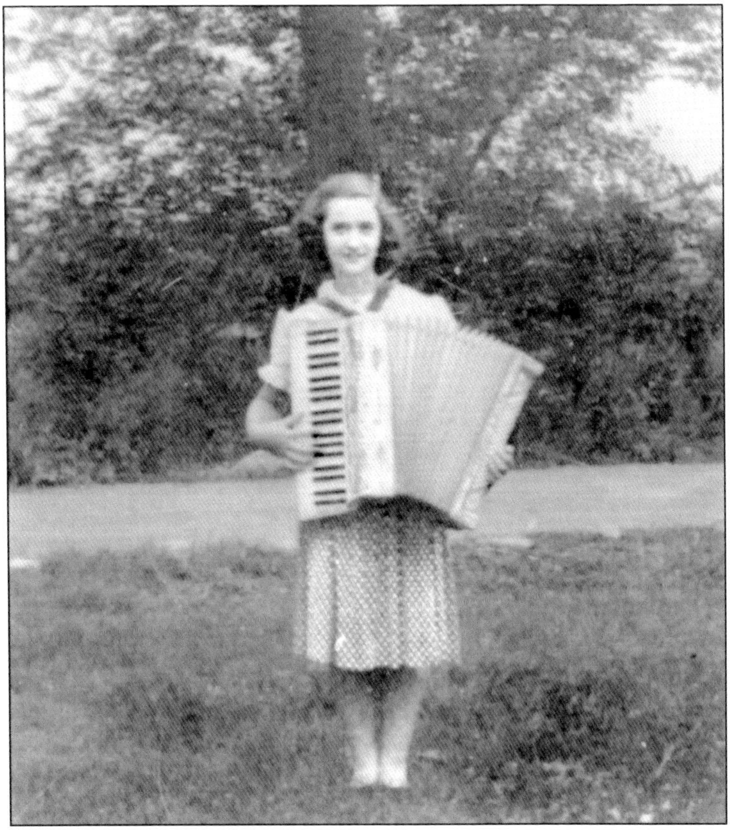

At one time, almost every child in the Paris area learned how to play the accordion. Marion (Grimminger) Wilson's mother bought this Italian accordion for her secondhand, and it far surpassed the tonal quality of other kids' new instruments in the area. She played it many years after that for recitals and family reunions. (Courtesy of Charlene and Junior Grimminger.)

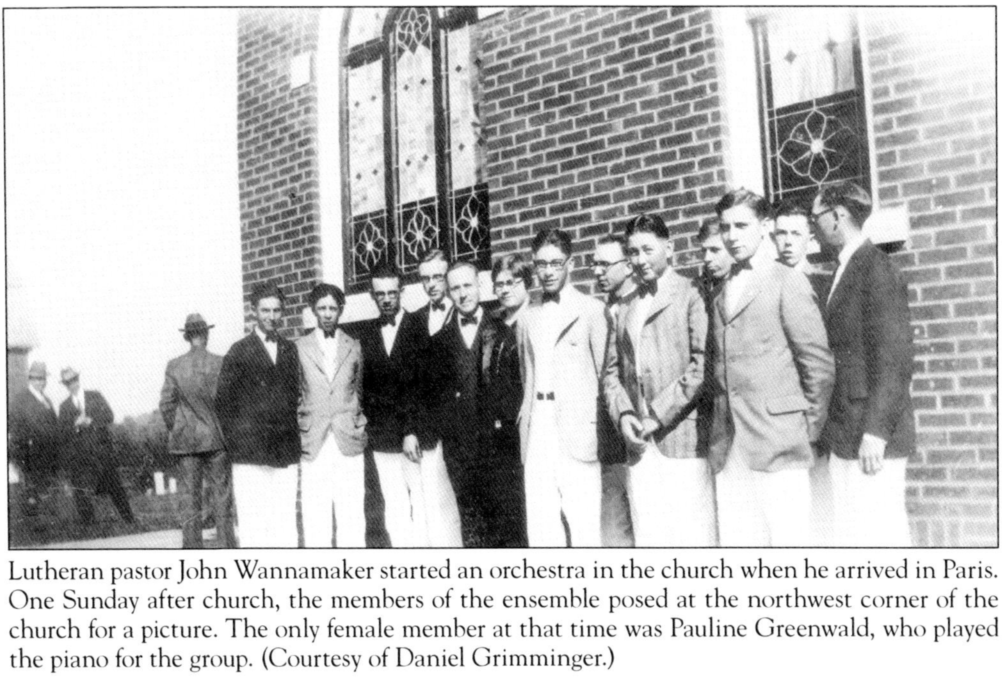

Lutheran pastor John Wannamaker started an orchestra in the church when he arrived in Paris. One Sunday after church, the members of the ensemble posed at the northwest corner of the church for a picture. The only female member at that time was Pauline Greenwald, who played the piano for the group. (Courtesy of Daniel Grimminger.)

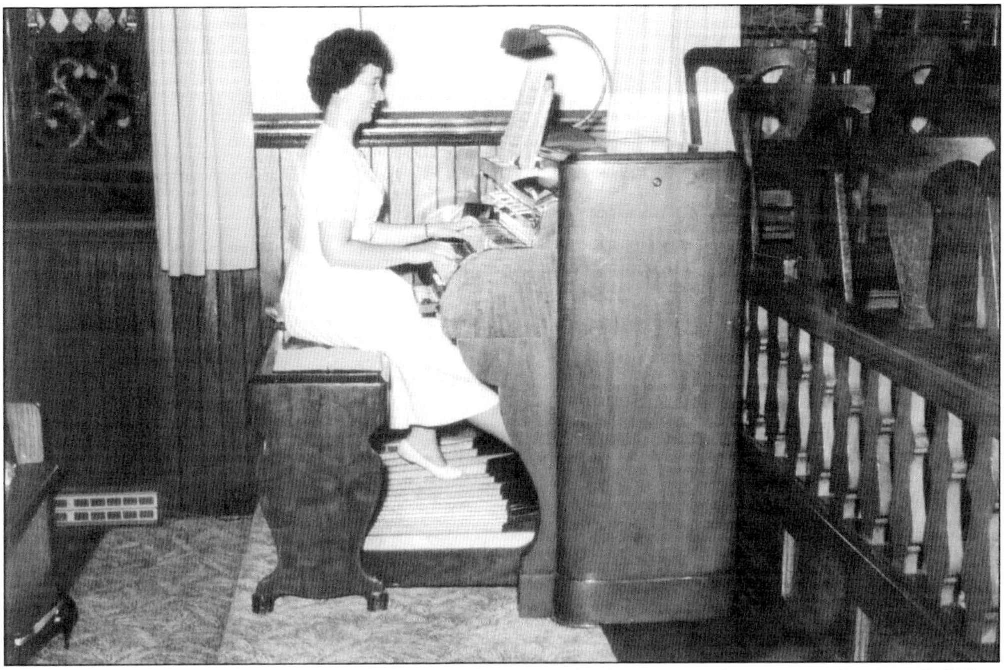

Marion (Grimminger) Wilson was also an accomplished organist, having studied with Edna Burget and at Mount Union College. Here she is playing in the Lutheran Church on the organ that they owned before the current Hillgreen and Lane pipe organ. Notice the chairs to the right that served as choir chairs. These were eventually moved to the basement for Sunday school and church dinners. (Courtesy of Charlene and Junior Grimminger.)

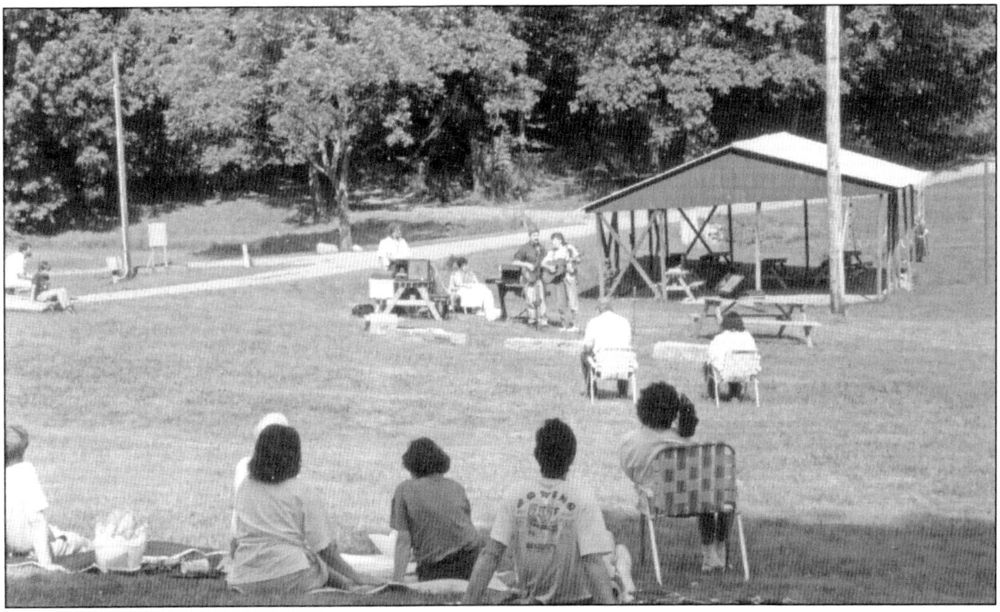

For a while in the 1990s, Bob and Ruth Fisher held "Gospel Music on the Grounds" of Hidden Valley Lake, normally on Saturday afternoons. The event was eventually discontinued for lack of interest. Shown here are some musicians and some of the audience seated on the grass in 1994. (Courtesy of Bob and Ruth Fisher.)

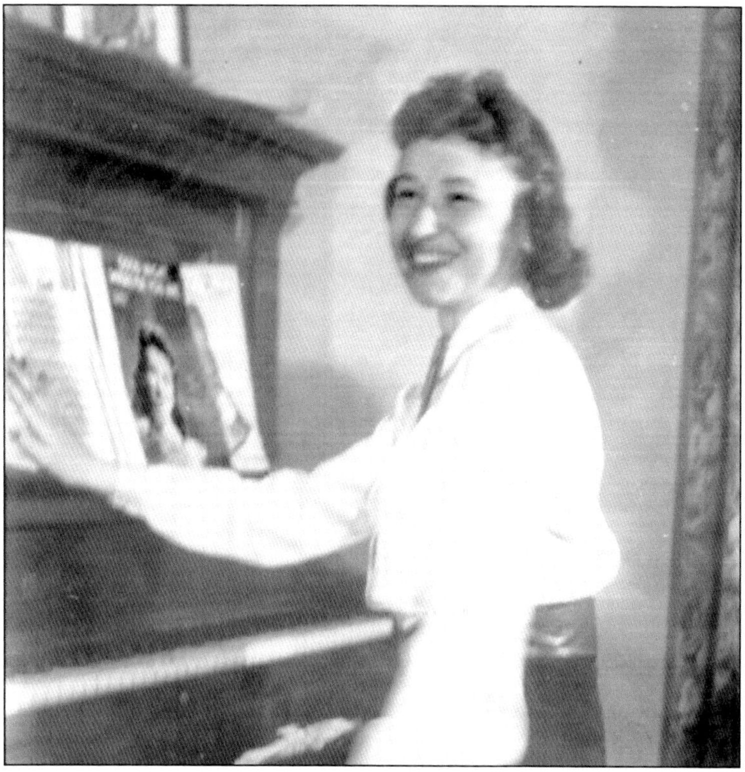

Betty Keith taught many piano students in the Paris community over the years. This picture was taken in 1947 for the McDowell Club of Canton of which she was a member. Her studio piano was her childhood instrument (now in the possession of the author); it was a player piano until her father gutted it to help his daughters learn how to play without pumping. (Courtesy of Carol Keith.)

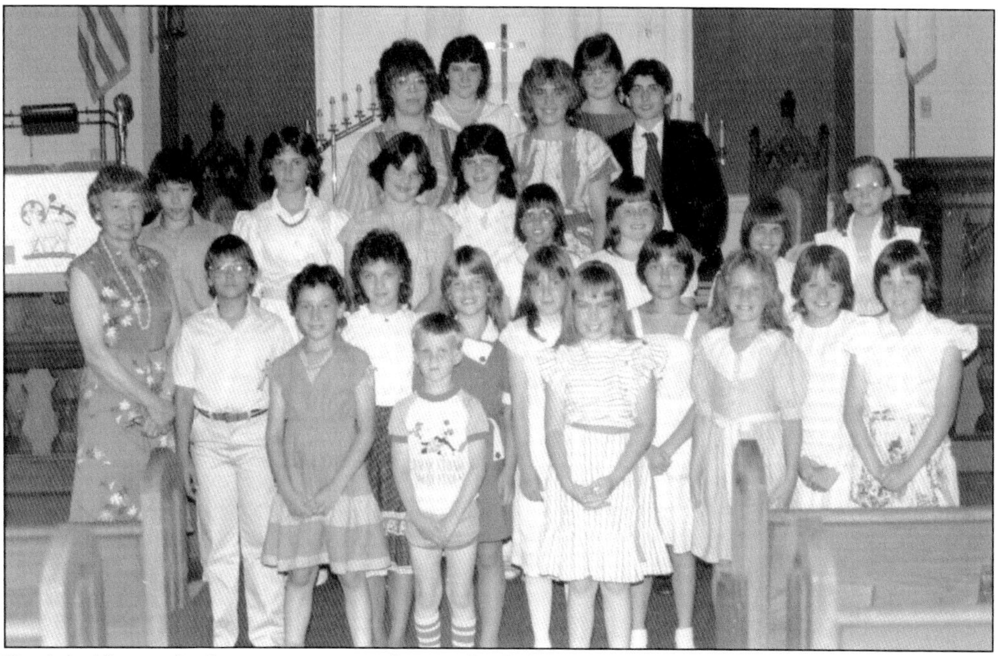

Keith held recitals almost every year she taught, believing that making music prepared students for life. This recital was held in 1985 at Israel's Lutheran Church in the village. Keith also taught for the Hammond Organ Studio in Alliance, and she played the organ and piano for Sunday school and church liturgies for the Lutherans. (Courtesy of Carol Keith.)

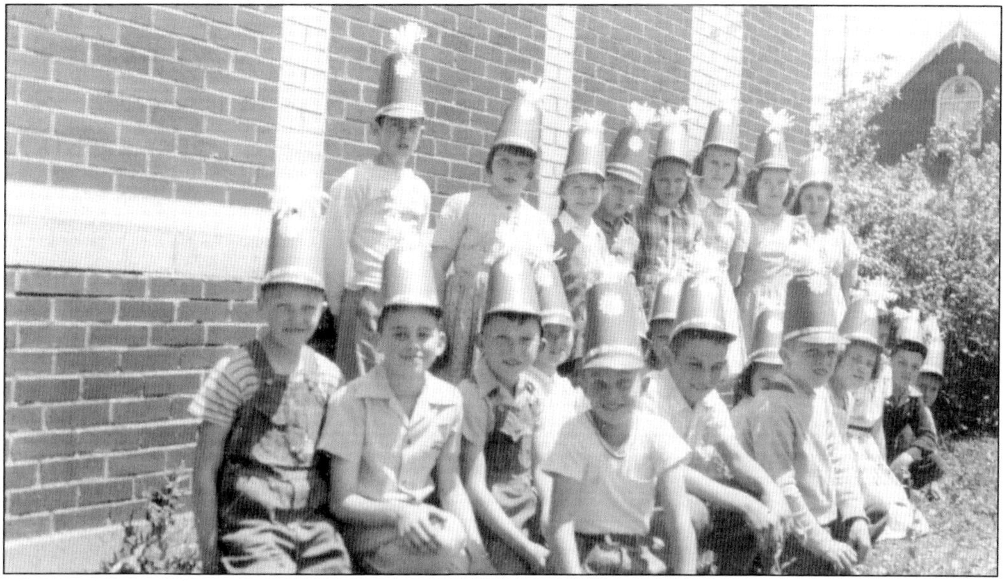

The students in the Paris School were fortunate to have a dedicated teacher in Mamie Stimmel. One of the things she did was teach them music. Pictured is her harmonica ensemble, called "Mamie's Mouth Organ Band" by some of its living members. The Lutheran Church building is visible in the background. (Courtesy of Charlene and Junior Grimminger.)

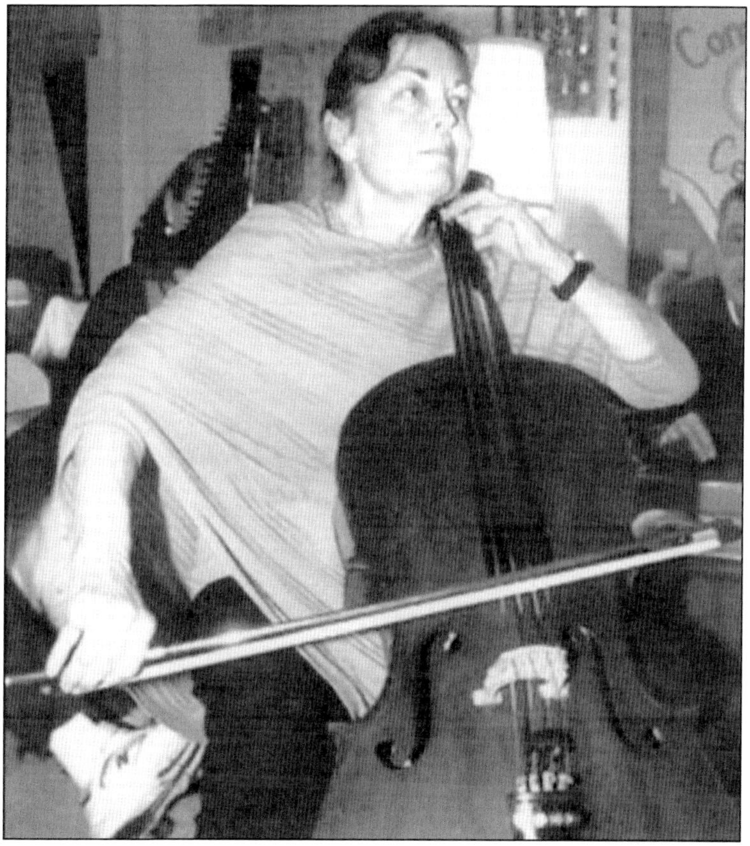

In recent years, Betty Onyett, a retired schoolteacher and accomplished cellist, started to hold music parties in her home (the old Kintner Store and post office on the west side of the square). Beginning with baroque music, the parties eventually shifted to emphasize folk music almost entirely. It was a tragedy when Betty died in her home, not to be found for over 10 days. (Courtesy of Daniel Grimminger.)

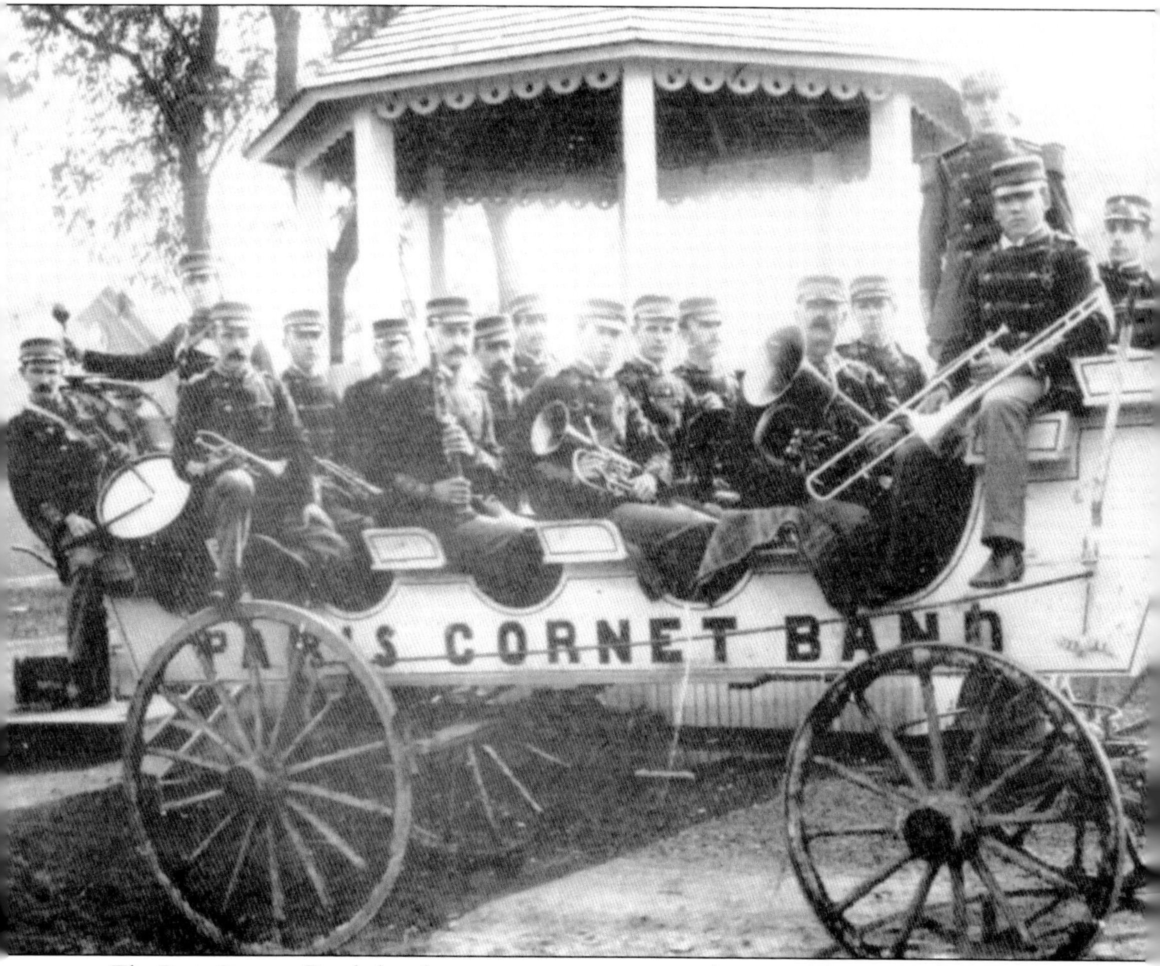

The Paris Coronet Band played at numerous events in northeastern Ohio. Here they are pictured on the same day that they played for a political rally at Augusta, Ohio, in 1896. Other photographs exist of the village square that show the band playing under the small white gazebo, which some called the bandstand. From this evidence, it is clear that Paris residents were not only musically literate by the end of the 19th century, but also that they were like many other Ohio and Pennsylvania communities and had community bands for the entertainment and elevation of the people. This picture was taken at the square looking southeast toward the Methodist Chapel. (Taken from *Paris, Ohio Sesqui-Centennial.*)

Six

Scenes in the Cemetery

In the Paris community cemetery, surrounding the old brick church, one can find some of the earliest settlers of the village. Paris founder Rudolph Bair is buried there. According to John Danner's book *Old Landmarks of Canton and Stark County*, Bair's grave was originally marked with a "walnut slab" but by 1904 it had "long since gone to decay." Danner thought at the time that "the citizens of Paris . . . owe it to themselves to erect a suitable monument over his resting place" (Danner, 65). A permanent concrete marker was eventually made and dedicated late in the 20th century to the town's founder. Other stones go back to the 1810s and 1820s; some in the south wing of the graveyard are much more elaborate, showing Victorian tastes; there are also two extant tombstones on the north side that bear German inscriptions. Many of the stones reveal how much 19th-century people admired nature and how they expressed their beliefs in God and social realities.

Parisians built a mausoleum in 1914, but they had to tear it down in the 1970s because water was seeping into the crypts and causing a stench and potential health issues. Pastor Donald Rice remembers the day of the demolition, claiming that some of the bodies and their coffins were in such bad shape that boards had to be slid under the remains and then rope was wrapped around them to prevent loss.

The combination of no official plot records and recent vandalism of stones by fast-moving lawn tractors, as well as a workday in the 1990s when men busted up stones that had fallen, indicates that Parisians should work to preserve the heritage of their ancestors.

In connection with the cemetery, it is valuable to remember that Homer Stier was the village undertaker. His ledger is a valuable reminder of life and death in the early 20th century. Stier's daughter Doris Myers told about the day that men made some funeral arrangements for a nonresident. At the time of the funeral, the guests arrived in white Klu Klux Klan hoods. Such things create an interesting historical account of the village.

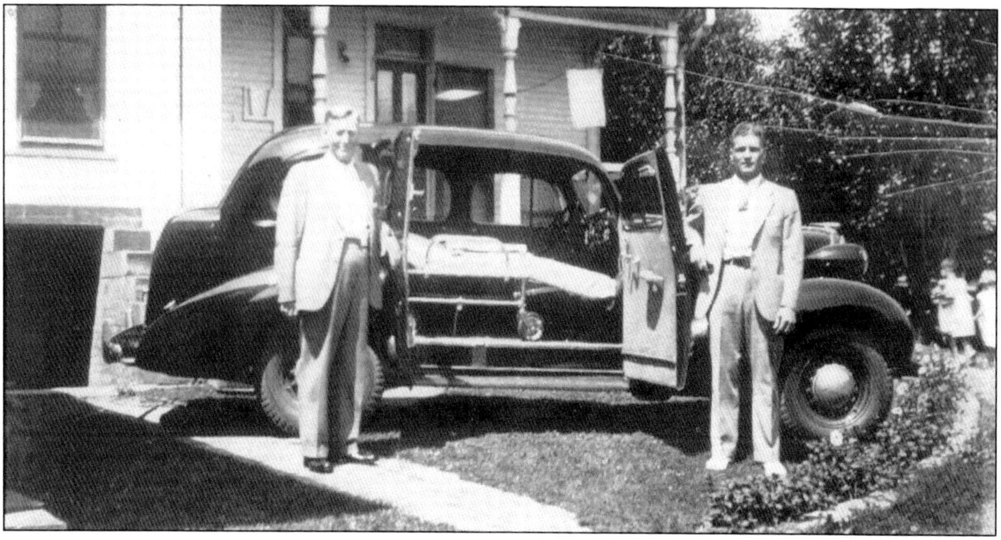

Homer and Howard Stier stand proudly on each side of their new hearse/ambulance for this picture. They were so proud of it that they took a second picture of the vehicle with the doors open. These pictures were taken outside of their funeral home, going down the hill east out of Paris on the right side (just before Pleasant Valley Road). For many years, they also had a horse-drawn hearse, which was housed in the barn on their property, but its whereabouts today are unknown. One person remembered a funeral in March of 1924 when "the horses were up to their knees in mud" as they pulled the old hearse (Gassman, 8). This new vehicle made transporting corpses much easier. (Courtesy of Vivian Myers Marty.)

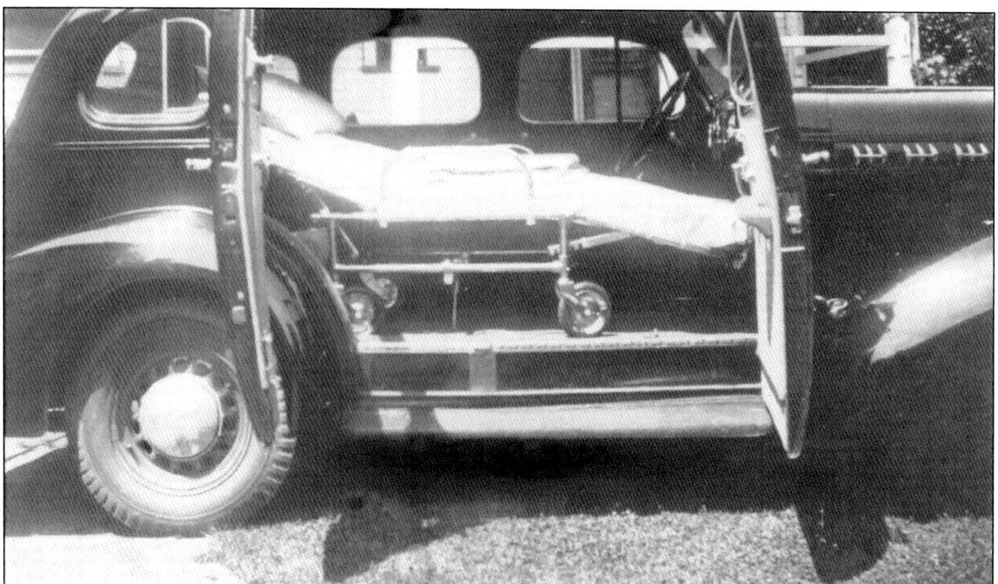

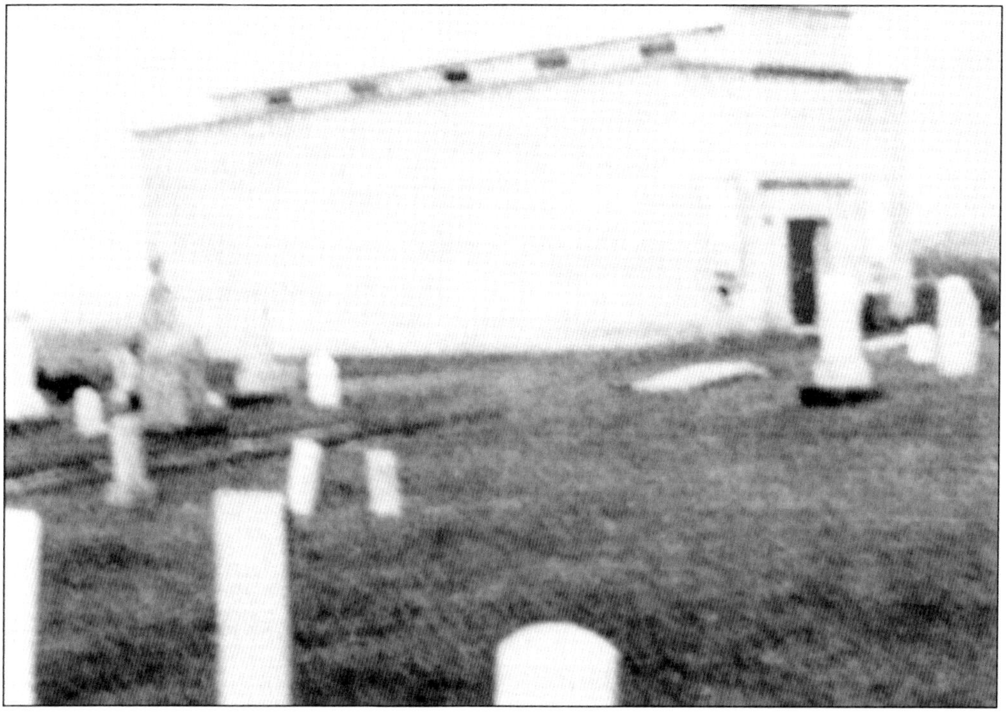

The mausoleum was erected in 1913 but torn down in the 1970s because the roof leaked and the corpses smelled. After the health department ordered its demolition, Howard Stier helped remove all of the bodies by sliding a wide board underneath the remains and wrapping the board to the remains with rope to prevent loss. This blurry image may be the only extant photograph of the mausoleum. (Courtesy of Daniel Grimminger.)

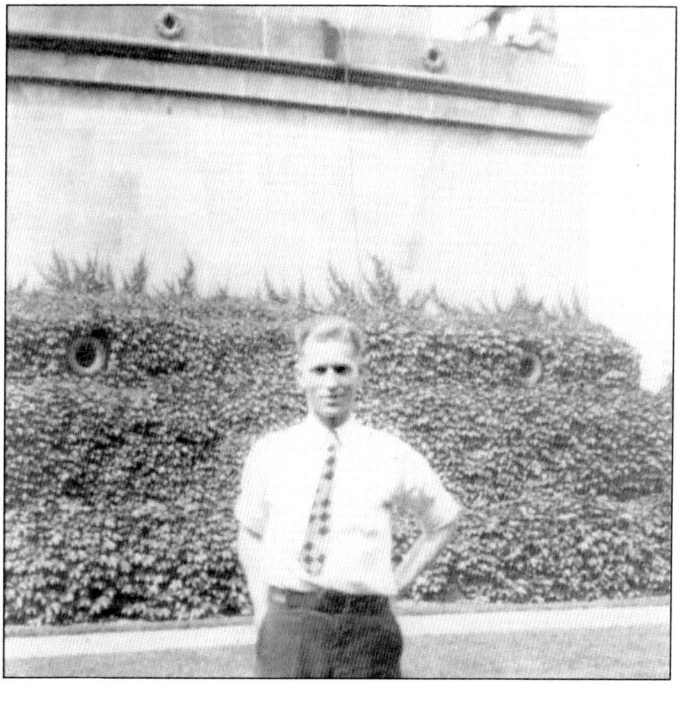

Howard Stier, who followed in his father's footsteps as an undertaker, poses here behind the Paris mausoleum. He moved the family funeral parlor business to Louisville, and it is now called "Stier-Israel Funeral Home." Many Parisians still make their funeral arrangements with Stier-Israel's. (Courtesy of Vivian Myers Marty.)

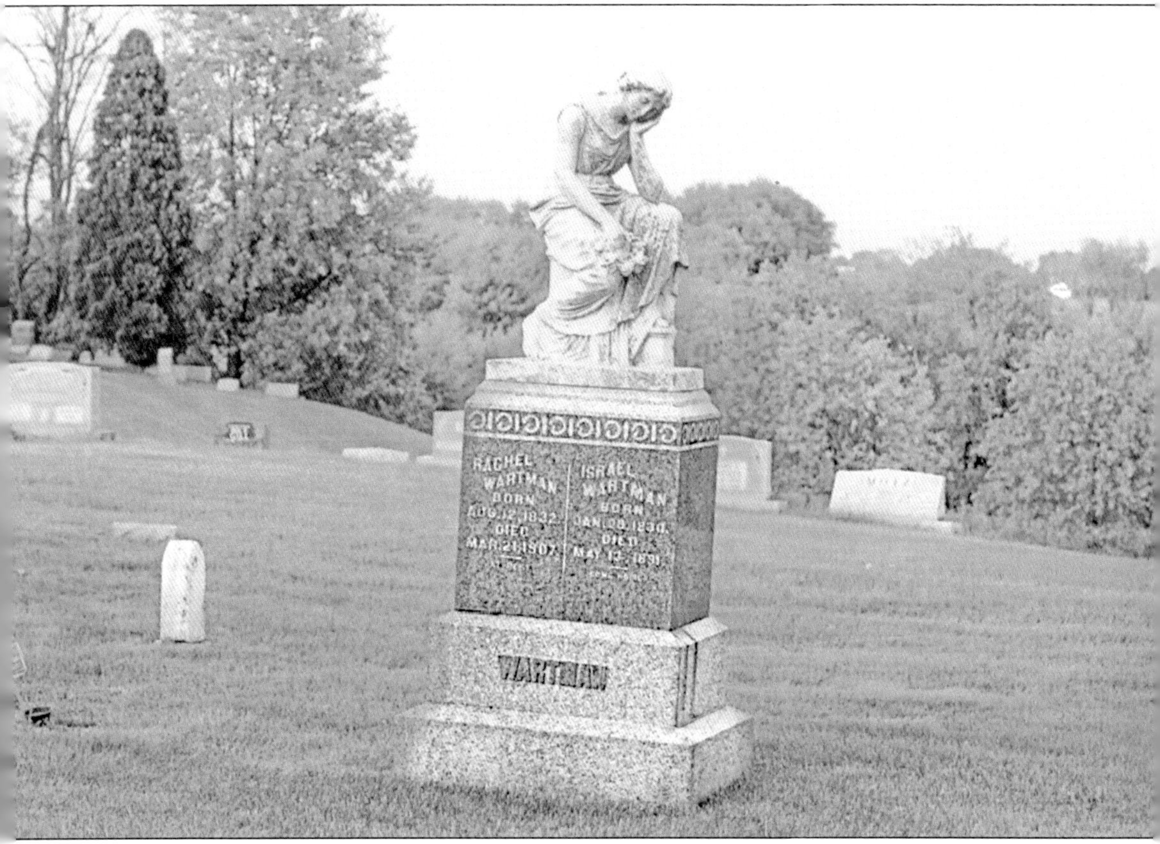

For years, the Israel (1830–1891) and Rachel (1832–1907) Wartman tombstone has graced the cemetery in its south wing. Its resting woman is reminiscent of the 19th century, when women were idealized for their femininity and beauty. The pedestal also recalls a past time when some Parisians were affected by religious Revivalism in the words, "Gone home" and "At rest." The south wing of the cemetery has other more elaborate stones, including three arch stones, one cannon-like stone, and an obelisk, that make this part of the cemetery imaginative and special. (Courtesy of John Miller.)

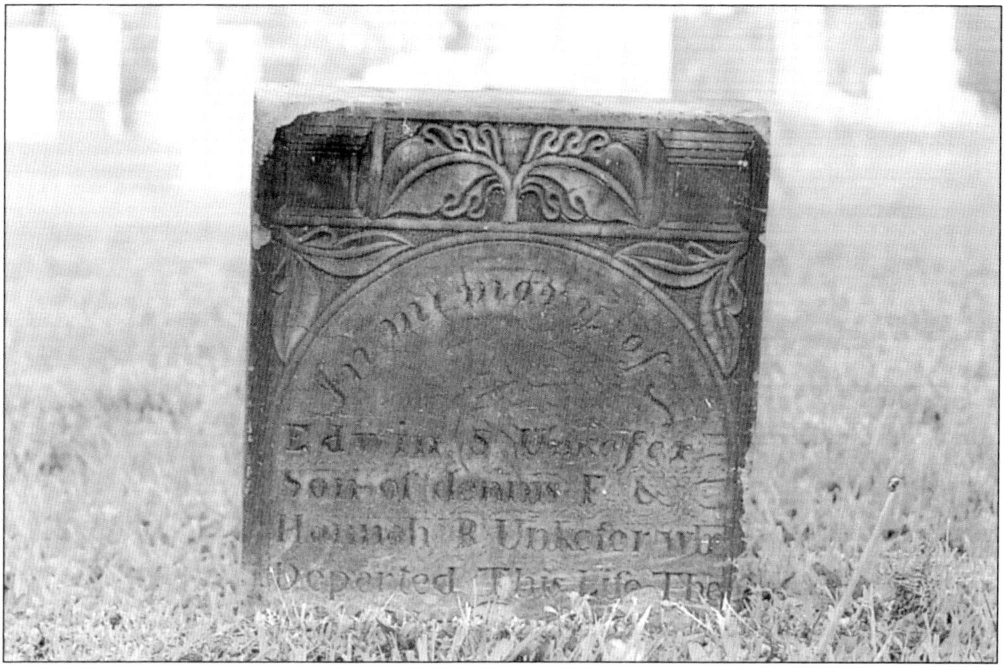

Some of the oldest stones in the cemetery were made from a more durable stone that turned black over time. This is one of the well-preserved examples of the earliest headstones. Notice the lovely leaf design that required a steady hand of the carver. Edwin S. Unkefer was part of one of the oldest Paris families. His relative, John Unkefer, kept the tavern at the square. (Courtesy of John Miller.)

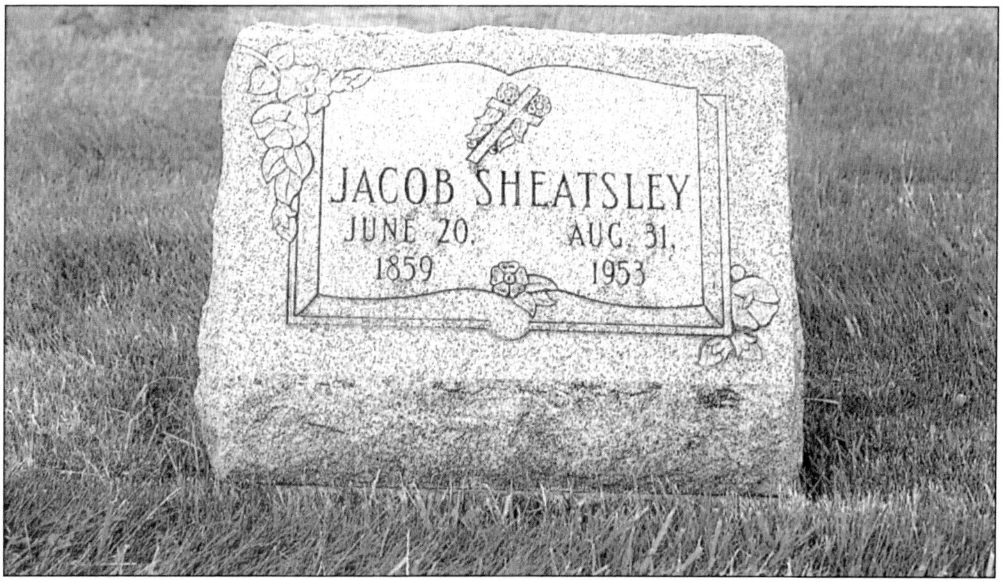

The Sheatsley family held an enormous place in the Paris community, but all of them have long since died, leaving no heirs to carry on their legacy. Jacob Sheatsley became a Lutheran pastor and served for some time in Columbus at Christ Lutheran Church on the edge of Capital University. (Courtesy of John Miller.)

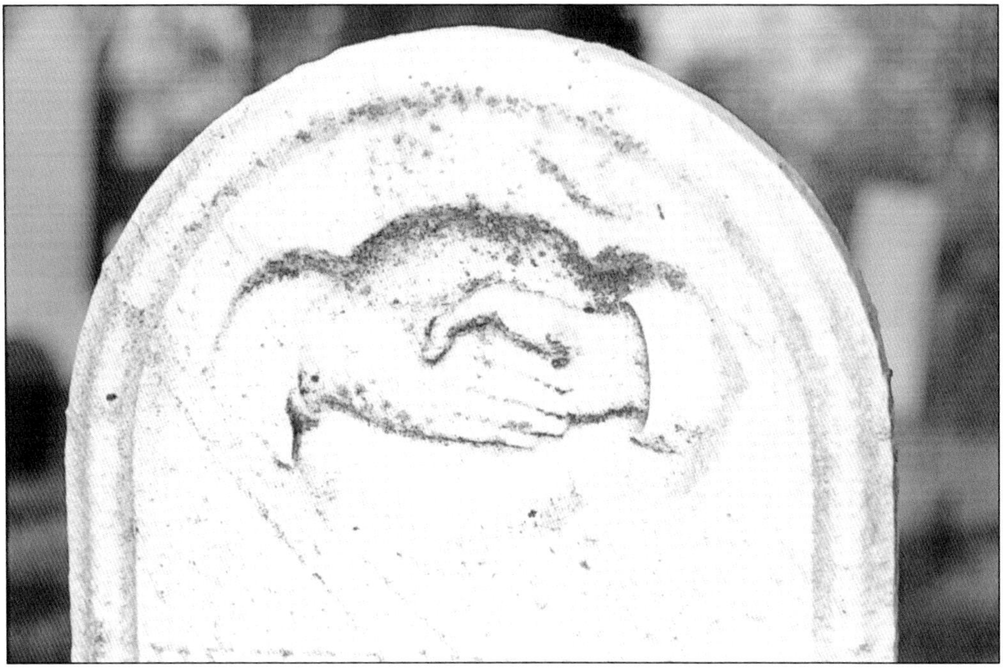

There are well over a dozen stones in the Paris cemetery with the "shaking hands" motif carved into the stone. This could have been symbolic of the bonds of marriage (as it often occurred on matching stones of husbands and wives), the union of the dead with God, a sign of farewell, or the reuniting of the deceased with loved ones after death. In one place, the multiple "handshakes" evoke images of a reunion or a gathering of friends. It is as if those buried here are able to offer their hospitality to visitors through their gravestones. (Courtesy of John Miller.)

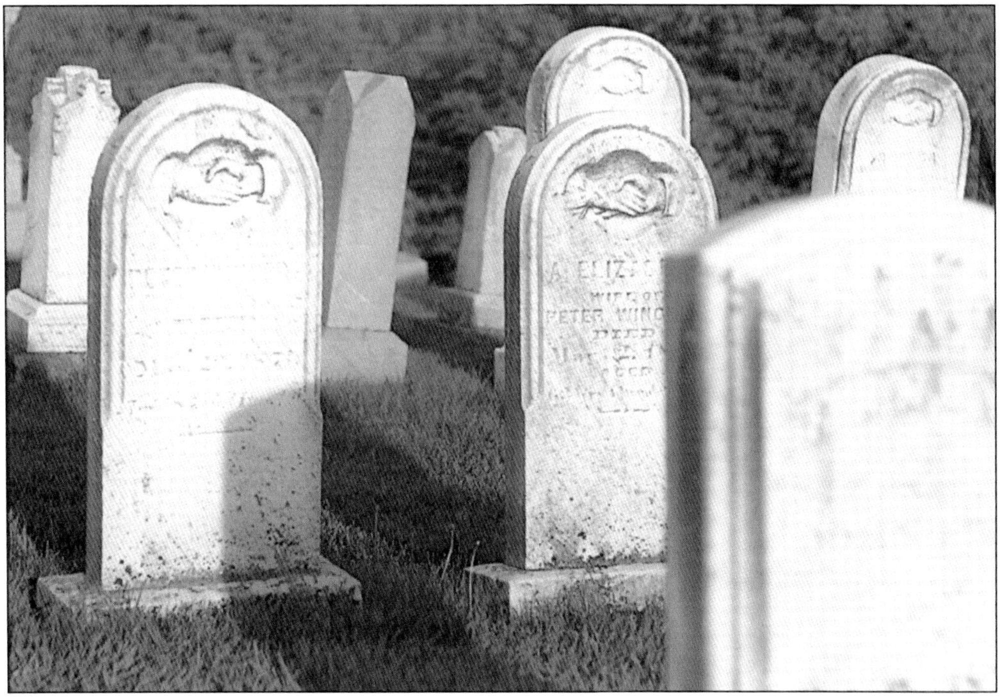

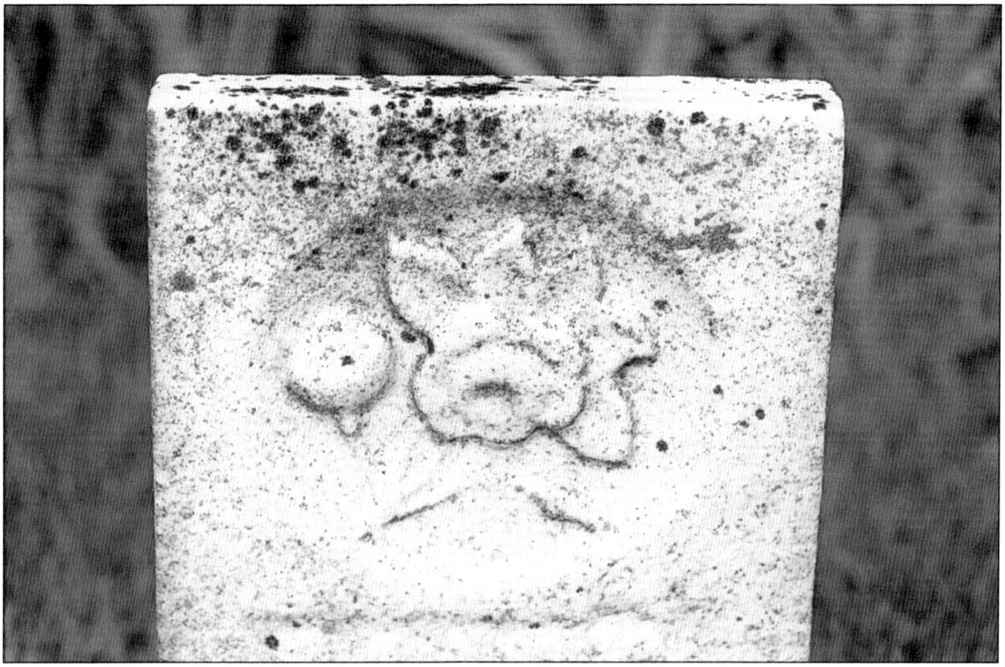

Nature played largely into the mindset of the people in the 19th century (known as the Romantic era). Flowers, wood, and animals were a large part of their lives. These stones show just two of many different floral ornaments on Paris tombstones. The first is just a sprig of flowers, while the second is a bouquet being held by a hand as if in a state of presentation. Other nature-themed stones in the graveyard make use of cement styled as logs and twigs (as in the Heim family stone), while others use animals like lambs (as in a Zinninger stone). (Courtesy of John Miller.)

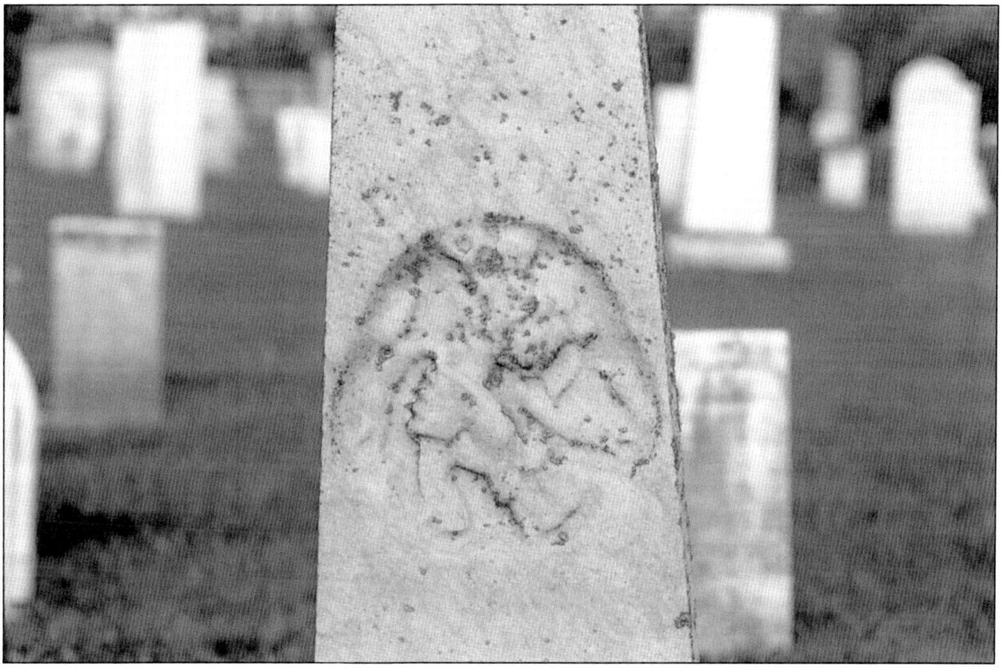

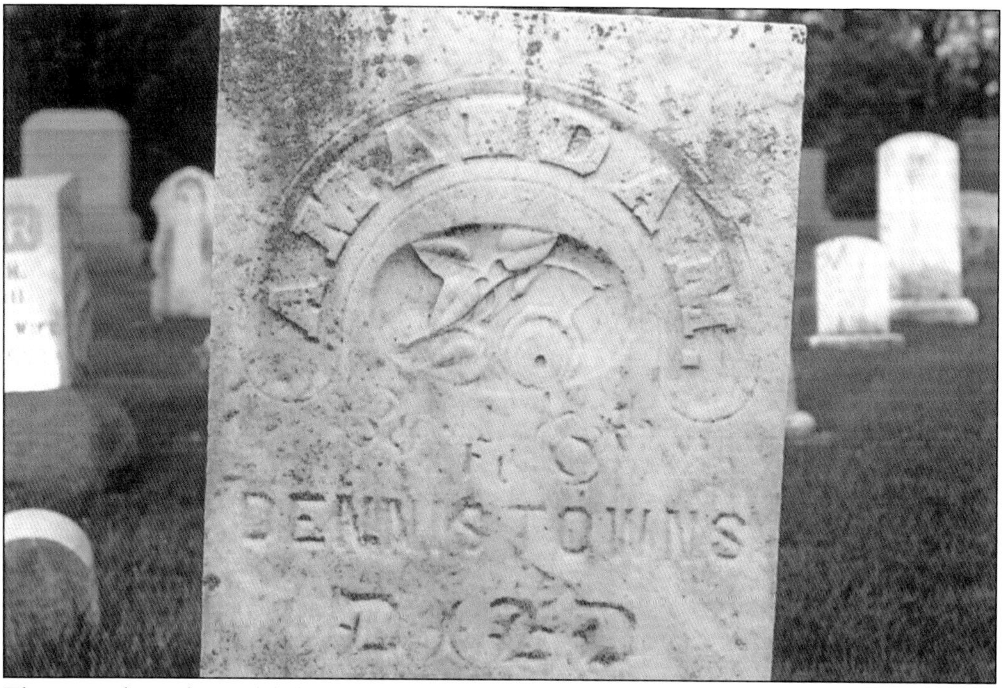

This stone has a beautiful floral motif, more leaves, and eloquent lettering for Amanda, wife of Dennis Towns, who was part of a family that no longer exists in the village or surrounding countryside. The marker is a reminder of such families that once played their part in the everyday workings of the town and of the English element that intermingled with Paris's German faction later in the 19th century. (Courtesy of John Miller.)

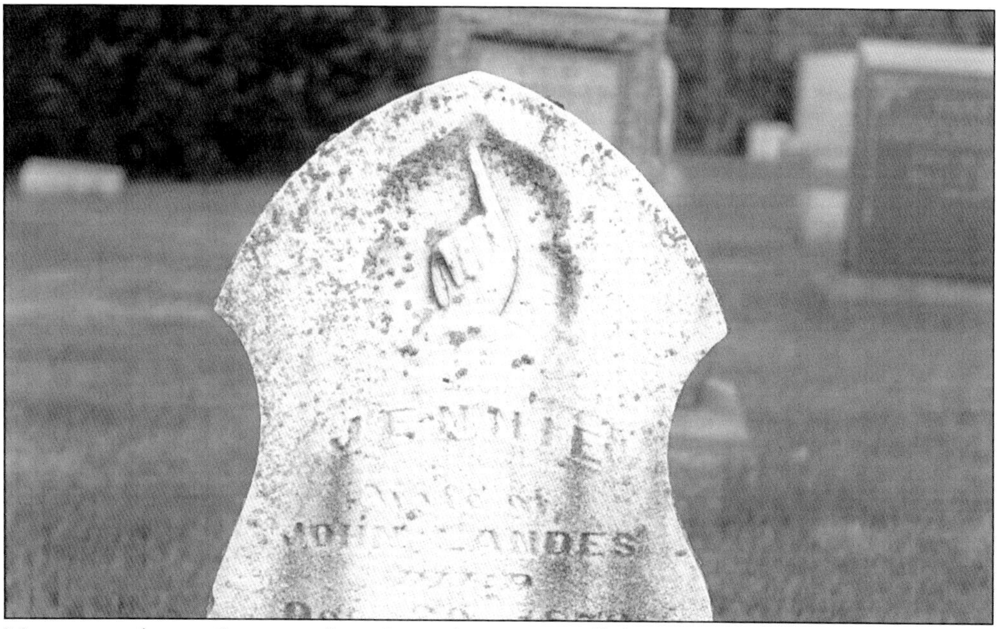

Many stones have a "pointing finger" motif meant to call the person viewing it to look to the things of heaven and to repentance. The upward direction of the finger also infers that the soul of the departed has gone to heaven. (Courtesy of John Miller.)

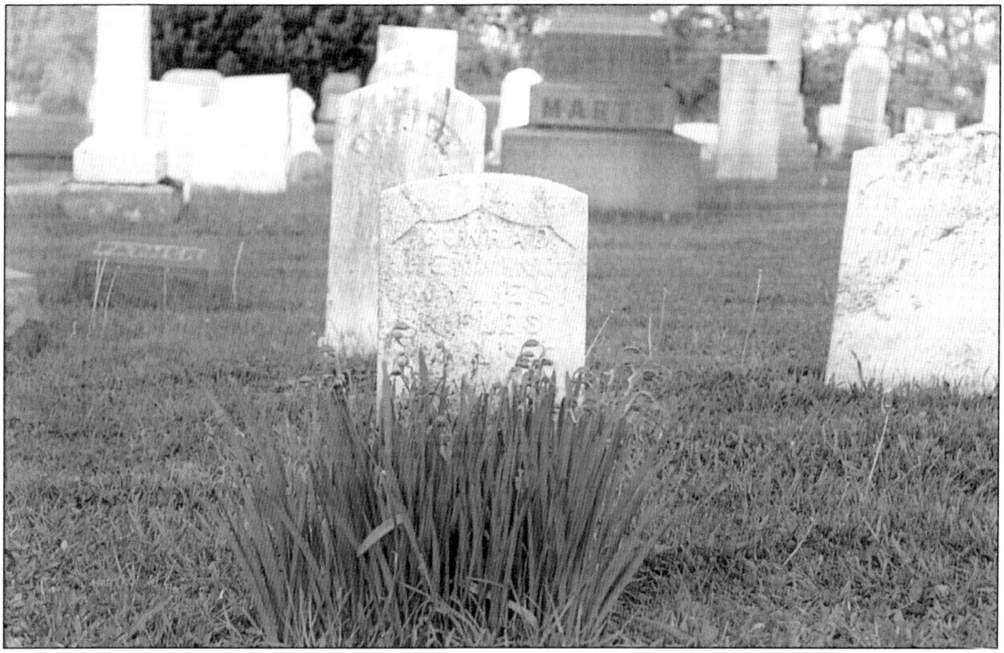

Conrad Henning was a Revolutionary War Veteran. He came to Paris in the spring of 1811 from Beaver County, Pennsylvania, where he had settled from his native Lancaster. He was the second schoolteacher of the village according to Danner's history. His grave place is not far from the east wall of the church building. (Courtesy of John Miller.)

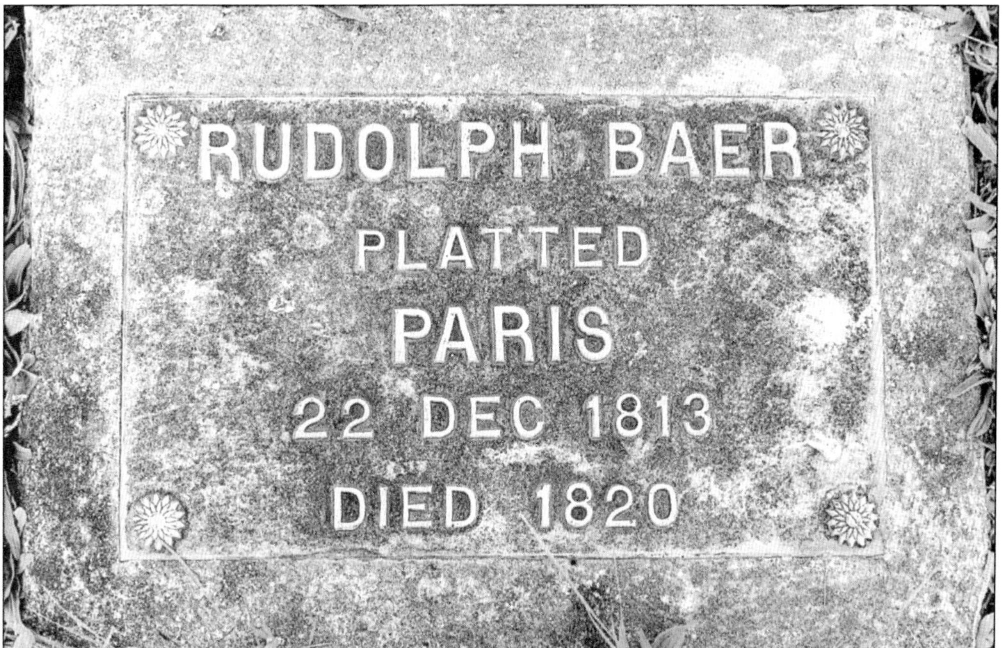

After many years of having no headstone, the people of Paris acknowledged Rudolph Bair (or "Baer" to use the German spelling) in the 1990s by placing a stone at his grave site. This replaced the original "walnut slab" that had been placed over his resting spot. (Courtesy of John Miller.)

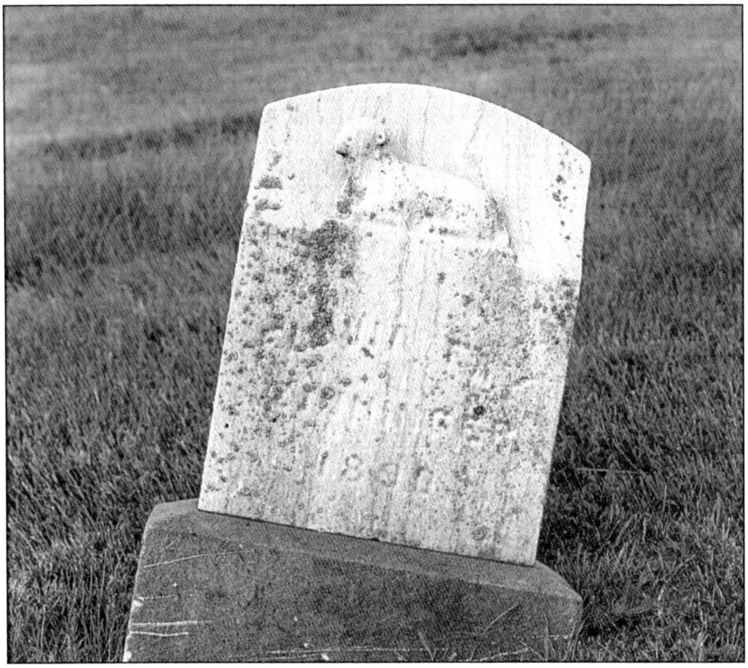

The lamb on this stone for a Zinninger brings to mind biblical imagery the early Parisians would have known and loved. In the setting of this cemetery where most people belonged to the union congregation ("Israel's Kirche"), the words of Psalm 114 (vv. 1–4) become more vivid, "When Israel came out of Egypt . . . Judah became God's sanctuary . . . the mountains skipped like rams, the hills like lambs."

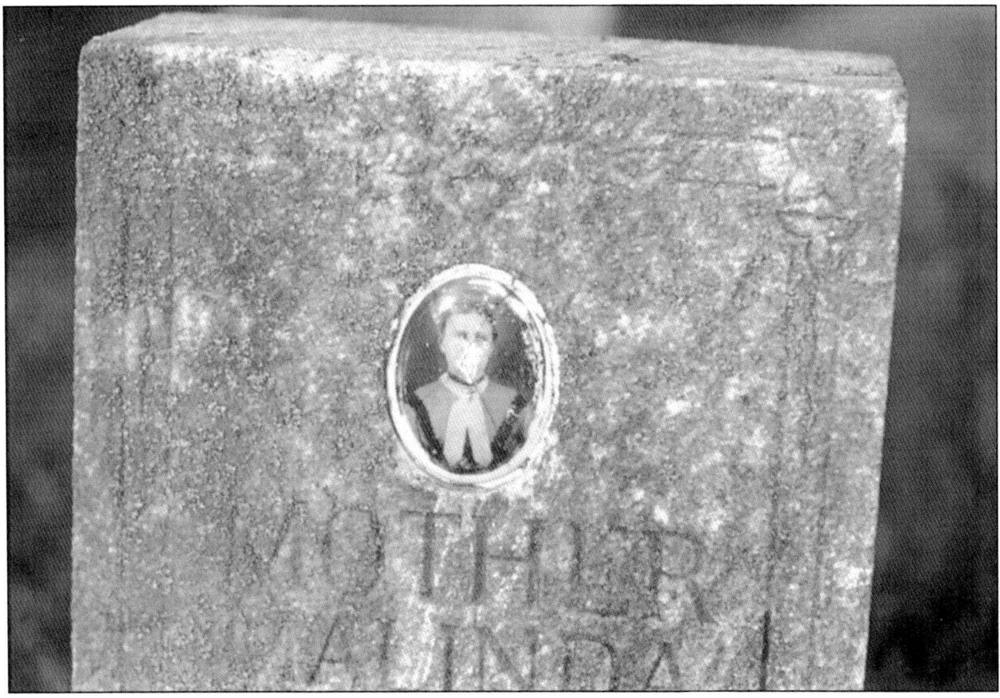

As is often the case, Malinda Sautters's (1855–1934) tombstone was erected by her descendants. What is remarkable about it is the small, medallion-shaped picture of Sautters on the front of the stone. This is the only stone with a real photograph of the deceased in the cemetery, however the image has been defaced at some point. The stone is located in the northeast side of the cemetery. (Courtesy of John Miller.)

Seven

Artifacts of Times Past

Material culture is an important aspect of understanding any village or people. Things like broadsides, architecture, art, and farm tools, among other things, take observers beyond book knowledge to the actual lived experience of a people. Items in Paris homes and owned by Paris families are no exception. Practical items tell people some of the most valuable things about everyday life in and around Paris.

Of particular interest is the printing trade in Paris. One history claims the first Democratic paper in Stark County was printed in Paris in 1828 by J. W. White "in the interest of [President] Jackson." This periodical was only printed there for six months, then in Canton, where it ceased to exist several months later (Kauffman, 149). David Huston, who also sold the union church coal, printed books: a German history of the United States for families and schools and an anti-Catholic tract.

Many other tradesmen existed in 18th-century Paris: silversmiths, potters, and others. Also, Ferdinand Brader, a Swiss immigrant, travelled through the Paris area sketching bird's eye–view farm scenes, and many of those numbered works exist in Parisian homes. They explain much about everyday life and a lifestyle that was simple, yet wholesome.

Several public artifacts remain as symbols of Paris. The cannon in the square is more than a sign of the past; it has served as a landmark for Paris residents and outsiders alike. It was brought from the South by B. M. Stier and John Oyer in 1888. It is now filled with cement, because some mischievous young men once shot it off, breaking windows of local homes. Artifacts of the local churches also explain much. The communion ware owned and kept by the Lutherans, for example, paints the picture of thousands of people who drank from the chalices because it was from those cups that the people believed they received God's grace. The worn "German silver" set reminds people today that finite things can convey infinite meaning.

These heirlooms fill the void of unrecorded history and collectively provide the "bigger picture" for those who live in a different time.

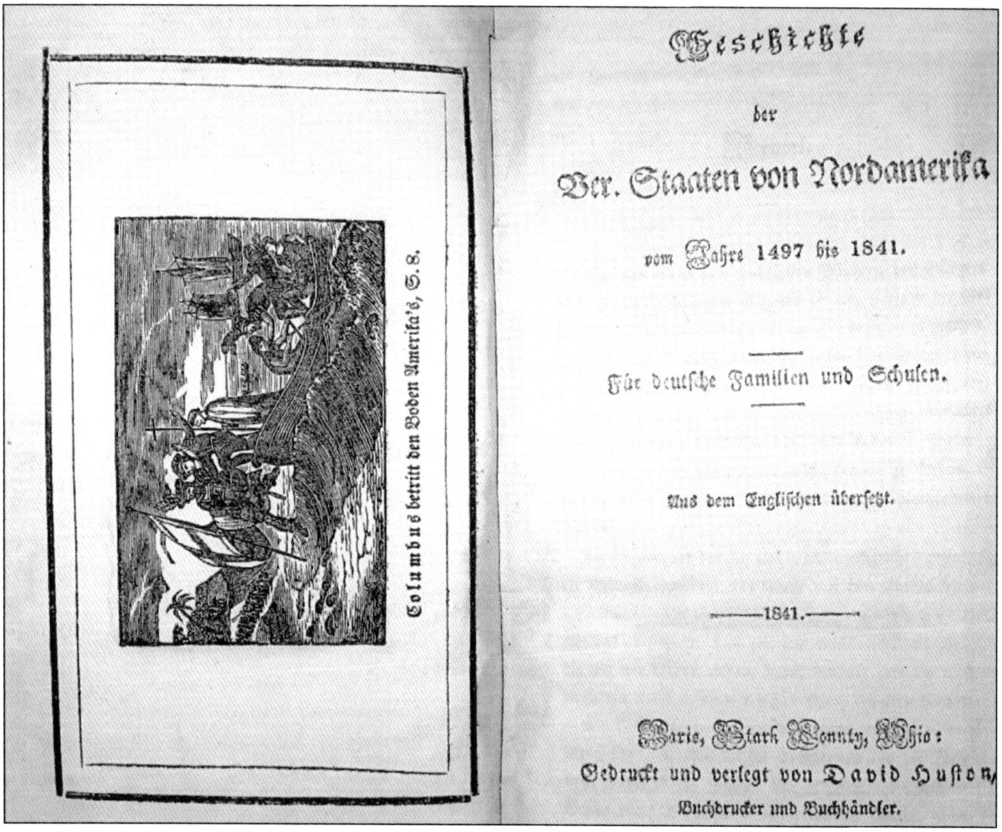

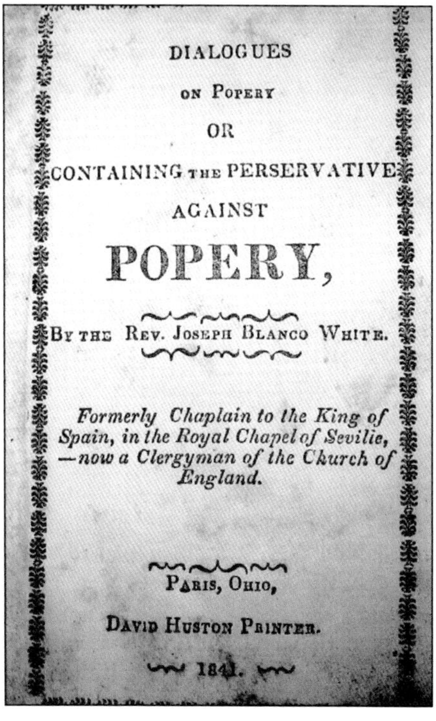

One of the oldest and most precious artifacts from Paris's heyday is this book printed by David Huston in Paris. Its title is best translated *History of the United States of North America from the Year 1497 to 1841. For German Families and Schools, translated from the English. 1841.* It is possible that this book served as a textbook in the Paris School; there are three extant copies. (Courtesy of Daniel Grimminger.)

The only other book known to have been printed in Paris was also from the press of David Huston. As one would expect, this is a religious book, an anti-Catholic tract. Unlike Huston's German history for homes and schools, this book has no woodcuts or other illustrations in it. David Huston also sold coal to the union church at least one winter. (Courtesy of Daniel Grimminger.)

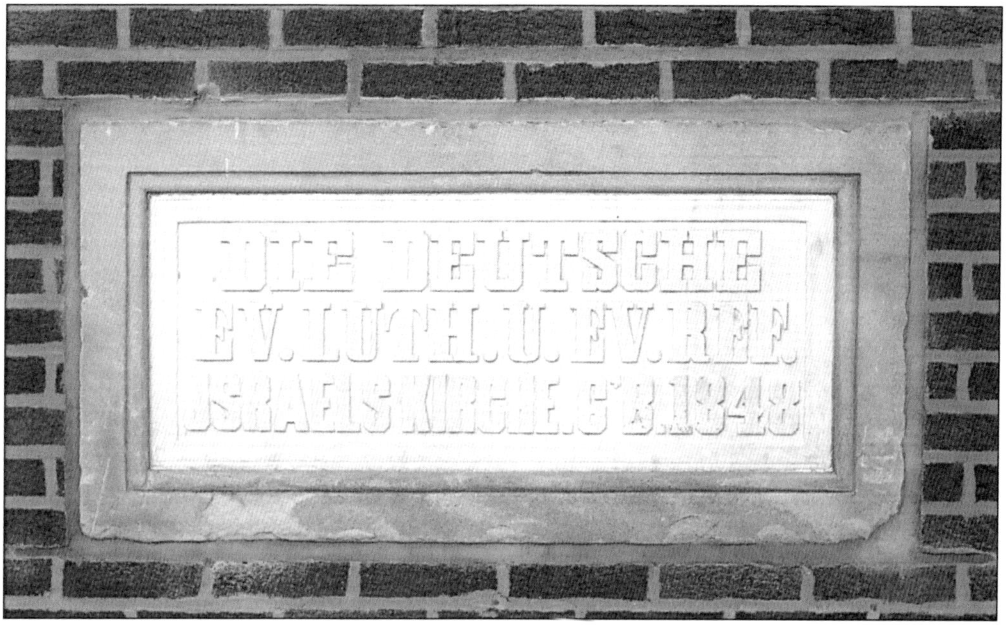

This German blessing stone is likely the first one for the Paris churches. Until recently, it was hidden in an old interior wall, originally the outside west wall. It shows some damage from removal, and its placement low on the new west wall is odd (it belongs above the entrance), but it is now visible to all, proclaiming that this was "The German Evangelical Lutheran and Reformed Israel's Church, built 1848." (Courtesy of John Miller.)

Communion use to be served in the German Union Church from this communion ware. Jay Lutz Sr. (1913–1995) told the author that when he was a child the Lutherans stopped using it on account of the tuberculosis scare. The common cup was then replaced by small glasses for each communicant. Also pictured is the last German pulpit Bible to be used by the union church. (Courtesy of Daniel Grimminger.)

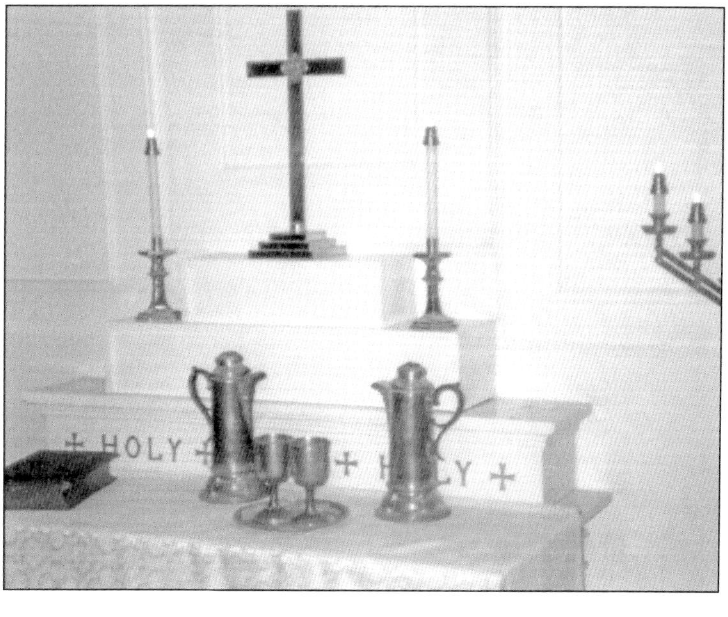

E. C. KINTNER

GROCERY, MEATS AND CONFECTIONERY

PHONE NO. 2

Paris, Ohio, ... 192.......

M ....

No. ....

MC CASKEY ALLIANCE O.

Reg. No............ Clerk.............. Account Forwarded

1	30 doz. eggs	.38	11	40
2				
3	7# [illegible]			32
4			11	08

This piece of ephemera is a part of a bill from the old Kintner store, showing the amount due to the Burgets for the eggs they sold the store for resale. At the Burget Farm Auction, there were many boxes full of this kind of ephemera, documenting not the huge accomplishments of a people, but their ordinary, everyday lives. (Courtesy of Daniel Grimminger.)

NOTICE.

OFFICE OF THE SECRETARY

Paris and Washington Townships Home Insurance Co.

You are hereby notified that the annual meeting of the Paris and Washington Townships Home Insurance Company will be held in the

Paris School House, Saturday, December 26, 1908, commencing at 12:30 o'clock.

At this time there will be a full Board of Officers elected; financial and other reports of the standing of the Company will be given Also business relative to the futuie welfaie of the Company may be transacted. You are earnestly requested to attend the annual meeting.

BY ORDER OF BOARD.

Respectfully, H H. SPONSELLER, Secretary.

Many residents of Paris and surrounding countryside were members of Paris and Washington Townships Home Insurance Company. This postcard was sent out to members in 1908 announcing a meeting to be held in the Paris schoolhouse the day after Christmas that year. (Courtesy of Betty Speakman.)

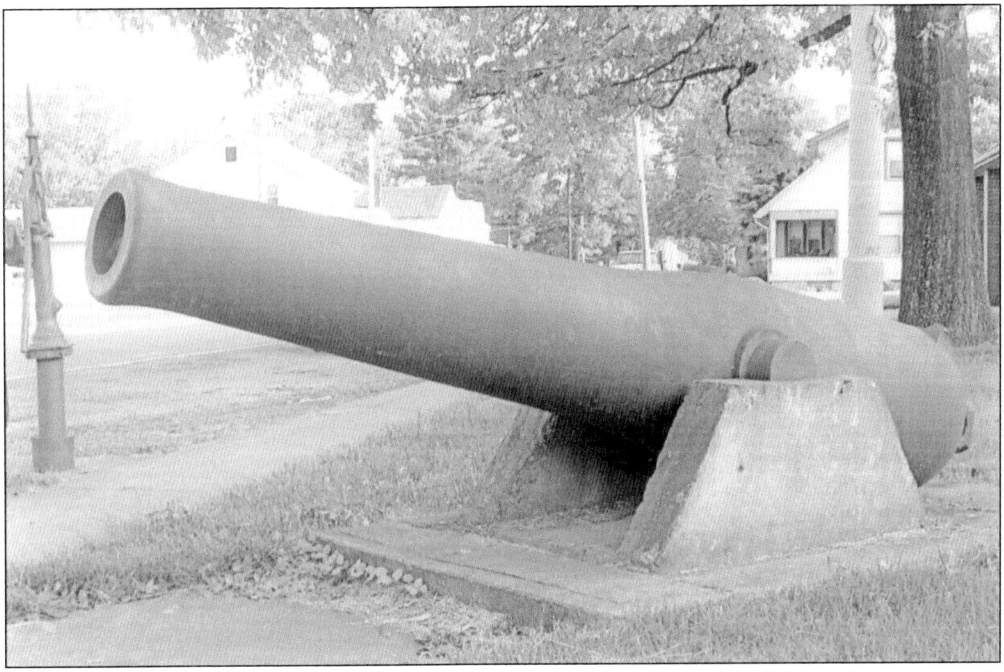

The cannon at the square of the village once sat perched on a mound back from the road; now it sits close to the street. It is by far the most recognized landmark of the village. Brought from the battlefields in the South by B. M. Stier and John Oyer in 1888, it was once fired by some Paris pranksters after which it was cemented shut. (Courtesy of Daniel Grimminger.)

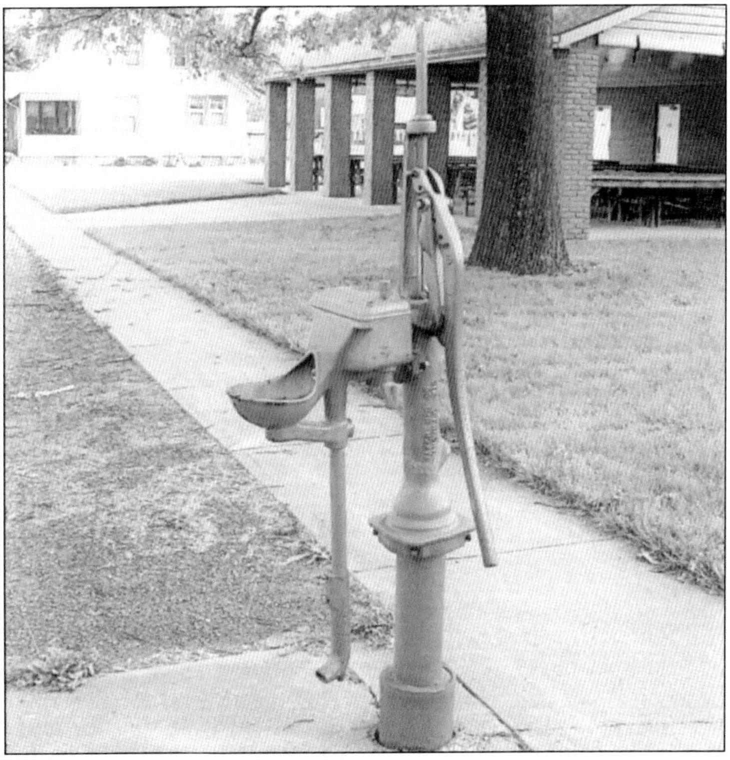

For many years, children would fill up water balloons, cool their feet, and of course drink from this red water pump, once painted dark green or black. For a time it was turned off in order to curb mischief. (Courtesy of Daniel Grimminger.)

Creek School

District No. 5

Paris Township, Stark County, Ohio

→ 1909-10 ←

LLOYD L. ECREMENT, Teacher

Pupils

BOYS

Harry Waltz		Ralph Stimmel
Earl Stimmel		Harry Lautzenheiser
Walter Bergert		Donald Sefert
Clark Snyder		David Walter
Albert Miller		Elden Walter
Walter Stuckey		Arla Snyder
Roland Hein	Lorin Waltz	Edwin Stimmel

GIRLS

Julia Sefert		Mamie Crowl
Floy Ramseyer		Freeda Miller
Ruth Ramseyer		Edith Ramseyer
Verda Bergert		Edna Bergert
Ruth Bair		Della Stuckey
Ruby Snyder	Vernice Bergert	Mabel Bair

Board of Education

I. A. Snyder, Pres.		E. C. Mong, Clerk
P. J. Walker	H. H. Sefert	C. E. Smith

William Bergert, Local Director

The Creek School existed on the creek that now runs through the Bomberger Farm just west of Paris. This is one page taken from a commencement booklet at the end of the 1909–1910 school year. The owner's father, Harry Lautzenheiser, as well as John "Edwin" Stimmel, are listed as pupils. Lloyd Ecrement, the teacher, had his picture on the front cover of the original booklet. (Courtesy of Lillian Munk.)

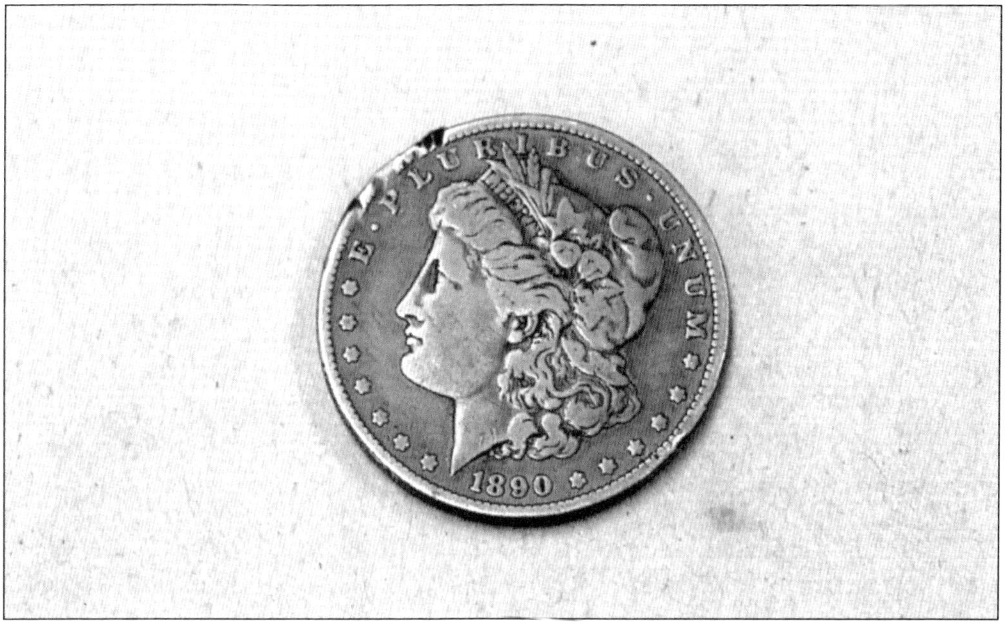

One of the most unique family heirlooms in the hands of Paris families is the "Valentine Mong silver dollar." Its marks tell the story of the day that he crossed the train tracks in Louisville and was struck by an oncoming locomotive. This coin was handed down through the Mong family to remind them of the fate of their ancestor, now buried beside the north wall of the Lutheran Church. (Courtesy of Steven Tibrea.)

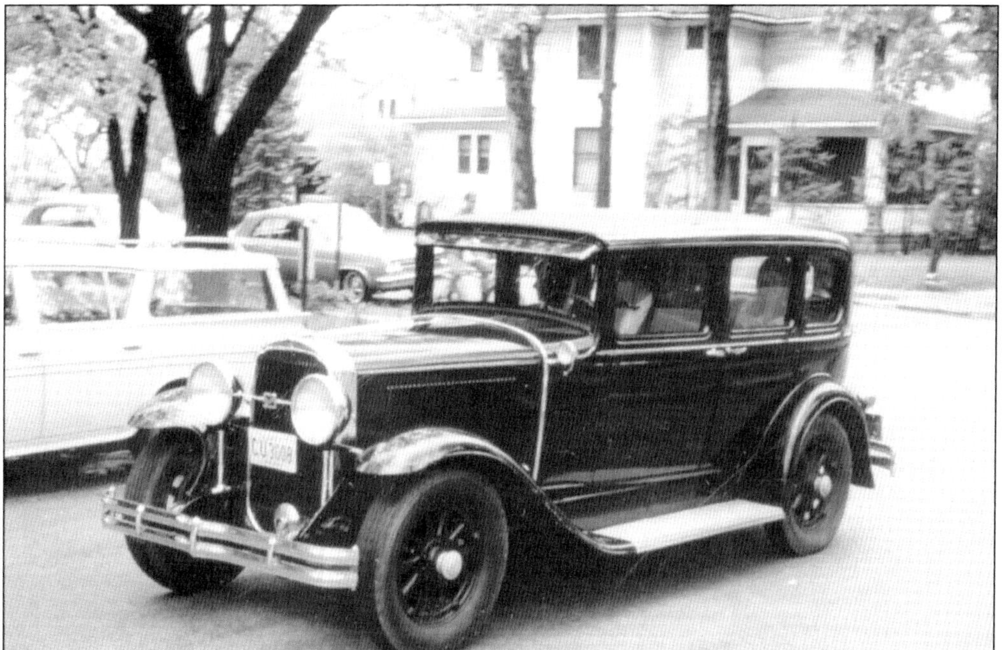

Wilbur Stuckey and his son Bruce restored this 1930 Buick after buying it from Walter Burget. Everything from the chrome to the upholstery was restored to make it look like it did the day it was originally purchased. (Courtesy of Kay Latham.)

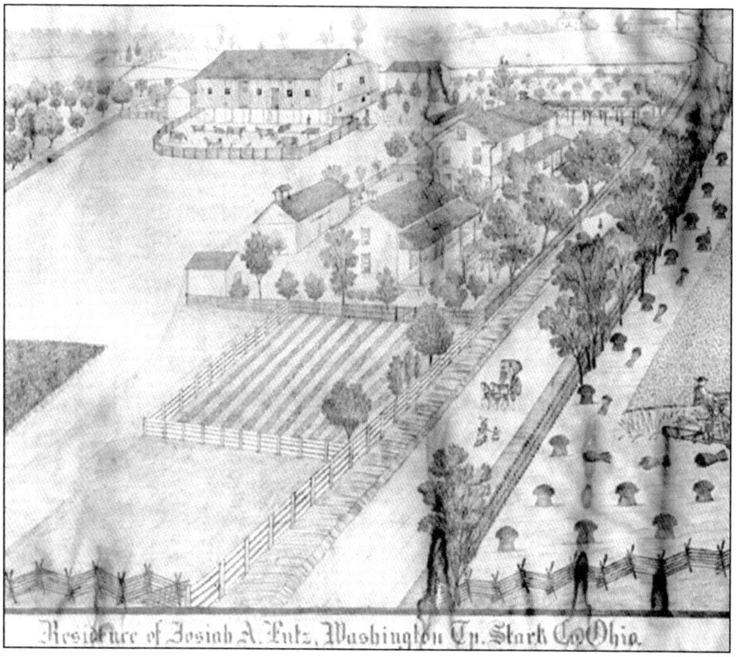

For many years, this sketch by Ferdinand Brader hung in the milk house of the Josiah Lutz (later Greenwald) farm. Its water stains and silverfish holes do not detract from its ability to illustrate historic agricultural practices, cooking, architecture, landscape, and leisure in the 1870s and 1880s. The street running in front of the house is Paris Avenue. This is a portion of a larger work. (Courtesy of Daniel Grimminger.)

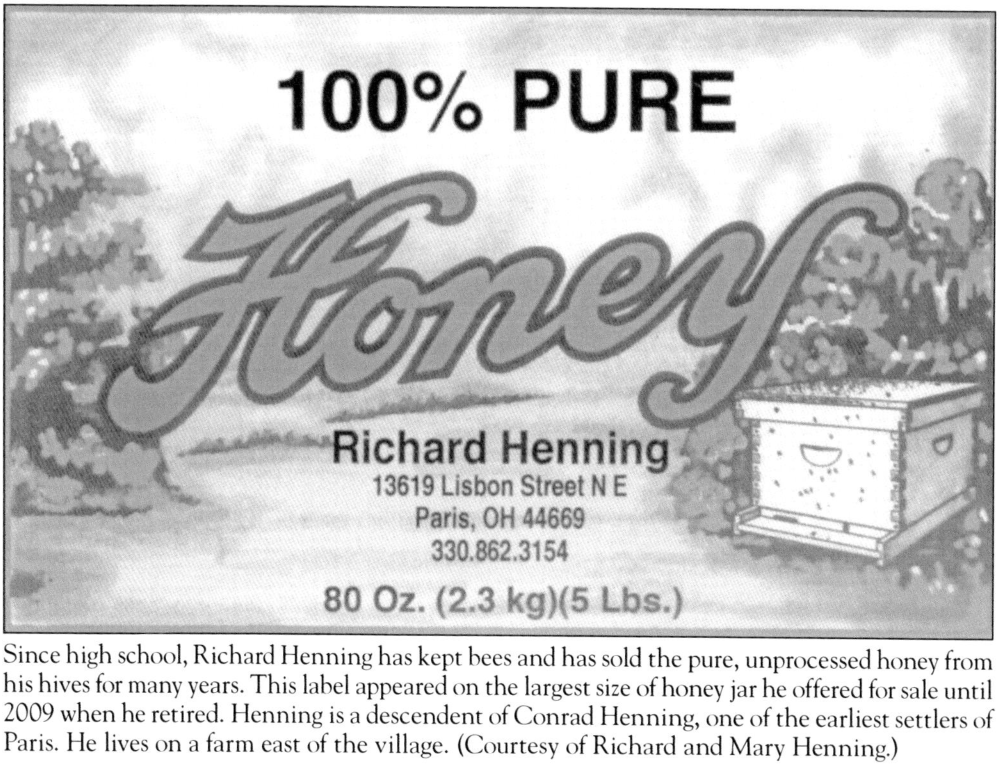

Since high school, Richard Henning has kept bees and has sold the pure, unprocessed honey from his hives for many years. This label appeared on the largest size of honey jar he offered for sale until 2009 when he retired. Henning is a descendent of Conrad Henning, one of the earliest settlers of Paris. He lives on a farm east of the village. (Courtesy of Richard and Mary Henning.)

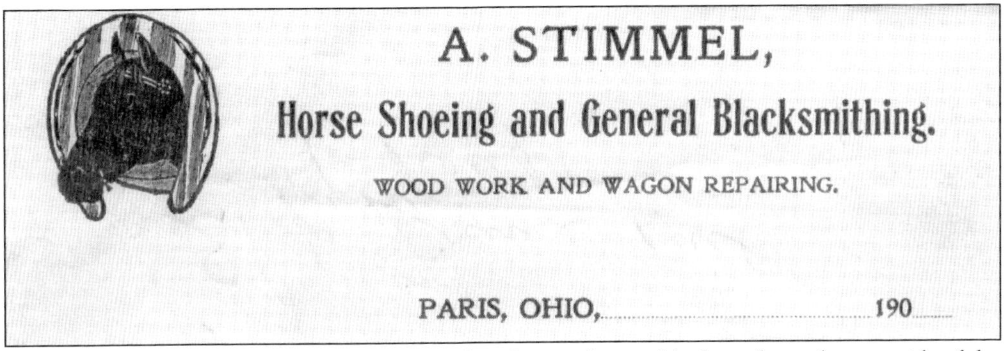

Betty (Stimmel) Speakman's grandfather Arthur Stimmel was a blacksmith on the west side of the village. His very distinct billhead shows a horse head within a horseshoe. As his billhead states, he would also do "Wood Work and Wagon Repairing" (Courtesy of Betty Speakman.)

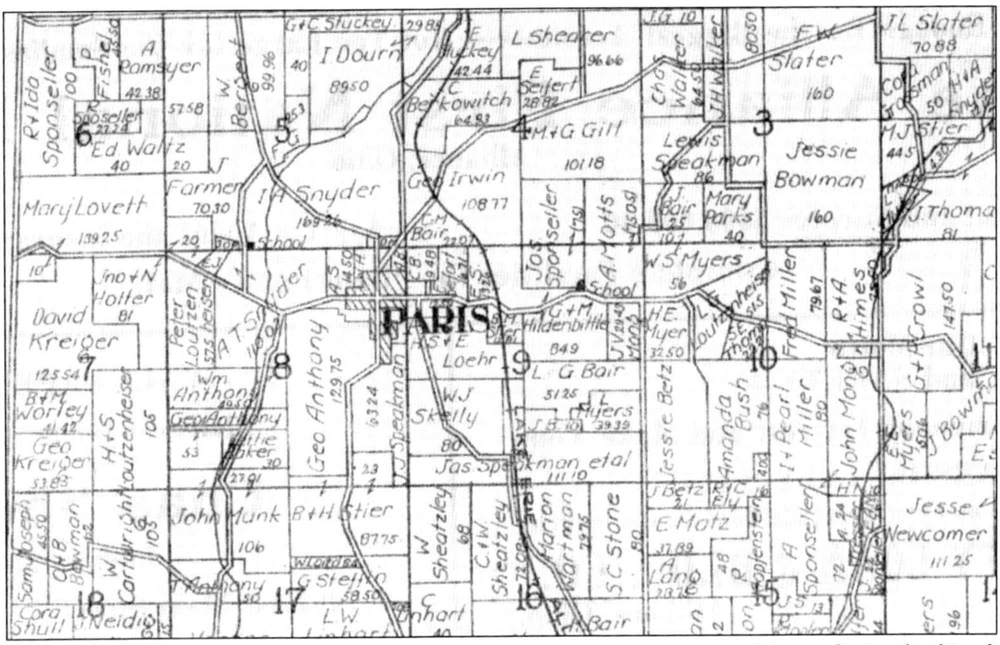

This plat record of the countryside surrounding Paris has been extracted from *Plat Book of Stark County, Ohio* (Rockford, Ill: W. W. Hixson, no date) around 1920. Some of the key family names from Paris Township are evident in this scan. (Courtesy of Kay Latham.)

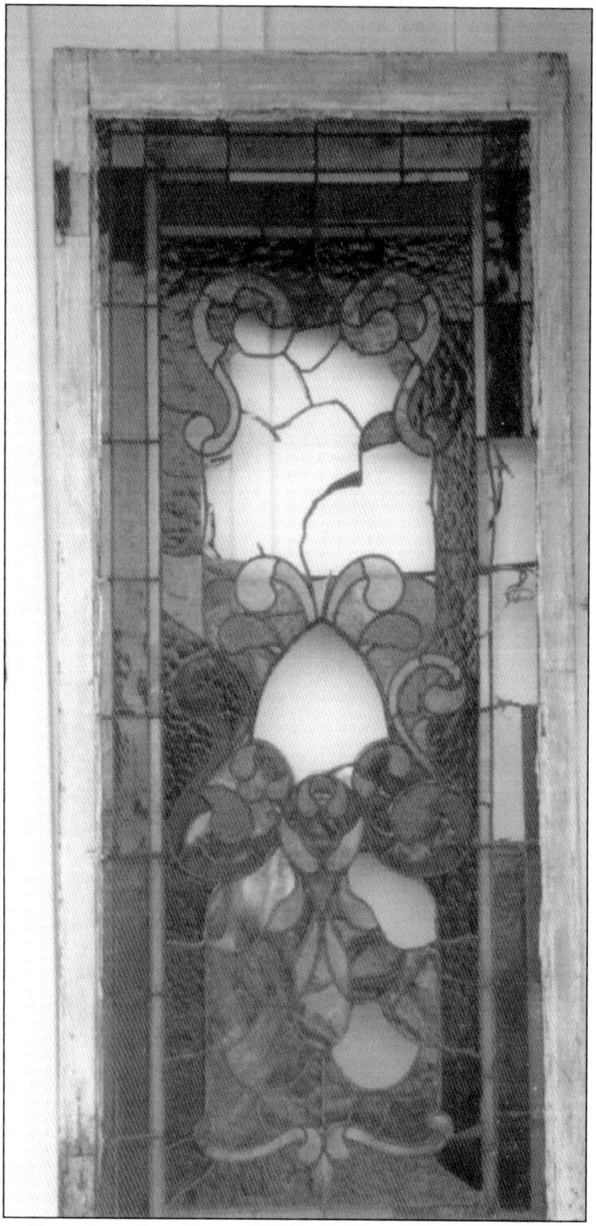

When the Lutheran Church replaced its old furnace in the 1990s, the trustees of the church found this window behind the old furnace. It was missing some panes of glass since the heat made the lead between the glass rubbery and brittle. Jay Lutz Jr. called the author to inform him what had been found and that it would be thrown on the trash pile if he did not care to have it. Later that day, Richard Mong loaded it on the back of his pickup truck and brought it to the Grimminger residence, where it was housed until it was restored by Studio Arts and Glass of Canton about six years later. According to Esther Schoner, this window used to be in the east wall of the Lutheran Church behind the altar. It had hinges on one side and was flanked by two small rectangular windows. When the church put in an apse, the windows were removed (even without permission, according to Doris Lutz) and a velvet curtain covered where they once were. (Courtesy of Daniel Grimminger.)

Bibliography

Bollinger, Theodore P., Henry Blosser, et al. *History of Saint John's Classis*. Cleveland: Central Publishing House, 1921.

Combination Atlas Map of Stark County Ohio. Philadelphia: L. H. Everts, 1875.

Danner, John. *Old Landmarks of Canton and Stark County, Ohio*, vol. I. Logansport, IN: B. F. Bowen, 1904.

Everts, L. H. *Combination Atlas Map of Stark County Ohio*. Philadelphia, 1875.

Gassman, Lois. *Memories*, unpublished manuscript, April 25, 1986.

Grimm, Hilmar. *Centennial History of Christ Lutheran Church, Bexley, Ohio 1978*. Columbus, OH: Pfeifer Printing Co., 1978.

Heald, Thornton. *The Stark County Story, being the First 76 Scripts covering the Years 1805–1874 on the Cities, Towns, and Villages of Stark County, Ohio*. Canton, OH: Stark County Historical Society, 1949.

Howells, Maud Marshall. "Paris, Once Metropolis—Boasted Five Hotels," *Canton Sunday News*. Sunday Morning, May 27, 1923.

Kauffman, William J., and Orrin F. Kauffman. *Atlas of Stark County Ohio, compiled from County Records and Actual Surveys*. Canton, OH: Map and Atlas Co, 1896.

Lehman, John H. A *Standard History of Stark County, Ohio*, vols. I and II. Chicago: The Lewis Publishing Company, n.d.

Paris, Ohio Sesqui-Centennial: Historical Souvenir Program, May 29, 30, 31, 1964.

Peter, P. A., and William Schmidt. *Geschichte der Allgemeinen Evang. Lutherischen Synode von Ohio und anderen Staaten*. Columbus: Lutheran Book Concern, 1900.

Portrait and biographical Record of Stark County: Containing Biographical Sketches of Prominent and Representative Citizens, together with Biographies and Portrait of all the Presidents of the United States. N.P.: Chapman Brothers, 1982.

Sheatsley, C. V. *History of the First Lutheran Seminary of the West, 1830–1930: Historical Sketch of the Theological Seminary of the Evangelical Lutheran Joint Synod of Ohio and Other States at Columbus, Ohio*. Columbus, OH: The Lutheran Book Concern, 1930.